ARE PERSONS PROPERTY?

For Liz and Eric

Are Persons Property?

Legal debates about property and personality

MARGARET DAVIES
Flinders University, Australia

NGAIRE NAFFINE
University of Adelaide, Australia

Ashgate

DARTMOUTH

Aldershot • Burlington USA • Singapore • Sydney

Published by
Dartmouth Publishing Company
Ashgate Publishing Limited
Gower House
Croft Road
Aldershot
Hants GU11 3HR
England

Ashgate Publishing Company
131 Main Street
Burlington VT 05401-5600 USA

Ashgate website: http://www.ashgate.com

British Library Cataloguing in Publication Data
Davies, Margaret (Margaret Jane)
    Are persons property? : legal debates about property and
    personality. - (Applied legal philosophy)
    1.Liberty 2.Human rights 3.Property
    I.Title II.Naffine, Ngaire
    342'.085

Library of Congress Control Number: 2001091401

ISBN 0 7546 2032 8

Printed and bound by Athenaeum Press, Ltd.,
Gateshead, Tyne & Wear.

Contents

Contents

Series Preface

The objective of the Dartmouth Series in Applied Legal Philosophy is to publish work which adopts a theoretical approach to the study of particular areas or aspects of law or deals with general theories of law in a way which focuses on issues of practical moral and political concern in specific legal contexts.

In recent years there has been an encouraging tendency for legal philosophers to utilize detailed knowledge of the substance and practicalities of law and a noteworthy development in the theoretical sophistication of much legal research. The series seeks to encourage these trends and to make available studies in law which are both genuinely philosophical in approach and at the same time based on appropriate legal knowledge and directed towards issues in the criticism and reform of actual laws and legal systems.

The series will include studies of all the main areas of law, presented in a manner which relates to the concerns of specialist legal academics and practitioners. Each book makes an original contribution to an area of legal study while being comprehensible to those engaged in a wide variety of disciplines. Their legal content is principally Anglo-American, but a wide-ranging comparative approach is encouraged and authors are drawn from a variety of jurisdictions.

Tom D. Campbell
Series Editor
The Faculty of Law
The Australian National University

Acknowledgements

We have incurred a number of debts during the writing of this book. We are grateful to the Australian Research Council for their financial support. We thank Kate Leeson for her assistance as researcher and often as advisor. Kathy Mack provided invaluable advice on the complete manuscript, and Tom Campbell has been an understanding and encouraging Series Editor.

Margaret Davies would like to thank Jane Knowler and Andrew Stewart for commenting on particular sections of the work, as well as David Lewis for research assistance.

Ngaire Naffine is grateful to the relevant publishers for permission to publish parts of her following works:

'The Legal Structure of Self-Ownership: Or the Self-Possessed Man and the Woman Possessed' (1998) 25, 2 *Journal of Law and Society* 193 (Blackwell Publishers, Oxford).

'"But a Lump of Earth": The Legal Status of the Corpse' in Desmond Manderson (ed) *Courting Death: The Law of Mortality* (London: Pluto Press, 1999), 95.

'When Does the Legal Person Die? Jeremy Bentham and the "Auto-Icon"' (2000) 25 *Australian Journal of Legal Philosophy* 80 (published by the Australian Society of Legal Philosophy).

'Are Women Legal Persons?' in Susan James and Stephanie Palmer *Visible Women: Essays on Feminist Legal Theory and Political Philosophy* (Hart Publishing, Oxford, forthcoming).

1 Persons as Property: Legal and Philosophical Debates

Are Persons Property?

The central question we pose in this book is 'Are persons property?'. There is perhaps a deliberate provocation intended in this simple inquiry — a provocation to lawyers and also a provocation to the political sensibilities of the citizenry at large. For it may seem that we are asking whether persons in the 'free' common law world are in some way still to be regarded as slaves, when surely our law and our society have long condemned slavery. Indeed the idea that persons are now all free and equal is supposed to be fundamental to modern liberal legal systems — the free person is not only the basic legal unit[1] but also the very *raison d'etre* of our law.

So were our question to have only this one meaning, were we only asking about the retention of explicit and legal forms of slavery, it would seem that there is necessarily only a brief reply to be given and hardly a book in it. For the short answer is that we do not recognise slavery; one person cannot own another. It is regarded as an abomination to commodify another human being in this manner.[2] The Western democracies outlawed slavery in the nineteenth century, though as Russell Scott has observed, it has 'not all disappeared from the Eastern world, nor from the African and South American continents'.[3] Indeed it seems that English common law never openly countenanced slavery, even though England was home to a number of slavers who derived immense wealth from a traffic in persons (English slavers wisely conducted their trade in other parts of the world).[4] As Rosemary Owens explains, 'In the famous *Sommersett's Case* [of 1772], English law decided against slavery, proclaiming its allegiance to the Enlightenment person and promising a protection for freedom'. In *Sommersett's Case*, it was concluded that there was no 'positive, or legislative, authorisation of slavery in England'.[5]

It could therefore be said with some confidence that Anglo-Australian law is in accord with the views of two of the leading philosophers of political and legal liberty, John Locke and Immanuel Kant, who, in different ways, both condemned the idea of treating other persons as property. According to Kant, 'a person cannot be property and so cannot be a thing which can be owned, for it is impossible to be a person and a thing, the proprietor and the property'.[6] Locke, too, was adamant about the importance of freedom from possession by others. In *The Second Treatise on Government* Locke begins his discourse on slavery by saying that

> The *Natural Liberty* of Man is to be free from any Superior Power on Earth, and not to be under the Will ... of Man ... not to be subject to the inconstant, uncertain, unknown, Arbitrary Will of another man.[7]

He goes on to say that :

> This *Freedom* from Absolute, Arbitrary Power, is so necessary to, and closely joyned with a Man's Preservation, that he cannot part with it, but by what forfeits his Preservation and Life together. For a Man, not having the Power of his own Life, *cannot*, by Compact or his own Consent, *enslave himself* to anyone ... No body can give more Power than he has himself; and he that cannot take away his own Life, cannot give another power over it.[8]

According to modern legal orthodoxy, Locke, Kant and modern law are *ad idem* in that the categories of person and property are now meant to be utterly separate and distinct. To be a person, it is said, is *precisely* not to be property. Thus it might be argued that the one concept negatively defines the other.

This may in large part be true, but in the course of this book we will suggest that, in a number of important respects, persons can still be rendered unfree and effectively reduced to something akin to the property of another in certain situations and under certain conditions. We therefore question the purity of the modern property/personality distinction, even when our starting question is interpreted in this way. Women in particular are still susceptible to certain forms of commodification. For example, as we see in Chapter Four, there have been well-documented recent instances of the autonomy of pregnant women being subordinated to the foetus, through the imposition of unwanted caesarian sections. The woman who is obliged to undergo major medical intervention for the benefit of 'another', her foetus, cannot be said to be a free person (whatever we think of the wisdom of her decision to refuse such treatment) and has even been characterised as a sort of faulty 'foetal container'.[9] She lacks the most fundamental common law right consistently asserted for all free persons, the right to exclusive control over her own body.[10] England's most senior judges have recently made just this point, while declaring a number of recalcitrant pregnant women legally incompetent to refuse surgery.[11]

Another way in which it may be said that modern law commodifies the person is at the end of life. When we die, our bodies acquire a status close to that of property and indeed in the United States a 'quasi-property' interest has been explicitly declared in the dead body (as we will see in Chapter Five). Also in the United States, it has been recognised that people have an alienable proprietary 'right of publicity' over their 'persona' (including their name, their image, and other recognisable aspects of their personality). Where this property has in fact been alienated, or where it becomes part of a person's estate after their death, it may truly be said that one person 'owns' an aspect of another. We will turn to this issue in Chapter Six. On a broader scale, the patenting of biotechnological processes and products based upon human genetic material may be characterised as creating property in human life. Although such a characterisation is highly controversial, and does not necessarily lead to the conclusion that any individual is in any way 'owned', human biotechnology patents do undeniably involve ownership of material closely connected with the human species. We will consider this controversy in Chapter Seven.

Consequently, it cannot be said that in the modern 'free world' persons are never the property of others. Slavery may be unlawful, but it is still possible to identify other ways in which persons continue to assume some of the incidents of property.

The Person as Self-Proprietor

However our question is susceptible of at least one other interpretation. If it is not taken to be a question about the legal currency of slavery, about whether one person can own another, it may be asking instead whether we are in some way our own property: whether persons are property in the sense that we are somehow the proprietors of ourselves. Certainly this was a welcome idea to Locke. For, although he rejected the idea that persons could be the property of others, Locke explicitly endorsed the idea that we own ourselves — our persons and our labours.

> Though the Earth, and all inferior Creatures be common to all Men,
> yet every Man has a *Property* in his own *Person*. This no Body has
> any Right to but himself. The *Labour* of his Body, and the *Work* of
> his Hands, we may say, are properly his.[12]

Locke famously employed the argument that we all naturally own
ourselves as a justification for private appropriation of the commons. As is
well known, Locke's view was that once we mix our labour (which we
own naturally) with an object in the commons, we gain property in it. Self-
ownership therefore provides a foundation for ownership of the external
world.

Hegel also developed an account of property that linked it to self-
ownership.[13] Hegel argued that in becoming a person one must put oneself
into the external world and then reappropriate the self through the
appropriation of objects in the world. Taking the world unto ourselves is
our method of completing our subjectivity and individuality, because it
involves the purely subjective person externalising their personality and re-
grasping it in the form of an external object. Property is 'embodied
personality',[14] that is, property is only property insofar as it is occupied by
a person's will. Property gives us the means of forming contractual
relations with others — through ownership we are able to recognise others
as owners, and exchange our property, and therefore our persons, in
contractual relationships. Property is therefore essential to the formation of
social relationships. At the same time, it is important to place Hegel's
account of property within the larger framework of his *Philosophy of
Right*. The acquisition of property for Hegel is only one preliminary
'moment' in the constitution of free subjectivity.

Hegel's account of the sovereign individual is therefore quite
different from Locke's. For Locke, the free and complete self-owning
individual labours and, through labour, becomes an owner. For Hegel, it is
only through the act of appropriation that a person realises their
subjectivity, and becomes free: 'Personality is that which struggles . . . to
claim the external world as its own'.[15] The person therefore does not start
as a self-owning entity.

Both personality and property in Hegel's account are complex
entities, formed dialectically. We begin, in Hegel's account, with pure
subjectivity and pure objectivity, which may appear to be a relatively
simple distinction between persons and the external world of objects.
However, persons become self-owning by externalising themselves
through the appropriation of objects. The person therefore becomes both

pure subject, and object.[16] Similarly, the object, which starts as a mere thing, having no end-in-itself, becomes invested with the will and spirit of the appropriator. As long as the person's will remains in the object, it is property. When abandoned, it returns to its former state of meaninglessness.

The Possessive Individual and Liberal Legal Philosophy

There is therefore a paradox to be observed here. The firm response to our first question was that persons are not property: to be a person is precisely not to be reduced to the property of another. And yet it has been said by influential Western thinkers that in some way we own ourselves, which logically necessitates a view of the person, or at least of parts of the person, as property, albeit one's own. If this is so, then the idea of the person is in fact deeply imbued with the idea of property. To be a person is to be a proprietor and also to be property — the property of oneself.

The concept of the person as self-proprietor, as we will see in Chapter Three, has a secure place within our modern liberal political theory and liberal jurisprudence. It has become a convenient way of highlighting the freedoms enjoyed by the modern individual, a sort of legal shorthand, a rhetorical device, which serves to accentuate the fullness of the rights enjoyed by persons in relation to themselves and to others. 'To be a full individual in liberal society', as Katherine O'Donovan observes, 'one must be an appropriator, defined by what one owns, including oneself as a possession, not depending on others, free'.[17]

The story of the emergence of modern law and its reliance on relations based on contract, as told by the legal historian, Henry Maine,[18] is the story of the man who quite naturally has property in his person, who has self-ownership. Thus he has the right to his capacities and to the products of his labours.

The appeal that the concept of property-in-self might hold to modern liberals, under the influence of Locke, is revealed by a brief inquiry into the etymology of the word 'property'. As Kenneth Minogue explains, '[t]he etymological root of the term (*proprius* — one's own), gives us the sense of the connection between property and what possesses it',[19] that is between the possessing subject and the object or thing possessed by that subject. Or as Gray and Symes put it, 'semantically, 'property' is the condition of being 'proper' to (or belonging to) a particular person'.[20] The properties of persons, the attributes they possess, render them distinctive.

That which is proper to a person delimits and individuates the person, marking the borders between him[21] and the rest of the world.[22]

If we examine the modern legal meaning of property, we can see its enduring appeal as a means of asserting the autonomy of the individual. Briefly, property describes a legal relationship *between* persons *in respect* of an object, rather than the relation between a subject and the objects possessed as property of the person.[23] A property right enables the proprietor to exercise control over a thing, the object of property, against the rest of the world. Property thus defines the limits of our sphere of influence over the world; it defines the borders of our control over things and so marks the degree of our social and legal power. The claim of property in oneself is an assertion of self-possession and self-control, of a fundamental right to exclude others from one's very being. It is a means of individuating the person, of establishing a limit between the one and the other: between thine and mine; between you and me.

In the modern legal literature, property and personhood have been connected in at least two ways. Property in things other than oneself has been said to enhance personhood, because it establishes an extended sphere of non-interference with one's person. Margaret Jane Radin, in a modern rendition of Hegel's thought, has called this 'property for personhood'.[24] Property and personhood have also been linked in a more intimate manner by the assertion that persons may also be said to have property in themselves. Common to both approaches has been a desire to show how property interests express and secure the autonomy of the individual and hence their very personhood.

Property for Personhood

Some Anglo-American interpreters of Hegel's explanation of property have tended to over-emphasise his explanation of the relationship between property and the person. To focus primarily upon this aspect of his *Philosophy of Right* is to neglect the fact that Hegel presents this as only one part of a much larger picture, incorporating relationships with others in moral life, through the family, and finally as part of the state.[25] However this limited reading of Hegel, which highlights his explanation of the role of private property in strengthening the personality, resonates strongly with modern liberal notions of the self. Property is seen as an extension of the person and as a means by which the person can relate freely and transparently with others. Property is seen to mediate our social relationships. According to Charles Reich, 'Property draws a circle around the activities of each private individual ... property performs the function of maintaining independence, dignity ... by creating zones within which the majority has to yield to the owner'.[26] To Alice Tay, 'Property is that which a man has a right to use and enjoy without interference; it is what makes him as a person and guarantees his independence and security'.[27]

Perhaps the leading theorist of property for personhood is Margaret Radin, who has used Hegel's account of the property/person relationship as a point of departure for her theory of property for personhood. Accordingly, she argues that in order 'to achieve proper self-development — to be a person — an individual needs some control over resources in the external environment'.[28] If property that is intimately connected to, and valued by, the person is taken away, then the person is concomitantly reduced as a person.[29] Indeed property is so important for personhood that 'certain categories of property can bridge the gap, or blur the boundary, between the self and the world, between what is inside and outside, between what is subject and object'.[30]

One of Radin's goals has been to develop a way of thinking about property which does not permit the commodification of persons as the property of others, and hence to counteract what she and others perceive as a tendency towards universal commodification, especially within the law and economics school of thought.[31] At the same time, she accepts that there is a relationship between persons and property. Radin therefore distinguishes between two types of property: property for personhood and fungible property. Property for personhood, as the term implies, is property that a person uses in their self-construction and self-identification. It is a relationship to an external thing that contributes to a person's feelings of well-being, freedom, and identity. The body is foremost in this category of external things, but Radin also mentions a person's primary place of residence, whether owned or rented, cars, and objects such as wedding rings, which may have a particular sentimental value. Fungible property is property that is interchangeable with any other, and exists mainly for wealth-creation. Radin argues that property which contributes to personality is socially more important than fungible property, and deserves greater legal protection. She also finds support in some US Supreme Court decisions, arguing that they reveal a judiciary that is more willing to protect personal property than fungible property.

The feminist dimension of Radin's work arises in what one commentator has described as her attention to 'the daily realities of human experience' and her acknowledgement of the 'tangible reality of gender and power'.[32] Although Radin's focus is not primarily on gender, she does attempt to locate property within real human relations, rather than in abstractions which may lead to universal commodification, including commodification of the female body. Whereas modern accounts of property emphasise the legal relationships between persons, Radin focuses upon the relationship between person and thing, attempting to strengthen this connection by arguing that the object is part of the person's identity. Like Hegel, Radin sees property not simply as an object that is owned by a subject, but as something that bridges the gap between object and subject. The subject finds herself in objects, and becomes object to herself in ownership.

Radin's analysis of property for personhood raises many interesting questions. For instance, what type and quantity of property would be regarded as property for personhood? One person may feel that *all* of the external objects which they have under their control — including six cars and three houses — are absolutely necessary to their self-perception and their worth as a human being. Another person may have what Radin considers to be a more 'normal' relationship to their property. Radin therefore distinguishes between personal property relationships that are genuine and those that are based on fetishism. She says

> We can tell the difference between personal property and fetishism
> the same way we can tell the difference between a healthy person
> and a sick person, or between a sane person and an insane person. In
> fact, the concepts of sanity and personhood are intertwined: at some
> point we question whether the insane person is a person at all.[33]

This method of distinguishing property for personhood from fetishism, or health from sickness, or sanity from insanity, raises an obvious question — who is included in the 'we' who makes such judgements?[34] And who is excluded? Given the legal and social histories of Western liberal democracies, which have often pathologised and de-personified women, it is surely wise to be cautious about any 'objective' means of distinguishing the normal from the deviant that relies primarily upon consensus. One person's normality might be another's fetishism.

Radin's account of property for personhood is intended to offer resistance to the commodification of the person, by distinguishing property which is essential to the person from property which is not. It is as though people have personal properties, which identify them and are intrinsically inalienable, as well as property, which is just fungible wealth. (What you have is what you are.) The person is not severable from their properties, and in particular from their body, and it would therefore not be possible to appropriate a person's properties, without commodifying or diminishing their person. In consequence, there must be some restriction on the free marketability of such property (or properties). The paradox within Radin's work is that it sets property against property. The self is understood as a function of property, and this propertied self is in turn expected to protect against the commodity form of the person.

Radin's thesis has been influential, but it has also had its critics.[35] Perhaps the greatest weakness of the thesis lies in Radin's acceptance of the view that personal identity is derived from relationships with objects, rather than with other subjects.[36] In her account, even the self becomes an object, because it finds itself in the external world of objects. In defending herself against her critics, Radin explains that her position is a pragmatic one:[37] she is not claiming that personality is always and inevitably a relationship to property, but rather that in the current (Western) social context, property and personality are in fact linked in this way. In her view, policy makers need to recognise this context, and use it to strengthen existing liberal rights.

Persons as Property

The idea that persons secure their personhood not only through property interests in external resources but also through property in themselves has also been stated in different ways. Paraphrasing the Lockean formulation, John Christman states that '[a] powerful way of expressing the principle of individual liberty is to claim that every individual has full "property rights" over her body, skills and labour'.[38] John Frow suggests that personhood plays a founding role as a category of property. In his view, the Western view of property 'is based on self-possession, a primordial property right in the self which then grounds all other property rights'.[39]

The modern interpreter of Locke, CB McPherson, has described the story of contract as the story of the rise of the 'possessive individual'.[40] The 'possessive quality' of the individual of modern liberal theory, according to McPherson, derives from his essential character as proprietor 'of his own person or capacities, owing nothing to society for them'.[41] As McPherson further explains:

> since the freedom, and therefore the humanity, of the individual
> depend on his freedom to enter into self-interested relations with

> other individuals, and since his ability to enter into such relations
> depends on his having exclusive control of (rights in) his own person
> and capacities, and since proprietorship is the generalized form of
> such exclusive control, the individual is essentially the proprietor of
> his own person and capacities.[42]

In this liberal interpretation of the person, ownership is all-defining. Thus the being who emerges as the central character of modern market society is no longer regarded as a part of a broader community but rather a discrete being: 'owner of himself'. Ownership is 'the critically important relation' which determines the realisation of freedom and one's 'potentialities'. Accordingly it is 'read back into the nature of the individual ... The human essence is freedom from dependence on the wills of others, and freedom is a function of possession'.[43]

Other analysts of liberal theory have provided similar accounts of its conception of the person as self-proprietor. Arneson sees the principle of self-ownership as 'foundational for one tradition of political liberalism running from Locke to Nozick'.[44] Or as Cohen, affirming Nozick, expresses it, the person 'possesses over himself, as a matter of moral right, all those rights that a slaveholder has over a complete chattel slave as a matter of legal right'.[45]

Certain liberal theorists have also been alert to the negative connotations of property-in-self. Immanuel Kant found the idea particularly troubling (and so rejected it) because it suggested to him a commodification of the person, the reduction of the human being to thing.

> Man cannot dispose over himself because he is not a thing; he is not
> his own property; to say that he is would be self-contradictory; for in
> so far as he is a person he is a Subject in whom the ownership of
> things can be vested, and if he were his own property, he would be a
> thing over which he could have ownership.[46]

The idea of property-in-self is, to many, still suggestive of an unsavoury and illiberal past when persons could be slaves.[47] As Margaret Davies has remarked, if persons can objectify their selves they become susceptible to objectification by others.[48] The new medical technologies, which have allowed for the removal of parts of the person without the total destruction of the person, and which have also generated enormous economic potential in those parts,[49] pose new possibilities of human commodification and so have revived the Kantian concern about regarding persons as property.[50] So to suggest that property-in-self is a means of expressing human autonomy is, paradoxically, also to threaten liberty.

The well-known Californian case of *Moore v Regents of the University of California* raises precisely this issue. John Moore was a patient of a David Golde at the University of California Medical Center, and was diagnosed with hairy-cell leukaemia in 1976.[51] Golde subsequently recommended that Moore have an operation to remove his spleen and Moore consented to this treatment. Before the operation was performed, Golde — who was aware that Moore's cells might have some scientific and commercial value — made arrangements with a co-researcher, Shirley Quan, to obtain samples of the spleen upon its removal. Their intentions in obtaining the samples allegedly had nothing to do with Moore's medical treatment. Rather they wished to use the tissue in their research. Moore made a number of trips from Seattle to Los Angeles for further treatment, and on these occasions further samples of blood and other tissue were taken. At no time did Moore consent to his tissue samples being used in research. Indeed, he was not even asked for his consent to the research on his tissue until much later. Golde developed a cell-line based upon Moore's cells in 1979, and the University of California applied for, and was granted, a patent on the cell-line in 1981. Commercial exploitation of the cell-line was negotiated between the University and two biotechnology companies (Genetics Institute Inc., and Sandoz Pharmaceuticals). Finally, Moore discovered the uses to which his body tissue had been put and sued Golde, Quan, the Regents of the University, Genetics Institute and Sandoz.

Moore alleged both breach of fiduciary duty (or lack of informed consent) and conversion. The claim of breach of fiduciary duty was readily accepted by the majority of the Supreme Court of California, which held that 'a physician must disclose personal interests unrelated to the patient's health, whether research or economic, that may affect the physician's professional judgement'.[52] The claim for conversion, however, was far more controversial. Conversion protects possession or, where possession has been willingly surrendered, it protects property. In this case, since Moore had consented to the removal of his tissue samples, the question was whether he still had an ownership interest in them after their removal. The majority decided he did not. In a separate concurring judgement, Arabian J objected in striking terms to any blurring of the boundary between person and property, saying that Moore was asking the court to 'to regard the human vessel — the single most venerated and protected subject in any civilized society — as equal with the basest commercial commodity'.[53]

While the majority refused to countenance any *self*-ownership by the plaintiff, the two minority judges both argued that a failure to protect a self-ownership interest in Moore's body would open the way for others to gain an ownership interest in it. Broussard J pointed out that a simple 'no-property' rule relating to any body parts is far too broad. He gave the example of a human tissue sample stolen from a laboratory after removal from a person. In such a case, the court would not in the least be troubled by a conversion action. Mosk J also pointed out that a refusal to recognise ownership of the body creates the more worrying possibility that it might be owned by another. Referring to the 'profound ethical imperative to respect the human body as the physical and temporal expression of the human persona' he was clearly troubled by the prospect that one person's body could be commercially exploited by others.[54] Mosk J's reasoning is, in essence, that it is possible to minimise commodification of the body by shoring up a person's own property in it. Self-ownership immunises against potential ownership by others. We will return to *Moore's Case* in Chapter Seven, where we will consider its implications for ownership of genetic resources.

While some have objected to the alienating, commodifying effects of possessive individualism, others have remarked on and challenged the unevenness of its original application. Indeed it may be said that much of the modern feminist movement has been, in one way or another, directed at the various forms of retention of the traditional status category of 'woman'. As we will consider in some detail in Chapter Four, the sexual and reproductive lives of women have never been charactersised by the freedoms of the possessive individual. And, as many feminists have remarked, the possessive individual is himself premised on the unfreedoms of women as sexual and reproductive beings.[55]

The Decline of Possessive Individualism: Reversion from Contract to Status?

While this book makes much of the idea of the possessive individual as a central character of modern Western law, we do not wish to overstate its influence. Not only does he fail in his role as a universal character (as feminists have shown), but it may also be said that his time of full flourishing has come and gone. The classical age of the free contractual legal individual, according to PS Atiyah (whose work we discuss in Chapters Two and Three) has undergone a partial reversal, although lawyers still tend to employ the 'conceptual apparatus' of the classical period. To Atiyah,

> So far as land is concerned, the absolute rights of ownership which were demanded and ... ceded during the eighteenth and nineteenth centuries, have largely disappeared again. The gradual extension of the rights of tenants at the expense of landlords, first in the case of agricultural land, and then in the case of urban housing, has steadily eroded the owner's powers over his lands.[56]

So too has disappeared the eighteenth century idea that the owner of land can do whatever he likes with it 'the absolute right of the owner to exploit and develop the land as he thinks best, has...entirely disappeared from English law'.[57]

Similarly, Atiyah notes that the eighteenth century idea that the individual determines and controls the market — that the market economy is basically an economic exchange of atomistic and free proprietors — has been eroded. 'It is today no longer the individual but the Government which largely allocates resources in the British economy', says Atiyah.

> Governments directly control, for instance, the resources to be invested in the nationalized industries, and in all the public goods and services directly supplied by the State or by other public bodies ... within the public system itself, the process of decision making on resource allocation is delegated to Committees or corporate bodies who do not function by market methods.[58]

In other words, administrative or government processes have taken over much of the legal activity which was formerly governed by individual contracts between private individual proprietors.

American law professor Charles Reich has also documented and condemned the impediments to the freedoms of the modern possessive legal individual. In his seminal essay, 'The New Property', Reich argued that the largesse now distributed by government and by the corporate sector has begun to assume a feudal quality in that rights over property are handed out in exchange for certain types of behaviour. To Reich, 'the right to possess and use government largesse is bound up with the recipient's legal status...hence the wealth is not readily transferable'. Thus 'individuals hold the wealth conditionally rather than absolutely [and] the conditions are usually obligations owed to the government or to the public and may include the obligation of loyalty to the government'. These obligations may be subject to change at 'the will of the state'.[59] Reich maintains that 'the combined power of government and the corporations...presses against the individual'.[60] In this account, the individual's freedoms to control his or her destiny have been greatly and inappropriately curtailed. The proprietor has suffered an erosion of sovereignty.

The Critique of Possessive Individualism

The problem of commodification implicit in the idea of the self-proprietor necessarily returns us to the first interpretation of our question, 'are persons property?', which at first blush we were inclined to answer in the negative. However, if we now accept that as modern liberals we do, after all, regard ourselves as self-proprietors, do we thereby make ourselves vulnerable to the objectification of others, that is, to some form of slavery? If we are willing to regard any part of ourselves as severable and consequently as 'a thing over which [we] could have ownership',[61] then perhaps we make it possible for others to make us their objects of property. This will be an important theme of this book.

   One of the earliest analysts of the divided, fetishised self was the young Karl Marx who described the alienating social and personal effects of modern market society. To the early Marx, modern industrial society depersonified and diminished the individual by wrenching from him[62] that which was most his own and which was essential for his full flourishing as a human being, that is his labour and its products. The parting of the individual from the products of his labours — taking from him what was naturally his — was to Marx a form of commodificiation of the person.[63]

   Early this century, the socialist historian RH Tawney in *The Acquisitive Society* objected to the dehumanising effects of the unequal possessive society, in which persons became the instruments of others (Kant's precise concern). In such a society, 'wealth becomes the foundation of public esteem, and the mass of men who labour, but who do not acquire wealth, are thought to be vulgar and meaningless and insignificant compared with the few who acquire wealth by good fortune...They come to be regarded, not as the ends for which alone it is worth while to produce wealth at all, but as the instruments of its acquisition'.[64]

However perhaps the most sustained critique of the idea of the person as proprietor this century comes from CB McPherson. In *The Political Theory of Possessive Individualism*, McPherson observed that '[t]he assumptions of possessive individualism are peculiarly appropriate to a possessive market society' and that the unfortunate consequence was the loss of cohesion derived from common class interests 'among all those with a political voice'.[65] Possessive individualism came at a considerable cost. For no longer was the person 'a moral whole, nor...part of a larger social whole'.[66] Moreover one's very humanity depended on ownership. As McPherson puts it, 'The individual in a possessive market society *is* human in his capacity as proprietor of his person'.[67]

Feminists have both supported and challenged the association of the personality with property. As Jennifer Nedelsky has commented, 'property looks to some like the perfect vehicle to power and autonomy and to others like the path to oppression'.[68] On the one hand, formal recognition of self-ownership for women has been seen to be an important element of the attainment of equal rights: a woman's person must be accorded the degree of respect and dignity which is attributed to the universal human (male) subject. Self-ownership — the idea that the person is inviolable and under the sole control of the self — is seen by some feminists to be a crucial element of recognition as a fully independent human agent and legal person. On the other hand, some feminists have criticised both the metaphor of self-ownership and the notion of property for personhood, arguing that, since property in a capitalist context is really about exploitation and power, it is important to oppose any strategy which might have the effect of reinforcing women's traditional status as objects of (men's) property. While she concedes that there are models of property which do not imply complete marketability,[69] Nedelsky argues strongly that the presumption of our capitalist world view is heavily in favour of commodification. It would therefore be difficult to carve out and maintain a non-commodity form of property-in-self. For Nedelsky, the better approach is to view persons in terms of their relationships with others, not as self-owners, or as territorially 'bounded selves'.[70] This is a view with which we have some sympathy, and to which we will return at the end of the book.

The Structure of the Book

From this brief survey, we can observe that the scholarship on the relationship between property and personality is complex and multi-disciplinary. In gathering material for this book, we have tried to make connections between a number of different fields of enquiry. We have studied mainstream (non-legal) philosophical analyses which address the justification for, and nature of, private property, and the nature of human identity and agency. We have also considered the formal jurisprudence of our topic, that is, theory which considers the legal notions of property and personality. In order to situate modern legal thinking about property and personality, we have also paid some attention to the historical development of these concepts, and to the different ways in which they have been related in legal history. Perhaps most obviously, we have analysed some of the many areas of law which directly or indirectly raise questions about persons regarded as property (of themselves, or of others). Finally, we have examined the ways in which, on a more abstract level, both property and a particular view of the person extend metaphorically into our language and social domain.

Although not formally divided into parts, there are three distinct sections in this work. Chapters Two and Three examine the philosophical, historical, and modern legal notions of property and personality. These chapters provide the theoretical foundation for the legal doctrinal analysis of the rest of the book. Chapters Four and Five focus upon some aspects of property in the *physical* person. These chapters examine the person/property division in entities which define the beginnings and ends of corporeal existence. Chapter Four considers the nature of the property/personality division in relation to women, especially their role as reproducers of the species, and in relation to the foetus as a potential legal person. Chapter Five attends to the end of our physical existence, to the legal personality of the testator and to the legal status of the corpse. Chapters Six and Seven also consider the frontiers of human existence, but at a more abstract level. The person is transformed into something abstract for the purposes of intellectual property law. Chapter Six looks at ownership of the public 'persona' (including the name, the image, and other identifying characteristics of a person). Chapter Seven is about the commodification and patenting of products derived from human genetic material.

The work is a joint project, one of the results of a collaboration on a project funded by an Australian Research Council Large Grant. From 1997 we have worked together on this project, and gained a (generally) shared understanding of our topic. However, apart from this introduction and the concluding chapter, we have contributed distinct sections to the book. Ngaire Naffine is the author of Chapters Three, Four and Five, and Margaret Davies is the author of Chapters Two, Six and Seven. This division reflects our research interests, which are (respectively) legal personality and the philosophy of property.

Notes

1   We appreciate that non-human beings and abstract entities can also be legal persons but our argument will be that a certain conception of the human being, as a free and possessive individual, provides the template for legal being.

2   Witness the vigorous condemnation of human commodification in the case of *Moore v Regents of the University of California* 793 P 2d 479 (Cal 1990), discussed below, and in Chapter Seven.

3   Russell Scott *The Body as Property* (London: A. Lane, 1981), 26–27.

4   See JH Baker *An Introduction to English Legal History* 3rd ed (London: Butterworths, 1990), 540–543.

5   Rosemary Owens 'Working in the Sex Market' in Ngaire Naffine and Rosemary Owens (eds) *Sexing the Subject of Law* (Sydney: Law Book Company, 1997), 123.

6   Immanuel Kant *Lectures on Ethics* L. Infield (trans) (London: Methuen and Co, 1930 ed), 165.

7   John Locke *Two Treatises of Government* Peter Laslett (ed) 2nd ed (Cambridge: Cambridge University Press, 1967, first published in 1690), *Second Treatise*, ch IV, para 22, 283–284.

8   Ibid, 284.

9   As Laura Purdy has argued in 'Are Pregnant Women Fetal Containers?' (1990) 4 *Bioethics* 273.

10   See for example the extended discussion of this right in *Marion's Case: Dept of Health v JWB and SMB* (1992) 66 ALJR 300.

11   See discussion in Chapter Four.

12   Locke *Two Treatises of Government, Second Treatise*, ch V, para 27, 287–288.

13   GWF Hegel *Philosophy of Right* TM Knox (trans) (Oxford: Oxford University Press, 1952).

14   Hegel *Philosophy of Right*, s51.

15   Hegel *Philosophy of Right*, s39. See also Drahos *A Philosophy of Intellectual Property* (Aldershot: Dartmouth, 1996), ch 4 'Hegel: The Spirit of Intellectual Property'.

16   The will 'becomes objective to me in property'; Hegel *Philosophy of Right*, s46.

17   Katherine O'Donovan, 'With Sense, Consent, or Just a Con? Legal Subjects in the Discourses of Autonomy' in Ngaire Naffine and Rosemary Owens (eds) *Sexing the Subject of Law* (Sydney: Law Book Company, 1997), 46.

18   See below, Chapter Three.

19   Kenneth Minogue, 'The Concept of Property and its Contemporary Significance' in *Nomos XXII: Property*, R. Pennock and J. Chapman (eds) (1980), 11.

20   KJ Gray and PD Symes, *Real Property and Real People: Principles of Land Law* (London: Butterworths, 1981), 7.

21   A central thesis of this book is that this individual is culturally male hence the deliberate use of the masculine pronoun.

22   This idea of 'the proper' and its relation to personhood has been explored by Margaret Davies in 'Feminist Appropriations: Law, Property and Personality' (1994) 3 *Social and Legal Studies* 365–391; see also Margaret Davies 'The Proper: Discourses of Purity' (1998) 9 *Law and Critique* 147.

23   Gray and Symes *Real Property and Real People,* 8.

24   Margaret Jane Radin, 'Property and Personhood' (1982) 34 *Stanford Law Review* 957, 959.

25   See, for instance, Hegel *Philosophy of Right*, s104.

26   Charles Reich, 'The New Property' (1964) 73 *Yale Law Journal* 733, 771.

27   Alice Ehr-Soon Tay, 'Law, the Citizen and the State' in Eugene Kamenka, Robert Brown and Alice Ehr-Soon Tay (eds) *Law and Society: The Crisis in Legal Ideals* (London: E. Arnold, 1978), 10.

28   Margaret Jane Radin *Reinterpreting Property* (Chicago: University of Chicago Press, 1993), 35.

29   This thesis has been vigorously criticised by Stephen J Schnably for its implicit conservatism. Radin, he says, assumes a consensus about the sanctity of the home (the most important type of property for personhood) and leaves unquestioned the political dimensions of this social ideal. See Stephen J Shnably, 'Property and Pragmatism: A Critique of Radin's Theory of Property and Personhood' (1993) 45 *Stanford Law Review* 347.

30   Margaret Jane Radin, 'The Colin Ruagh Thomas O'Fallon Memorial Lecture on Reconsidering Personhood' (1995) 74 *Oregon Law Review* 423, 426.

31   A prime target of Radin's criticism is Richard Posner. See his *Sex and Reason* (Cambridge, Mass: Harvard University Press, 1992), for an attempt to analyse sex and sexuality in economic terms.

32   Catharine Pierce Wells 'Pragmatism, Feminism, and the Problem of Bad Coherence' (1995) 93 *Michigan Law Review* 1645, 1662.

33   Radin *Reinterpreting Property*, 43.

34 Radin does recognise this as a potential problem, but believes that an 'objective moral consensus' can provide a standard for such judgements. *Reinterpreting Property*, 43.

35 Shnably 'Property and Prgamatism'; Jeanne Schroeder 'Virgin Territory: Margaret Radin's Imagery of Personal Property as the Inviolate Feminine Body' (1994) 79 *Minnesota Law Review* 55.

36 Although Radin does not present her case as based upon a complete acceptance of Hegel's account of the property-personality relationship, it is interesting to note that for Hegel relationship with others in morality and ethical life overtakes the simple property-person relationship.

37 See Radin *Reinterpreting Property*, ch 1.

38 John Christman, 'Self-Ownership, Equality and the Structure of Property Rights' (1991) 19 *Political Theory* 28.

39 John Frow, "Elvis' Fame: The Commodity Form and the Form of the Person' (1995) 7 *Cardozo Studies in Law and Literature* 131, 149.

40 CB McPherson *The Political Theory of Possessive Individualism: Hobbes to Locke* (Oxford: Clarendon Press, 1964).

41 McPherson *The Political Theory of Possessive Individualism*, 3.

42 Ibid, 261.

43 Ibid, 3.

44 Richard Arneson, 'Lockean Self-Ownership: Towards a Demolition' (1991) 39 *Political Studies* 36.

45 GA Cohen 'Self-Ownership, World-Ownership and Equality' in Lucash (ed) *Justice and Equality Here and Now* (Ithaca, New York: Cornell University Press, 1986) 108, 109.

46 Kant *Lectures on Ethics*, 165.

47 As Courtney S Campbell has suggested, 'the property paradigm' is shadowed by 'the historical legacy of chattel relationships with persons, especially women and children, and slavery'. 'Body, Self, and the Property Paradigm' (1992) 22(5) *Hastings Center Report* 34, 36.

48 Davies 'Feminist Appropriations', 381.

49 See for example *Moore v Regents of the University of California* 793 P2d 479 (Cal 1990) (*Moore's Case*).

50 There is an extensive and rapidly expanding literature on body parts as property which encompasses a heated debate about the commodification of the person. See for example Lori Andrews 'My Body My Property' (1986) 16(5) *Hastings Center Report* 28; Roy Hardiman 'Toward the Right of Commerciality: Recognising Property Rights in the Commercial Value of Human Tissue' (1986) 34 *UCLA Law Review* 207; Michelle Bourianoff Bray 'Personalizing Personalty: Toward a Property Right in Human Bodies' (1990) 69 *Texas Law Review* 209; Courtney Campbell 'Body, Self, and the Property Paradigm' (1992) 22(5) *Hastings Center Report* 34; Roger Magnusson 'The Recognition of Proprietary Rights in Human Tissue in Common Law Jurisdictions' (1992) 18 *Melbourne University Law Review* 601; Stephen Munzer 'Kant and Property Rights in Body Parts' (1993) 6 *Canadian Journal of Law and Jurisprudence* 319; Brian Hannemann 'Body

Parts and Property Rights: A New Commodity for the 1990s' (1993) 22 *Southwestern University Law Review* 399; Paul Matthews 'The Man of Property' (1995) 3 *Medical Law Review* 251; Danielle Wagner 'Property Rights in the Human Body: The Commercialisation of Organ Transplantation and Biotechnology' (1995) 33 *Duquesne Law Review* 931.

51   The statement of facts is summarised from the judgement of Panelli J, in the majority: *Moore v Regents of the University of California* 793 P2d 479 (Cal 1990), 480–481.

52   Ibid, 483.

53   Ibid, 497 per Arabian J.

54   '[O]ur society acknowledges a profound ethical imperative to respect the human body as the physical and temporal expression of the human persona. One manifestation of that respect is our prohibition against direct abuse of the body by torture or other forms of cruel or unusual punishment. Another is our prohibition against indirect abuse of the body by its economic exploitation for the sole benefit of another person. The most abhorrent form of such exploitation, of course, was the institution of slavery. Lesser forms, such as indentured servitude or even debtor's prison, have also disappeared. Yet their specter haunts the laboratories and boardrooms of today's biotechnological research-industrial complex. It arises wherever scientists or industrialists claim, as defendants claim here, the right to appropriate and exploit a patient's tissue for their sole economic benefit — the right, in other words, to freely mine or harvest valuable physical properties of the patient's body'. Ibid, 515–516 per Mosk J.

55   Perhaps the best known and most influential account of this dependency status of the possessive individual is to be found in Carole Pateman's *The Sexual Contract* (Cambridge: Polity Press, 1988). See also Ngaire Naffine *Law and the Sexes: Explorations in Feminist Jurisprudence* (Sydney: Allen and Unwin, 1990).

56   Patrick Atiyah *The Rise and Fall of Freedom of Contract* (Oxford: Clarendon Press, 1979), 727.

57   Ibid, 729.

58   Ibid, 717.

59   Reich 'The New Property', 770.

60   Ibid, 773.

61   Kant *Lectures on Ethics*, 165.

62   Marx was essentially concerned with the plight of the male worker.

63   See Istvan Meszaros *Marx's Theory of Alienation* (London: Merlin Press, 1970) for a sustained analysis of Marx's view of the commodified person.

64   R H Tawney *The Acquisitive Society* (Brighton, Sussex: Wheatsheaf Books, 1982,1st ed 1921), 37.

65   McPherson, *The Political Theory of Possessive Individualism,* 273.

66   Ibid, 3.

67   Ibid, 271.

68   Jennifer Nedelsky 'Property in Potential Life? A Relational Approach to Choosing Legal Categories' (1993) 6 *Canadian Journal of Law and Jurisprudence* 343, 350.

69   Radin's 'property for personality' is one such model. Another, discussed at length by Nedelsky, is a view of property in the self as suggesting a caretaker or custodianship relationship. Nedelsky rejects this as a possibility — not because it is theoretically unattractive, but because it is unrealistic in a capitalist world.

70   Jennifer Nedelsky 'Property in Potential Life?'; 'Law, Boundaries, and the Bounded Self' in Robert Post (ed) *Law and the Order of Culture* (University of California Press, 1991). See also Ngaire Naffine 'The Body Bag' in Ngaire Naffine and Rosemary Owens (eds) *Sexing the Subject of Law* (Sydney: Law Book Company, 1997), 79.

2 From *Dominium* to 'Thin Air': Concepts of Property

Introduction

The Roman concept of *dominium* has been a defining idea in the history of European and Western notions of property. Although common law property rights have always been more limited, contextual, and relational than *dominium*, the Roman concept has nonetheless served as a benchmark against which lesser notions of property have been measured. In addition, something akin to *dominium* has had a powerful symbolic function both within the legal and socio-political arenas as the most absolute and ideal expression of property, thus strengthening the notions of property as sovereignty, and of the person as absolute owner of the self. Starting with the Roman category of *dominium*, this chapter traces the historical development of various concepts of property and tenure, and explores aspects of the relationship between property and legal personality. We will briefly examine the English feudal system and the expansion of the domain of private property commencing with the gradual collapse of that system. Finally, we will consider modern philosophies of property. Examination of civil law concepts of property, which were the direct inheritors of Roman law, is unfortunately beyond the scope of the chapter.

The primary purpose of the chapter is to illustrate the historical nature of the concept of property and, in so doing, to consider the connection of the concept of property to political and economic discourses throughout legal history. In sketching the heritage of different concepts of property, we will suggest that the modern legal, philosophical, and cultural characterisations of property each incorporate different and sometimes contradictory components from our legal history. Specifically, we will argue that the rhetoric of self-ownership has tended to draw upon a fairly simple notion of property involving actual possession, the right to control and exclude, and the sovereignty of mind over bodies, a theme which will be further developed in Chapter Three.

The Significance of Property

The nature of property, and its relationship to the socio-political order, has attracted an enormous amount of attention in a variety of academic disciplines, especially philosophy, politics and law. It has also, perhaps to state the obvious, played a crucial role in non-academic political and legal discourse, and has been at the centre of many major social upheavals and revolutions. Property concerns the relationships between human beings and all things — physical or conceptual — which can be made into resources.[1] It therefore also intimately concerns the structure of the social relationships between people.

In liberal legal thought, one of the primary methods human beings have of relating to the world's physical and abstract resources is by appropriating them. Much of the world of objects is owned by individual legal persons (including corporations and other artificial legal persons). Fundamental to our law is a distinction between subjects, who are individual entities holding rights and duties, and objects, which are external to the person, incapable of having rights, and defined by the fact that they are owned, controlled or dominated by legal subjects. Of course, the distinction is not always rigorously maintained. Prior to the twentieth century, a woman could be a legal subject for some purposes, such as her criminal liability, but was still legally controlled by her husband or father. Slaves, children, people with mental disabilities, and arguably animals have been (and in some instances still are) in this ambiguous position of having some rights or immunities of their own,[2] while also being subjected to the legal control of another.

These are issues which we will consider further in Chapter Three, but several matters need to be mentioned at this point. First, the distinction between the legal subject and the legal object of rights is most under stress where human beings are regarded as not completely deserving of full human status. This tension is to be expected given that Western beliefs about the world only ascribe spirit to animate beings, and generally only to human beings. Within our predominantly liberal mode of thought, there is little question of regarding the inanimate earth or heavens as anything other than a resource for current or (occasionally) future generations,[3] although, as we will see, this has not always been true of Western society. That which is outside the category of the human has little or no moral status. Moreover, since political and social supremacy has been largely determined by race, class, and gender, it is unsurprising that some human beings have historically been accorded fewer rights than the bundle envisaged by the standard human ideal.

Second, the category of property is sufficiently flexible in modern law to make any bright line between person and property difficult to maintain. There are many borderline cases of 'objects', such as the foetus, the image, a person's genetic information, and body parts, which do not fit easily into either category. The fundamental liberal distinction between person and property is therefore very difficult to delineate clearly.

The individual human being, or legal person created in the image of a human being, is the cornerstone of the concept of property assumed by liberal legal thought. This individual is distinguished both from other individuals, and also from the world of objects, which, because they are objects, may be appropriated. However, it would be wrong to claim that the philosophies of individualism and humanism simply precede and determine private property. The reverse is equally true, that is, the concept of property gives shape and meaning to individualism.[4] As we saw in Chapter One, the person and property, as the two fundamental elements of the liberal world order, are mutually constituting. The creation and protection of private property buttresses the impression we have of the separate human entity, just as the individual lays claim to ownership and control of her or his self and environment.

Debates about the nature and political significance of property have taken a number of forms. First, there is a large philosophical literature concerning the moral, economic, or political justification of property. This commentary asks whether there is a natural right to private property, or whether the economic interests of society will be served by respecting private property.[5] A smaller, but nonetheless equally complex body of legal literature concerns the jurisprudence of property. Over the past hundred years, lawyers have debated the status of 'property' as a legal concept. In particular, they have questioned whether it is essentially different from other legal categories, and whether it has intrinsic characteristics or is comprised of a 'bundle of rights' which are distinct and severable.[6]

Several critical traditions, both within and outside the discipline of law, consider property in a historical and political setting. Such work does not always engage with the substantive arguments which are advanced in favour of the recognition of property as a natural right, nor with the technical legal debates over the concept of property in law, but rather considers the significance and political consequences of the concept and institution of property within its historical, social and ideological context. Traditionally it is Marxist thought which poses the most sustained and detailed theoretical critique of the institution of private property. However, feminist critiques of property have also posed a strong challenge to established notions of property, by showing how they metaphorically reinforce gender stereotypes.[7] The restrictions on women owning property, which have persisted until recently, have also provided a point of departure for feminists concerned with the nature and distribution of property. The literature concerning property is therefore large, complex, and lacking distinct boundaries, and we have not attempted to be comprehensive in our coverage of it. In this chapter, we have concentrated upon those aspects of the scholarship which have a direct bearing upon the relationship of persons and property.

As many legal commentators have noticed, the term 'property' is used popularly to designate an object which a person owns, as in 'this car/pen/table is my property'.[8] Such a usage tends to emphasise a particular concept of property and particular types of objects which can be owned, and which might be said to possess at least three characteristics: first, that property relates to a physical thing; second, that it has to do with a unique relationship between a person and an object; and third, that property is typically about physical things which we possess.[9] The clear implication of the usual claim that an object is a person's 'property' is that the owner, and no-one else, has the right to deal with it as she or he pleases.

It is usual at this stage in a commentary on property to observe that the popular concept is not the same as the technical legal concept, for the following reasons. Property is not a thing, but rather a right which a person has in relation to a thing. That right is often said to be *in rem*, as opposed to *in personam*, meaning that a property right, unlike a contractual right, is enforceable against the whole world, and not against a particular person or class of persons.[10] Therefore property is not a relationship between a person and a thing, but rather a relationship between persons with respect to things.[11] Moreover, as any lawyer knows, property is not necessarily about physical things, does not depend upon the right to possession (though it may be derived from actual possession),[12] and nearly always stops far short of the absolute right to deal with an object as one chooses.

It would be very easy to dismiss so called 'popular' conceptions of property as unsophisticated, non-technical and of little relevance to an inquiry about the nature of property. Such a rejection of the popular may indeed be required of formalistic legal approaches which deal with (in theory) precise categories and with an institution which is supposed to be entirely a creation of positive law, but it fails to recognise that the discourse of property takes place on many levels and in many registers.

Dominium: The (Nearly) Ideal Form

The Roman concept of *dominium* is frequently invoked as an absolute and indivisible recognition of property rights, often in order to contrast the relative and divisible property constructions of the common law. Although Roman *dominium* and its civil law derivatives are in this way conceptually opposed to the property notions of the common law,[13] Roman *dominium* has also undoubtedly exerted some influence on the common law concept of property — on both the formulation and exposition of the law and, in liberal thought, on the ideological evocation of (a certain kind of) property as a political and social necessity.

Several different types of ownership were legally recognised at different stages of the Roman civilisation. At its height, *dominium* named only the greatest of the possible interests and 'implie[d] a Roman owner of a Roman thing acquired by a Roman process'.[14] It was therefore limited by *who* could own (a foreigner or slave could not), by the *class* of thing which was owned, and by the *process* by which the thing was acquired. That is, title was acquired by the formal processes specifically laid down by Roman, or civil, law, as opposed to the more general methods of so-called '*ius gentium*'.[15] Ownership by non-Roman citizens of non-Roman lands, or according to transfers made in a non-civil law form, gave rise to lesser sorts of interests.[16]

Lee notes that by the time of Justinian's *Institutes,* 'these distinctions had become unimportant'. For instance, originally the status of Roman citizen was confined to citizens of the precincts of Rome itself. In 212 AD, Roman citizenship became more generally available throughout the Empire, meaning that the class of people who could hold *dominium* was also greatly expanded.[17] The distinctions between types of property did not, however, disappear altogether as a result of such reforms. Usufructuary rights were still common, as were 'servitudes' (the equivalent of common law easements), and both of these types of interest are discussed at some length in the *Institutes*.[18] Subject to the existence of one of these lesser interests, *dominium* comprised essentially the right to use, dispose of, destroy and otherwise control an object in the most extensive fashion recognised by the law.[19] Although *dominium* was the ultimate title, it was evidently not absolute. The owner of land was then, as now, restricted not only by any rights of use held by others, but also by various laws protecting the interests of neighbours and the requirements of agriculture.[20] Even so, *dominium* was essentially indivisible and its derivatives in the civil law jurisdictions are relatively inflexible or 'rather stolid' asGray and Symes have put it.[21] The absolute character of *dominium* then, may be said to refer not so much to the level of rights conferred, but rather to the fact that such rights were basically unitary. Lesser rights could not simply be carved at will out of *dominium*.[22]

This schematic description of *dominium* belies the complexity of its historical development, a few features of which are worth mentioning.[23] *Dominium* is said to derive from the familial structure of early (pre-historical) Roman society in which the *paterfamilias* of the household group (which extended well beyond the limits of the modern nuclear family) had a general power (*patria potestas*) over all household elements essential to the rural economy, including his wife, other free family members, slaves, animals, and land.[24] *Patria potestas* was not a right of ownership as such, but rather a general undifferentiated political, economic, and personal authority.[25] Authority over persons and authority over things were not clearly distinguished because both were integral to the early rural economy; nor was lordship distinguished from ownership. Although the *paterfamilias* may have *effectively* owned the household, such ownership did not have a distinct conceptual existence as a property right, but was rather the result of the general power.

Diósdi explains that the movement from the generalised power (which united personal, political and economic relations) to the more specific concept of ownership occurred as a result of several social and economic changes which took place between the third and second centuries BC.[26] First, the number of slaves increased (due to expansion of Roman territory, and wars) and therefore they were no longer regarded as an integral part of the household, but rather as economic resources or things.[27] Secondly, the *economic* value of free family members decreased as a direct result of the increasing economic reliance on slaves: free family members therefore became institutionally and conceptually separated from the things of economic value. Third, a growing commercial, as opposed to peasant, economy, meant that the economic world was expanded beyond the confines of the traditional household. Therefore, the *res mancipi* —

those things originally having particular value as integral to the peasant economy — lost their primary economic status. Other factors which, according to Diósdi, influenced the consolidation of *dominium* as a concept include the development of a legal distinction between ownership and possession, rising individualism, and increasing awareness of Greek scientific and philosophical habits of abstract thought.[28]

One of the most interesting aspects of the story of the early development of the Roman concept of property is that it appears to have arisen over several centuries as a result of a gradual separation of the realm of persons from the realm of fungible things.[29] By the time the great legal treatises of Gaius and Justinian appeared, the distinction was completely entrenched, and was reflected in the legal distinction between the law of persons and the law of things. Slaves occupied an ambiguous position as both human and property,[30] although throughout the Classical period, the rights of slaves were strengthened.[31] We can see that personality and property crystallise as opposites from the socio-economic changes which liberated some people from their subservience to the economic demands of the household to which they belonged (presumably at first from the more wealthy and powerful families) while reducing other human beings to a primarily fungible status. At the same time, the domain of economically valuable things extended well beyond the agriculturally useful. Put very simply, both the rights of the person and property rights over objects were derived from the general power of *patria potestas*.

Although the person and property are construed as opposites within modern legal thought, as they essentially were within the developed Roman system,[32] they are still metaphorically and ideologically bound together as aspects of an exclusionary, controlling, and categorising power. Today, the person legally *cannot* be the property of another and that which is property cannot be a person (although we will explore cases where this is not so clear cut). However, socially some human beings have been effectively owned and objectified, in particular women and children. And, as we have indicated in Chapter One, the ideal of the person rests upon a symbolic and sometimes actual construction of the person as the property of the self, that is, as a 'possessive individual'. Although it would be impossible to trace thoroughly the development of these ideas of person and property from ancient sources, it is interesting to note the mutuality of their early formation.

One further matter to note about the history of the Roman concept of ownership is the increasing differentiation between the idea of the *dominus* as master or political superior, and that of *dominus* as owner, which helped to sharpen the legal definition of *dominium*. It is questionable whether political superiority has ever *effectively* been separated from ownership, as we will see in the next chapter. Ownership confers power over others, and power over others is often expressed as a denial of the other's self-ownership, even where equality and autonomy are explicitly asserted. However, the development of a modern liberal idea of the person as free, equal and individual, regardless of the status conferred by property, required a separation of the concepts of (public) political superiority and (private) relationships of property. We can see some early signs of this distinction, although within a different political context, in Roman law.

Feudal Properties

Feudal societies also lacked a sharp distinction between personal and political power. The feudal political structure was comprised of a socio-economic hierarchy headed by the king: political and social status were essentially the same thing, and such status was fixed by one's relationship to a system of estates in land.[33] Here again, the power of ownership and that of lordship were not clearly distinguished, although the situation was arguably more complicated than under Roman law, the reason being that any feudal lord, barring the king, was also the tenant of another.

Making complete sense of a feudal concept of property is an almost impossible task because of the doctine of tenure, which made all land holding conditional upon the performance of a service.[34] David Seipp's historical research indicates that the term 'property' was not used in relation to land by legal practitioners and judges in the thirteenth-century Year Books, the earliest reports of cases available in England.[35] Although both *proprietas* and *dominium* were used to refer to land by the twelfth and thirteenth century treatise writers, notably Glanvill and Bracton, this usage was possibly derived from Roman texts, rather than reflecting the state of the common law.[36] The term 'property' was used to refer to goods and domestic animals, and occupied a much more marginal place in legal, economic, and political organisation than it does today.[37] By contrast, land, or real property, is now often taken as the archetypal case of property, even though the economic significance of land is arguably in decline.[38]

In feudal England, then, land itself was not clearly 'property' and certainly not in the modern sense, although there was a multitude of actions — possessory or as of right (that is, the assertion of some title greater than possession) — relating to various rights arising from land.[39] One of the most obvious reasons for the non-proprietary character of land was that the rights and responsibilities of both lords and tenants of land in the feudal system were so structured that no-one could reasonably be said to have the extensive rights in relation to land which would amount to property or ownership. Taking a full conception of property as our benchmark, land simply did not qualify. For instance Baker comments:

> Feudal tenure was the antithesis of ownership as we know it. Before the advent of the common law, the tenant enjoyed few of the privileges which we now attribute to an owner. He could not do what he liked with the land. He could not sell it without the lord's consent. He could not pass it on to others by will [at first the succession was at the discretion of the lord, and later determined by custom], and there was no legally enforceable right of succession in his family after his death.[40]

Similarly, the immediate lord of any tenant was not an 'owner' of the land because he (or occasionally she) was the tenant of someone else, if only the king, and had certain obligations which arose from the land itself. 'Only the king was not a tenant; but no king after William I had the kind of control exercised in the 1070s, and no one thought of the lord king as being in any meaningful sense owner of all the land in England'.[41] By contrast, 'owners' of land are no longer tied to it, nor owe such structured duties to others. However, modern legislative controls, reflecting a rising environmental consciousness and even the resurgence of claims to customary 'landrights',[42] suggest that the era of relatively unfettered property in land is well and truly over.

The feudal relationship to land was therefore not one of 'ownership', but was more akin to guardianship or custodianship. This was entirely in keeping with the teaching of the medieval theologians, who regarded human beings as the stewards of the earth's resources.[43] As Atiyah observes:

> In medieval times the very concept of absolute ownership was scarcely recognised: it would have been repugnant to the nature of

that society to admit that a man was absolutely free to do what he
wanted with his property, as it was repugnant to think that a man
was free to do anything at all. In that sort of world men were not
absolutely free; they owed duties to their feudal lord, to their fellow
men, to the Church, to God; and their 'tenure' of property was a
transient thing. A man in possession of property was the temporary
custodian of it rather than an owner; property was a 'responsible
office' carrying duties as well as rights.[44]

Even now, at the height of capitalism, the notion of custodianship,
particularly custodianship of land,[45] has not fully disappeared, and still
provides the occasion for conflict between landowners (or even tenants)
wishing to assert full and exclusive control of a tract of land, and those
concerned with maintaining the vestiges of common rights. For instance,
the British Parliament has been attempting to find some balance between
landowners and the 'ramblers' whose aim is to preserve the ancient rights
of way.[46] In some cases, even more extensive common 'landrights' are
being claimed.[47] Of course, the more widely recognised landrights
campaigns concern dispossessed and indigenous peoples. In Australia,
customary rights have been asserted by the Aboriginal people, and have
resulted in a formal recognition of 'native title', a constructed form of
common property which challenges both the doctrine of tenure and notions
of private property as individually owned and fully alienable.[48]

Towards the Absolute: Blackstone and Beyond

By the eighteenth century, property had changed completely. Land holding
had been transformed, becoming much more like the 'property' recognised
by modern law. Ownership and political power were in the process of
being philosophically distinguished by a nascent liberalism. Of course, a
distinction between property ownership and political power was not
formally established until the granting of 'universal' suffrage.[49] Because
property *is* a form of power over others,[50] it is debatable whether (public)
political power and (private) property can ever be separated in practice.
Clearly, however, between the thirteenth and the eighteenth centuries some
major social, legal, economic, and political movements took place, which
completely changed the nature of the formal and symbolic relationship
between persons and property. These changes centred upon the rise of

'possessive individualism',[51] that is, upon an increasing consciousness of the distinctness of each self-owning human entity as the primary social and political value.

As Atiyah explains, the rise of the concept of the free individual was accompanied by the rise in the concept of absolute and freely-held property.[52] Feudal persons were not defined by their relationships to *property,* as we currently understand it,[53] but rather by their position within a system of estates and tenures in land. The rise of freely-owned property as a significant economic and socio-political determinant and the rise of the possessive individual were parallel movements. Indeed, Atiyah makes it clear that the autonomous individual possessed of the capacity to make free political, social, and economic choices, *presupposed* an individual free of the obligations of tenure, and who was able to deal with the primary economic resource — the land — in a relatively unconstrained fashion.[54] The free person presupposed the existence of land holding unconstrained by feudal tenures. It is interesting to observe some parallel here with the history of the Roman idea of *dominium.* As we noted above, the division between persons and property/things gradually congealed into distinct areas of law from a common origin. Similarly, the transition from feudal to modern law involved the liberation of persons from feudal estates, and the conceptualisation of land as being transferable in ways other than those laid down by the doctrine of tenure.

It would be too ambitious to attempt to explain, in any detail, the complex changes in the socio-legal order which facilitated what Maine called the movement from 'status to contract'.[55] This would, in any case, take us too far into the depths of legal history, which is not our principal concern. Suffice it to say that relationship to land, and therefore personal identity, was gradually freed from the 'suits and services' which defined feudalism.[56] The consequence was that it became possible to imagine a free individual with fairly full property rights. Eventually this imagined person turned into a social and legal reality. It became possible to contract out of one's feudal obligations which were in turn largely abolished.[57]

A crucial step in the process of freeing the individual from the land, and the land from the system of tenure, was the statute *Quia Emptores* (1290) which stated that 'from henceforth it shall be lawful for every freeman to sell at his own pleasure his lands and tenements, or part thereof'.[58] Simpson explains that the statute protected the economic interests of the lord and 'is a striking illustration of the lack of importance which by this time was attached to the personal relationship of lord and tenant; lords were more interested in protecting their incidents than in selecting their tenants'.[59] The development of the 'use' meant that it was possible to bypass the common law rules of inheritance which meant that land was not subject to testamentary disposition, but automatically descended to the heir.[60] In 1540, the *Statute of Wills* made it possible to devise land by will in the same way that it was devisable *inter vivos*. Effectively, real property was increasingly analogised to chattels as fully 'propertisable'. (However, primogeniture continued to apply to real property in cases of intestacy until the nineteenth century.)

The commodity status of land was further strengthened by the enclosure movement. Enclosure of what was previously common land took place by private agreement from the sixteenth century, and by parliamentary intervention from the late eighteenth century.[61] The gradual submersion of custom under the weight of the more flexible legislative order resulted in a weakening and, eventually, the virtual elimination, of the complex system of common rights which provided basic support for the majority of people. Thus land was separated from the person, and the person was separated from land, opening the way for land ownership, and an altogether more extensive notion of property.

William Blackstone is, almost without fail, cited in discussions of the concept of property, partly because of his importance as a legal commentator in a critical period in English legal history, and also because of the striking way in which he declared in his *Commentaries on the Laws of England* an absolute conception of property, which by this time clearly applied to land, goods, and animals, as well as to a range of other (for instance incorporeal) things. Blackstone's *Commentaries* are widely regarded as a great distillation of the social and legal consciousness of the eighteenth century. Although aspects of the *Commentaries* may not have been entirely legally accurate, and thus have been strongly criticised, the work blended the growing ideology of individualism with prevailing legal ideas, becoming enormously influential as an authoritative statement of law.

Blackstone famously described property as 'the sole and despotic dominion which one man claims and exercises over the external things of the world, in total exclusion of the right of any other individual in the universe'.[62] In one condensed thought, this evocation of the absolute brings together the elements of exclusion, individual sovereignty, immediate relationship to external things, the limiting of objects, and assured individual identity in the figure of the 'one man'. Whether such a description of property has ever been fully reflective of the law is open to some debate. It is clear, for instance, that there have *always* been some restrictions on the things which can be owned, the uses to which they are put, and even the degree and means of exclusion which may be exercised.[63]

Nevertheless, Blackstone's idealised form of property, evoking Roman *dominium*, suggests at the very least a symbolism of property which persists in modern popular, ideological, and economic discourse. The idea of property as private sovereignty is exceptionally widespread,[64] and has been of immense influence in shaping Western political institutions. It is also, not coincidentally, reflected in the symbolism of the person as distinct, bounded and self-determining. In essence, as we saw in the last chapter, the right to private property is seen to ensure the security of the individual against the potential excesses of the state and, more broadly, the ability of each individual to control his destiny and to engage in public life on an equal footing with others. Thus private property is said to erect a boundary or 'area of non-interference' which is essentially an extension of the person into the external world and represents a zone of absolute freedom. Such a view is strongly represented in the work of such modern liberals as Charles Reich and Isaiah Berlin.[65] Of course, the trouble with the private sovereignty conception of property is that such sovereignty is never truly private, since property brings power not only over things, but also over other people and thus reaches well beyond the confines of a person's own self.[66] The notion of an inviolable private realm, still largely based on a patriarchal familial order, has also resulted in State blindness to violence within the domain of private property.

Hohfeld and the Crisis of Property

Blackstone's 'sole and despotic dominion' therefore encapsulates one predominant view of the rights supposedly associated with private property. By contrast to this very strong and specific notion of property, which owes as much to Roman law and the emerging liberal consciousness as it does to the common law, it is sometimes now said that property is suffering an identity crisis.[67] This assertion does not refer to any measurable breakdown in private ownership, but rather to the fact that the current legal conception of property appears to be more fluid, more adaptable, and less definable than it once was. Certainly Blackstone's 'sole and despotic dominion' no longer represents a widely held legal view of property, even though it is still probably the dominant understanding of property in social and political discourse.[68] The rights afforded by property are no longer absolutely distinguishable from those offered by other legal categories; property no longer carries a clearly-identifiable set of incidents; it is no longer regarded as an inviolable frontier between the private person and others (notably the State); and it refers to an increasingly complex and abstract array of objects. Of course, to state that a concept or an institution is in crisis does not necessarily signal a decline, but may rather indicate a reorientation, an expansion, a reconstruction. Certainly it suggests a negative or disaggregating tendency, but not necessarily a destructive one.[69]

The origin of the modern understanding of property as 'disaggregated' is generally traced to two articles by Wesley Newcombe Hohfeld, published in 1913 and 1917.[70] Hohfeld's distinct contribution to property theory was to conceptualise property as nothing more than a relationship between persons. Put simply, property is not a unique and pre-legal bond between a person and a thing, but rather a bundle of legal rights and obligations. In the terminology which has been characteristic of property theory, Hohfeld argued that a right *in rem* (against the world) is only different from a right *in personam* (against a particular person) because it gives rise to a greater number of corresponding duties.[71] Property in an object is not primarily a right to it. The right is only secondary to, or derivative of, the fact that every other person has a duty not to interfere with the owner's enjoyment of the object. The *right to the thing*, which an owner might feel that she has, is really composed of the legal duty which everyone else has not to interfere with the object of property. The point is that whatever the owner's emotional attachment to the object, or her moral justification of her ownership of it, legally speaking, property is only the cumulative effect of legal obligations between people.

The pre-eminent twentieth-century positivist Hans Kelsen has explained the idea of property as a mere construction of positive law:

> Since the law as a social order regulates the behaviour of individuals in their direct or indirect relations to other individuals, property, too, can legally consist only in a certain relation between one individual and other individuals. This relation is: the obligation of these other individuals not to disturb the first one in his disposition over a certain thing. What is described as the exclusive

'dominion' of an individual over a thing is the legally stipulated exclusion of all others from the disposition over this thing. The dominion of the one is merely the reflex of the exclusion of all the others.[72]

Therefore the structure of property as understood by post-Hohfeldian property theorists is rather like the structure of subjectivity or the structure of meaning as understood by postmodern theorists.[73] It is an *effect* of relationships, or of a system of signs, not an already-existent category, and still less a unique or original bond between an intentional being and an object. Property has no positive content other than that which is conferred by law. We could even say that its positive content is merely an illusion which derives from negative legal relations.[74] This content takes the form of a number of possible incidents of ownership (such as the rights to possession, use, enjoyment, alienation),[75] none of which are *necessary* to the legal recognition that a right is a property right. We can, after all, own something without having the immediate right to possess, enjoy, or use it, for instance, land or an object which is leased to another. We may even own a thing without having any right to alter it (heritage property) or to transfer it (prescription drugs).

The Hohfeldian view is most compatible with a fairly thorough legal positivist approach which asserts that law is nothing more than an artificial human construction with no necessary moral or natural content.[76] By contrast, the idea that property might consist, to some degree, in a relation between a person and a thing tends to lead the analysis of property beyond the confines of positive law, because it places emphasis upon what may be a particular individual's attachment to a thing, rather than upon an agreed legal relationship. The Hohfeldian and positivist views regard any special relation between a person and their objects as outside the domain of law. An emotional, moral, or need-based attachment would be irrelevant to the concerns of positive law, which is concerned solely with shared human constructs. Our legal relationship to a thing is therefore only derivative of such constructs.

The positivist nature of the Hohfeldian account is therefore reasonably clear, although it would be overstating the case to claim that positivism and the Hohfeldian view are co-extensive. Many accounts of property have attempted to ground, explain, or justify positive law by reference to some extrinsic (natural or socially conditioned) bond between person and thing. For instance, the idea of first occupancy as a 'natural' justification for property is sometimes said to provide a reason for the weight given by common law to actual possession.[77] Some theorists have tended to regard ownership as a natural relationship or a natural right, one which ought to be reflected in and protected by law, or which gives credence to the positive law structure of private property, and which exists in principle regardless of particular legal provision.[78] By contrast, the positivist view is that properly *proprietal* relationships are constructed purely by law. Jeremy Bentham went so far as to say that 'Property and law are born together, and die together. Before laws were made there was no property; take away laws, and property ceases'.[79]

Is property then, nothing but a legal fiction? From the point of view of a positivist, who looks to the law's own constructions to ascertain the nature of its concepts, rather than to any external social or moral arena, the case is a compelling one. Kevin Gray, for instance, claims that property is a category wholly constructed by law and, like any other legal category, is a fiction. That is, it does not reflect, but rather constructs, its objects.[80] Law itself is said to rest upon a 'legitimate fiction' or, more accurately, the fiction of legitimacy.[81] According to Kelsen, positive law gains its legitimacy by virtue of the fact that we act *as if* it had objective or factual existence.[82] As a category entirely constructed by law, property depends entirely upon this fiction. (Clearly the person is also a legal fiction, as we will see in the next chapter, being nothing more than a bundle of rights, legal capacities, and responsibilities.[83]) However, to describe property as a fiction is not an attempt to demolish or even deconstruct property as a category.[84] It is, rather, to demystify the idea that property has some natural existence independent of the law and of state enforcement of ownership regimes. It does not eliminate property, but rather liberates property from its traditional constraints. As Gray comments:

> If 'property' is not a thing but a power relationship, the range of resources in which 'property' can be claimed is significantly larger than is usually conceded by orthodox legal doctrine. (This is indeed the source of both the greatest challenge and the greatest danger confronting the law of property in the 21st century.). . . By lending the support of the state to the assertion of control over access to the benefits of particular resources, the courts have it in their power to create 'property'.[85]

If 'property' is constrained only by the limits of prevailing ideas about which resources can morally be taken out of common circulation, then it has the potential to intrude even further into human relationships.[86] Moreover, if it is not composed of a number of necessarily-joined incidents, but is rather a bundle of separable sticks, then any legal relationship resembling one of the incidents or sticks might be taken to be a proprietal relationship. Jeanne Schroeder has argued that one consequence of this potential 'disaggregation' of property is that the language of ownership can be used in increasingly abstract ways to refer to any right.[87]

Therefore the so-called 'identity crisis'[88] of property is itself an ambiguous and politically indeterminate phenomenon. It may signal the death of property rights, or the death of a unique and individuated concept of property. It may simply recognise the completely constructed nature of a property right, or some fluidity in the potential objects of property. It may even suggest the liberation of property from its traditional conceptual constraints, leading to its uncontrollable dissemination as idea, metaphor, and legal relationship.[89] It is undeniable, however, that the rhetoric of property has significant political purchase, and that the modern flexibility of the concept enables it to be deployed in a multitude of ways, many of which we will consider in later chapters. The successful characterisation of a thing as an object of property, a process which takes place in everyday language, in law, and in political discourse, can be of immense strategic value both in engineering and retarding social change.

Metaphorical Extensions: Property and Power

As we have seen, the development of liberal philosophy depended on the notion that each man is owner of himself, and therefore can command external resources, but cannot be owned by another. Yet the law was slow to extend this principle to those who were not regarded as fully capable, or whose interests were suppressed in order to maintain the economic and political power base of the privileged white man.[90] Such formal legal recognition is now fairly uniform in the liberal West, and yet social relationships are still extensively constructed around the idea of property (where property is basically Blackstonian private sovereignty). Consequently, the claim of self-ownership is still a strategically powerful argument and is frequently invoked to counteract the social control of some people by others. It might also be surmised that actual patterns of ownership are indirectly influenced by notions of the typical self-owner, who is also the ideal owner of external resources (including social ownership of other people).

It is this social power which positivist property theory tends to deny in its efforts to delineate a purely legal concept of property. Positivist property theory is analytically useful in clarifying the *legal* source of property claims. However, precisely because it defines law and property in a positivistic fashion — that is, as owing their existence purely to a set of factual, state-based, institutions — positivist theory contributes little to a broader understanding of the social function of the idea of property. It does not help us to appreciate what its political potential might be and, most importantly, how the legal and non-legal domains interact in ways completely beyond the comprehension of positive law. Such questions are defined out of existence by positivist theory, making it all the more necessary to ask them. It is therefore important to consider the interrelationship of a law constructed as autonomous and the social environment in which it is situated, not only because law is a culturally-specific institution, but also because it is necessarily read and interpreted in the context of social relationships and presuppositions. A brief overview of some feminist scholarship on the gendering of the institution and concept of property will help us to explain what we mean.

It is uncontroversial to say that, even within the liberal West, actual ownership is very largely the preserve of men, and that male power and the power over others conferred by property are mutually reinforcing.[91] This is not to suggest that all economic divisions align solely, or even primarily, with gender, because clearly property also divides individuals and communities along the lines of their class, race and political position within a global economy.[92] However, one of the central social distinctions related closely to the idea and the fact of private property is that of gender. The liberation of the person from socially-imposed status did not originally extend to women. The current gendered distribution of property, and the political and private power it brings, is at least partly due to the former legal incapacity of married women, whose property passed to their husband upon marriage. Women remained legally defined by their relationship to a man or a family until the passing of the various Married Women's Property Acts.[93]

However, a more complex set of social and legal relationships underlie the fact of a gendered division of property. As we indicated in

Chapter One, the notion of self-ownership is itself gendered. Because property is typically seen as territorial, closed, and inviolable, conceptions of self-ownership more closely reflect perceptions of the male body, rather than the female body, which is supposedly lacking in such clear frontiers. As both Ngaire Naffine and Jennifer Nedelsky have illustrated,[94] women have to reassert constantly the principle of bodily integrity, rather than have it taken for granted. In socially-prevalent metaphors of heterosexual sex, women are represented as surrendering their boundaries, and, according to Naffine, this view of sex is reflected in law.[95] We will explore the gendering of the concept of self-possession further in Chapter Four. Moreover, self-ownership requires a conceptual division between the self as subject and the self as a physical object. Since women are under-represented as active agents in language, law, political discourse, and the symbolic order generally, 'self'-ownership for women appears irregular.[96] We may also observe that, where self-ownership is seen to be enhanced by ownership of external objects, those who own more will have an enhanced personality. To put none too fine a point on it, the wealthy have more 'personality' and more rights over others (even if such rights are characterised as 'private', they are still backed by the state). If the poor in our society are valued less as persons than are the wealthy, it is, as Tawney and McPherson both indicated, because personality and personal value are both strongly associated with ownership. Arguing that property augments personality may only exacerbate this perception, to the clear detriment of women and other groups over-represented in lower socio-economic strata.

Problems of unequal distribution of resources are not only indicative of oppression on the basis of sex. In 'Whiteness as Property', Cheryl Harris illustrates the economic value and the exclusionary mentality characteristic of notions of racial superiority. Her argument is that historically in the United States, whiteness became 'property'. As slaves, Black people were the objects of property and could not themselves be proprietors; whiteness was accorded status, privileges, rights, and immense value; and the borderline between whiteness and blackness was policed rigorously. As slaves, Black people did not own themselves, and, in any case, their persons were accorded far less social and legal value. Whiteness was an exclusive territory characterised by its legal purity. Although, as Harris says, some persons with more than a drop of Black blood could be considered white, the legal definitions were designed to ensure a strict delimitation of a territory of whiteness that no-one could enter who did not satisfy the blood requirements laid down by law.

Harris comments that 'whiteness and property share a common premise, a conceptual nucleus, of a right to exclude'.[97] 'In effect', she says, 'the courts erected legal "No Trespassing" signs'.[98] The metaphors of purity, boundary, and territorial exclusion are thus evidenced in the legal concept of whiteness that underpinned much of the history of race relations in the United States. Harris goes further than this, however, and argues that property in whiteness is still very much a part of the social context of law.

Conclusion

This chapter has traced some of the significant developments in the legal concept and political context of property, from Roman law to the present. Although detail has been sacrificed in order to contain a very complex story to a single chapter, several important themes have emerged.

We have seen that property is not an internally coherent concept which may be objectively described. It is rather a complex and plural concept, formed from a number of historical practices, legal principles, and political, social and economic ideals. The legal idea of property is strongly connected to liberal political ideals and to positivist legal theory, but different concepts of property emerge in different political contexts. Many of these concepts are evident in modern socio-legal debate about the nature of property. For instance, the current resurgence of the notion of custodianship in certain non-indigenous contexts is reminiscent of an embedded, but largely forgotten, idea of the common law. Antithetical as common custodianship might seem to modern notions of private property, it is interesting to reflect on the fact that the common law has historically recognised such a concept. And although *dominium* does not adequately reflect the common law understanding of property, it nonetheless has a strong hold on the legal imagination. We have also seen that the power of the concept of property extends well beyond its recognition by law. Property is a metaphor which underpins our construction of our selves and our social position.

Notes

1   We use the word 'resource' here loosely. An object of property need not be useful, nor of general (marketable) value. In practice, if a person claims a

property right, the object does have some value to that person, if to nobody else.

2   Clearly animals do not have 'rights' in the sense of having any legal standing to protect their interests. However, they have protectable interests in the sense that neglect of, or cruelty towards, animals is generally prohibited, these interests being protected by a third party. See, for instance, the *Prevention of Cruelty to Animals Act* (SA).

3   Cf. Irene Watson 'Indigenous People's Law-Ways: Survival Against the Colonial State' (1997) 8 *Australian Feminist Law Journal* 39; 'Power Of The Muldarbi, The Road To Its Demise' (1998) 11 *Australian Feminist Law Journal* 28.

4   CB MacPherson *The Political Theory of Possessive Individualism: Hobbes to Locke* (Oxford: Clarendon Press, 1964); Jennifer Nedelsky 'Law, Boundaries, and the Bounded Self' in Robert Post (ed) *Law and the Order of Culture* (Berkeley: University of California Press, 1991).

5   For instance, see John Locke *Two Treatises of Government* Peter Laslett (ed) 2nd ed (Cambridge: Cambridge University Press, 1960, first published 1690) *Second Treatise*; GWF Hegel *The Philosophy of Right* (TM Knox trans, Oxford: Oxford University Press, 1952, first published 1821); Robert Nozick *Anarchy, State and Utopia* (Oxford: Basil Blackwell, 1974); Jeremy Waldron *The Right to Private Property* (Oxford: Clarendon Press, 1988). An excellent article which surveys critically much of the literature and places the debate about justification within a concrete political setting is Jeremy Waldron 'Property, Justification, and Need' (1993) *Canadian Journal of Law and Jurisprudence* 185.

6   Wesley Newcombe Hohfeld 'Some Fundamental Legal Conceptions as Applied in Judicial Reasoning' (1913) 23 *Yale Law Journal* 16; 'Fundamental Legal Conceptions as Applied in Judicial Reasoning' (1917) 26 *Yale Law Journal* 710; Thomas Grey 'The Disintegration of Property' (1980) XXII *Nomos* 69; Charles Reich 'The Individual Sector' (1991) 100 *Yale Law Journal* 1409; Pavlos Eleftheriadis 'The Analysis of Property Rights' (1996) 16 *Oxford Journal of Legal Studies* 31; Alain Pottage 'Instituting Property' (1998) 18 *Oxford Journal of Legal Studies* 331; Brendan Edgeworth 'Post-property? A Postmodern Conception of Private Property' (1988) 11 *University of New South Wales Law Journal* 31; Carol Rose *Property and Persuasion: Essays on the History, Theory, and Rhetoric of Ownership* (Boulder: Westview Press, 1994); JE Penner *The Idea of Property in Law* (Oxford: Clarendon Press, 1997); Jeanne Schroeder *The Vestal and the Fasces* (Berkeley: University of California Press, 1998); Janet McLean (ed) *Property and the Constitution* (Oxford: Hart Publishing, 1999).

7   See in particular Ngaire Naffine 'The Body Bag' in Ngaire Naffine and Rosemary Owens (eds) *Sexing the Subject of Law* (Sydney: Law Book Company, 1997), 79; Nedelsky 'Law, Boundaries, and the Bounded Self', 162–189; Margaret Davies 'Queer Persons, Queer Property: Self-Ownership and Beyond' (1999) 8 *Social and Legal Studies* 327.

8   Hohfeld 'Some Fundamental Legal Conceptions as Applied in Judicial Reasoning' (1913).

9   At common law, the offence of larceny, for instance, concerned the removal of tangible objects.

10   This is generally true but a right *in rem* is not the same thing as a proprietary right. For instance, the right to bodily security is a right *in rem*, but it is not legally considered to be a property right. Of course, our entire project centres on the somewhat shadowy legal and rhetorical characterisation of human entities such as the body.

11   See also, for a brief description of the civil law position, FH Lawson (ed) *International Encyclopedia of Comparative Law Vol VI: Property and Trust* (Tübingen: JCB Mohr, 1978), 8.

12   Property may be derived from possession when a person finds an object, or in the case of adverse possession of real estate, which eventually will result in the original owner being barred from reclaiming possession — that is, when the period of limitation of actions has expired. See Carol Rose 'Possession as the Origin of Property' (1985) 52 *University of Chicago Law Review* 73, reprinted in Carol Rose *Property and Persuasion.*

13   See eg, KJ Gray and PD Symes *Real Property and Real People: Principles of Land Law* (London: Butterworths, 1981), 21.

14   Such title is formally called '*dominium ex jure Quiritium*'. RW Lee *The Elements of Roman Law* 4th ed. (London: Sweet and Maxwell, 1956), 111.

15   The distinction is explained in Justinian's *Institutes* Book I, Title II; see JAC Thomas *The Institutes of Justinian* (Amsterdam: North Holland Publishing Co, 1975). In contrast to modern thinking, which tends to distinguish between international law and natural law (the latter attracting widespread scepticism), in the ancient world, natural law and the universal law of peoples (*ius gentium*) were generally regarded as the same thing.

16   See Lee *The Elements of Roman Law,* 111. Such interests were, according to Lee, '1, ownership by peregrines; 2, ownership of provincial lands; 3, the so-called "bonitary ownership"'. The latter could, for instance, be the result of the situation arising where a thing which was supposed to be transferred by a particular process, was in fact transferred differently. Thomas explains that provincial lands were owned by the Roman state, although they were privately leased from the state, and could be transferred according to the *ius gentium*; JAC Thomas *Textbook of Roman Law* (Amsterdam: North Holland Publishing Co, 1976), 135. The distinction between Roman and provincial land was eliminated in several stages.

17   Lee *The Elements of Roman Law,* 111; Thomas *Textbook of Roman Law,* 136.

18   Book II, Titles III and IV, in Thomas *The Institutes of Justinian,* 85–90. See also David Johnston *Roman Law in Context* (Cambridge: Cambridge University Press, 1999), 67–70.

19   Dominium is sometimes characterised as '*ius utendi fruendi abutendi*' or 'the right to use, take the fruits of and abuse property': Thomas Glyn Watkin *An Historical Introduction to Modern Civil Law* (Aldershot: Dartmouth, 1999), 228.

20   Thomas *Textbook of Roman Law,* 133–134.

21   See eg, Gray and Symes *Real Property and Real People: Principles of Land Law*, 21.

22   An exception to this indivisibility of title appears to be the so-called 'bonitary' ownership, which arose if a *res mancipi* (slaves and beasts of burden, Italian land, and country servitudes/easements over Italian land) was transferred by mere delivery (*traditio*) instead of by one of the prescribed legal forms (mancipation or *cessio in iure*). However, a bonitary owner could achieve *dominium* by good faith possession of the thing for a defined period of time (*usucapio*). Lee *The Elements of Roman Law*, 119–124; Thomas *Textbook*, p. 136. Again, Justinian's abolition of the distinction between *res mancipi* and *res nec mancipi*, made the concept of bonitary ownership redundant.

23   For reasons of economy, this is a very simplified account, which omits as much as possible the technical terms used by the historians. An interesting summary of scholarly debates surrounding these matters is to be found in György Diósdi *Ownership in Ancient and Preclassical Roman Law* (Budapest: Akadémiai Kiadó, 1970). See also Charles Reinold Noyes *The Institution of Property: A Study of the Development, Substance, and Arrangement of the System of Property in Modern Anglo-American Law* (London: Longmans, Green and Co, 1936), ch 1 'The Organization of Early Roman Society'.

24   Noyes says that the term *potestas* was applied only to human beings, however, Diósdi claims that the word was also used to refer to chattels; Noyes *The Institution of Property*, 78; Diósdi *Ownership in Ancient and Preclassical Rome*, 54.

25   David Johnston *Roman Law in Context*, 30.

26   Summarised from Diósdi *Ownership in Ancient and Preclassical Roman Law*, 132–133.

27   Lee states the history quite succinctly: 'In the earliest times there were few slaves and the slave was a member of the household. Plutarch in his Life of Coriolanus tells us that in those days (5th cent. B.C.) the Romans treated their slaves with much consideration, for they worked and lived with them on equal terms. When Rome began to extend her conquests outside Italy and to engage in distant wars there was a vast increase in the slave population ... In town and country alike slave labour replaced free labour': *Elements of Roman Law*, 48–49.

28   Ibid, 133–134.

29   See generally Lee *Elements of Roman Law*, 46–60; see also Peter Birks 'The Unacceptable Face of Human Property' in Peter Birks (ed) *New Perspectives in the Roman Law of Property: Essays for Barry Nicholas* (Oxford: Clarendon Press, 1989).

30   Although classified within the law of persons, slaves were also property, like animals. 'Slaves were property. They were bought and sold like other goods. Slave dealers had a bad reputation: the seller of a slave was required to warrant that the slave was free of defects; eventually this warranty was implied in the contract of sale ... Much the same regime applied to cattle'. David Johnston *Roman Law in Context*, 42.

31   Ibid, 43.

32   Of course, a slave was not a complete non-person, but rather both person and property. See Chapter Three for further discussion of the status of slaves.

33   See RH Graveson *Status in the Common Law* (London: Athlone Press, 1953). See also our discussion in Chapter Three, below.

34   For a detailed discussion, see AW Brian Simpson *A History of the Land Law* 2nd ed (Oxford: Clarendon, 1986, first published 1961), ch 1 'Tenure'.

35   David Siepp 'The Concept of Property in the Early Common Law' (1994) 12 *Law and History Review* 29.

36   Seipp notes that Bracton made little distinction between land and other things, and that the same law of ownership could be applied to both categories of things; Siepp 'The Concept of Property in the Early Common Law', 35–37. The point is also made by FW Maitland and Frederick Pollock in *The History of English Law Before the Time of Edward I* (Cambridge: Cambridge University Press, 1898), 2.

37   This is not to say that moveables were not of economic significance. Clearly they were.

38   Forms of real property are, of course, still of immense economic significance. Real property has, however, clearly been displaced by less scarce commodities, in particular, by forms of intellectual property.

39   Seipp says that the Year Book actions for moveable things claimed property, while those for land claimed right (*dreit*). The action for possession (*seisin*) could be used for either land or moveables; Siepp 'The Concept of Property in the Early Common Law'.

40   Baker *Introduction to English Legal History*, 262. A somewhat different view is expressed by Pollock and Maitland in *The History of English Law Before the Time of Edward I*, 3–6. See also Bede Jarrett *Social Theories of the Middle Ages 1200–1500* [1926] (London: Ernest Benn Ltd., 1966), 130–131; Geoffrey Samuel 'The Many Dimensions of Property' in McLean (ed) *Property and the Constitution*, 40–63, 52.

41   Baker *Introduction to English Legal History*, 263.

42   A recent example of restrictions on land use from South Australia is provided by the amendments to the *Development Act*, which compels land owners to gain permission from a local council before lopping or felling trees over a certain size; *Development (Significant Trees) Amendment Act 2000*; *Development Act 1993*, s4; *Development Regulations 1993*, s6A.

43   Human beings were also regarded as stewards of their bodies for God, rather than owners of the body. Such a view of the body is still reflected in some attitudes to euthanasia.

44   Patrick Atiyah *The Rise and Fall of Freedom of Contract* (Oxford: Clarendon Press, 1979), 86.

45   William Lucy and Catherine Mitchell 'Replacing Private Property: The Case for Stewardship' (1996) *Cambridge Law Journal* 566.

46 The *Countryside and Rights of Way Bill 2000* is an attempt to ensure rights of way are available to specified 'public access' areas. See also the Ramblers' Association internet site at http://www.ramblers.org.uk/.
47 For instance, an organisation called 'This Land Is Ours' (TLIO), more radical than the Ramblers' Association, aims to promote discussion and activism in favour of common land rights in Britain. Much of the activism of the group centres on countering the takeover of countryside by developers, and attempting to ensure that development is ecologically and socially appropriate. In addition to environmental concerns, a serious claim to common rights in land underlies these protests. See, for instance the TLIO Website at http://www.oneworld.org/tlio/index.html which provides a number of interesting links to current and historical activist groups involved in asserting such land rights.
48 *Mabo v Queensland* (No 2) (1992) 175 CLR 1; *Wik Peoples v Queensland* (1996) 187 CLR 1. These cases represent a departure from the doctrine of tenure because they recognise a form of title, beneficial or allodial title, which is not derived from a Crown grant. See Brendan Edgeworth 'Tenure, Allodialism and Indigenous Rights at Common Law: English, United States and Australian Land Law Compared After Mabo v Queensland' (1994) 23 *Anglo-American Law Review* 397; John Devereux and Shaunnagh Dorsett 'Towards a Reconsideration of the Doctrines of Estates and Tenure' (1996) 4 *Australian Property Law Journal* 30; Lee Godden 'Wik: Feudalism, Capitalism and the State. A Revision of Land Law in Australia?' (1997) 5 *Australian Property Law Journal* 162.
49 The British *Reform Acts* of 1867 and 1884 extended the male franchise, but the vote was only available to those male owners or tenants who held land of sufficient value. The *Representation of the People Act* 1918 (UK) gave the vote to men who were 21 and women who were 30, and who occupied a residence. The minimum age for women voters was reduced in stages. In Australia, propertyless male subjects gained the vote from 1856 onwards.
50 See Kevin Gray and Susan Francis Gray 'Private Property and Public Propriety' in McLean *Property and the Constitution*, 13.
51 Macpherson *The Political Theory of Possessive Individualism*; see our discussion in Chapter One.
52 Atiyah *The Rise and Fall of Freedom of Contract*.
53 Even though a feudal tenant did not have 'property' in land and did not simply own it, it is nonetheless usual in modern commentaries to speak generally of estates in land in the middle ages as property: see eg. CMF McCauliff 'The Medieval Origin of the Doctrine of Estates in Land: Substantive Property Law, Family Considerations and the Interests of Women' (1992) 66 *Tulane Law Review* 919; Charles Reinold Noyes *The Institution of Property*, 221–284.
54 Atiyah *The Rise and Fall of Freedom of Contract*.
55 Henry Sumner Maine *Ancient Law: Its Connection with the Early History of Society and its Relation to Modern Ideas* (London: John Murray, 1930).
56 Jarrett *Social Theories of the Middle Ages*, 134.
57 Jarrett *Social Theories of the Middle Ages*, 141.

58   Quoted in Simpson *A History of the Land Law*, 54.

59   Ibid, 54–55.

60   The developed rules of inheritance are explained in some detail by Simpson *A History of the Land Law*, 57–63.

61   For discussion of the social and economic consequences of the enclosure movement see MJ Daunton *Progress and Poverty: An Economic and Social History of Britain 1700–1850* (Oxford: Oxford University Press, 1995), ch 4 'Open Fields and Enclosures: The Demise of Commonality'; and Michael Turner *Enclosures in Britain 1750–1830* (London: Macmillan, 1984).

62   William Blackstone *Commentaries on the Laws of England, Vol 2: Of the Rights of Things* (University of Chicago Press, 1979, reprint of 1st ed 1765), 2.

63   For instance, land can be subject to compulsory acquisition by governments; there are limits to the use of force in defence of property (just as with defence of self, but arguably more stringent with defence of property).

64   See, for example, Morris Cohen 'Property and Sovereignty' (1927) 13 *Cornell Law Quarterly* 8.

65   See Charles Reich 'The New Property' (1964) 73 *Yale Law Journal* 733; Charles Reich 'The Individual Sector'; Isaiah Berlin 'Two Concepts of Liberty' in Isaiah Berlin *Four Essays on Liberty* (Oxford: Oxford University Press, 1969).

66   Kevin Gray and Susan Francis Gray argue that there are domains of 'private' property, such as shopping malls, enclosed residential areas, and companies providing public infrastructure services, which have a 'quasi-public' character. They suggest that these forms of property ought to be subject to different legal controls than property which does not have a public interest dimension. See Gray and Gray 'Private Property and Public Propriety, 11.

67   James Penner *The Concept of Property in Law*; Charles Donohue 'The Concept of Property Predicted From its Past' in Pennock and Chapman (eds) *Property*, 28, 46.

68   Jeremy Waldron comments: 'Private property — the idea of one person being in charge of a resource and free to use or dispose of it as she pleases — remains a powerful concept in our social thought even though legal technicians would want to substitute a much more complex and variegated description.' Waldron 'Property, Justification, and Need', 188.

69   For discussion on the effects of the 'disaggregation' of property, see Carol Rose *Property and Persuasion*, 278–282; Jeanne Schroeder *The Vestal and the Fasces*.

70   Wesley Newcombe Hohfeld 'Some Fundamental Legal Conceptions as Applied in Judicial Reasoning' (1913); 'Fundamental Legal Conceptions as Applied in Judicial Reasoning' (1917).

71   Hohfeld states that 'the supposed single right in rem correlating with "a duty" on "all" persons really involves as many separate and distinct

"right—duty" relations as there are persons subject to a duty', Hohfeld 'Fundamental Legal Conceptions as Applied in Judicial Reasoning', 743. An excellent modern explanation and defence of Hohfeld's position is to be found in Pavlos Eleftheriadis 'The Analysis of Property Rights'; see also Alain Pottage 'Instituting Property'. Modern critiques of Hohfeld are less common, but two, from completely different perspectives, include JE Penner *The Idea of Property in Law* and Jeanne Schroeder *The Vestal and the Fasces.*

72   Hans Kelsen *Pure Theory of Law* (Berkeley: University of California Press, 1967), 131. Cf. Kelsen's views on legal personality, discussed below, Chapter Three.

73   For an introductory account of the postmodern approach to the questions of meaning and subjectivity see Margaret Davies *Asking the Law Question* (Sydney: Law Book Company, 1994), chs 7 and 8.

74   Ferdinand de Saussure *Course in General Linguistics* (New York: Philosophical Library, 1959), 120, summarised in Davies *Asking the Law Question*, 233–234.

75   Tony Honoré 'Ownership' in AG Guest (ed) *Oxford Essays in Jurisprudence* (Oxford: Oxford University Press, 1961), 107–147.

76   See Kelsen *Pure Theory of Law*; HLA Hart *The Concept of Law* 2nd ed (Oxford: Clarendon Press, 1994, first published 1961).

77   For an overview of the use of possession in law, see Carol Rose *Property and Persuasion*, ch 1 'Possession as the Origin of Property'.

78   In fact, our language betrays this as a very common idea: for instance we might say that the law 'fails to protect private property' or that a particular legal system 'does not recognise private property rights', implying that the property comes first, and then the law, which is either adequate or inadequate to the pre-legal rights.

79   Jeremy Bentham *Theory of Legislation* CK Ogden (ed) (London: Kegan Paul, Trench, Trubner, and Co, 1931), 113.

80   Kevin Gray 'Property in Thin Air' [1991] *Cambridge Law Review* 252.

81   Jacques Derrida 'Force of Law: The "Mystical Foundation of Authority"' (1990) 11 *Cardozo Law Review* 919.

82   Kelsen's basic norm became in his later work 'a genuine or "proper" fiction (in the sense of Vaihinger's philosophy of As-If) whose characteristic is that it not only contradicts reality, since there exists no such norm ... but is also self-contradictory'; Kelsen *General Theory of Norms* (Oxford: Clarendon Press, 1991), 256.

83   'The physical or juristic person who "has" obligations and rights as their holder, is these obligations and rights — a complex of legal obligations and rights whose totality is expressed figuratively in the concept "person".' Kelsen *Pure Theory of Law*, 173; see also Lon Fuller *Legal Fictions* (Stanford, California: Stanford University Press, 1967).

84   In an influential article Thomas Grey argued that the 'substitution of a bundle-of-rights for a thing-ownership conception of property has the ultimate consequence that property ceases to be an important legal category in legal and political theory'. T. Grey 'The Disintegration of Property', 81.

85   K. Gray 'Property in Thin Air', p. 299.
86   For instance, certain economic theory (and in particular certain strands of law and economics) have a tendency to attach a commercial value to even the most intimate aspects of human relationships: see for instance, Richard Posner *Sex and Reason* (Cambridge, Mass.: Harvard University Press, 1992).
87   Schroeder *The Vestal and the Fasces*. See also Charles Donohue 'The Future of the Concept of Property Predicted from its Past'.
88   See, for example, the opening comments in Penner *The Idea of Property in Law*, 1.
89   Jeanne Schroeder has emphasised this danger of the 'disaggregation' theories particularly well in *The Vestal and the Fasces*.
90   See above, note 49.
91   It is not possible here to review the extensive feminist literature which connects male power with the power associated with property. Such literature includes socialist and Marxist feminism, as well as feminist work which explores metaphorical and ideological constructions of gender. See, for instance, Michèle Barrett *Women's Oppression Today: Problems in Marxist Feminist Analysis* (London: Verso, 1980); Carol Pateman *The Sexual Contract* (Oxford: Polity Press, 1988); Jennifer Nedelsky 'Law, Boundaries, and the Bounded Self'.
92   Cheryl Harris 'Whiteness as Property' (1993) 106 *Harvard Law Review* 1707–1791; see also Patricia Williams 'On Being the Object of Property' (1988) 14 *Signs: Journal of Women in Culture and Society* 5.
93   The first British Married Women's Property Act was passed in 1870. Similar legislation was passed in all Australian states between 1870 (Victoria) and 1892 (Western Australia).
94   Nedelsky 'Law, Boundaries, and the Bounded Self'; Naffine 'The Body Bag'.
95   Naffine 'The Body Bag'; 'Possession: Erotic Love and the Law of Rape'.
96   Luce Irigaray has suggested the development of a regime of specific rights for women in order to combat this lack of legal subjectivity, a position which has been convincingly rebutted on the grounds that it would simply entrench (hetero)sexual difference in law. See Irigaray *je, tu, nous: Toward a Culture of Difference* (New York: Routledge, 1993), especially ch. 10 'Why Define Sexed Rights?'; See also the excellent commentary by Nicola Lacey *Unspeakable Subjects: Feminist Essays in Legal and Social Theory* (Oxford: Hart, 1998), 212–218.
97   Harris 'Whiteness as Property', 1741.
98   Ibid.

3 The Nature of Legal Personality: Its History and its Incidents

Introduction

In the last chapter, we observed that the concept of property and its relationship to the socio-political order have attracted considerable scholarly attention, both in politics and law. It may therefore come as a surprise to discover that this is not true of the concept of 'legal personality',[1] even though the person may be regarded as the most fundamental unit of law, and the only other legal category into which legal matter can be placed. As we know, modern law generally insists on the distinctiveness and separation of the categories of persons and property. The two concepts have an important negative interdependence: as a rule, that which is a person cannot be property; that which is property is stripped of personality. Whereas modern legal theorists have sought, at length, to elucidate the concept of property, comparatively little time has been expended on the companion concept of legal personality. This is remarkable given the importance of the concept to our daily lives, both as citizens and as legal actors. In this chapter, we consider the history of the concept of legal personality, and the modern characteristics of the legal subject.

To be visible in law, and thus to have legal standing, to attract legal rights and to assume legal obligations, one must be a legal person. If a being is not a person in law,[2] she can be treated as a species of property: she can be bought and sold. It is because animals are not legal persons that their owners, almost with legal impunity, can destroy them. The offences against the person are not designed to afford legal protection or dignity to the family pet. Closely allied with the legal concept of the person is the moral concept of person. For, to be a legal person is also to have moral standing, which is why animal liberationists have argued for the legal personhood of the non-human primates — it is thought that with legal standing comes moral standing.[3] The argument also runs the other way. That which is thought to have moral standing is more likely to be made the subject of legal rights. Thus the growing recognition of the intelligence and sociability of the higher primates has served to strengthen the case for ape rights.

To be a legal person is also to be recognised as an active participant in the *polis*. As one legal analyst has remarked about the former denial of personhood to Afro-Americans, it was more than just a matter of 'legal standing; it involve[d] considerations both of the fundamental legal and political concept of membership within a liberal society and the fundamental scope of understanding of civil ... rights and liberties'.[4]

Notwithstanding the immense practical significance of legal personality, both as a political and jurisprudential topic, the study of legal personality as it applies to human beings has fallen into desuetude. The heyday of legal theory of persons was the 1920s and 1930s when it was still considered an important field of study.[5] Since then it has waned in importance and the law of persons has ceased to hold a discrete place in common law theory, unlike the law of property. As Richard Tur observes, 'the law of persons is not a clearly delineated area'[6] and it is no longer afforded a discrete place in the teaching or scholarly study of jurisprudence. In the common law countries, it is rare to find the Law of Persons (the old Roman title for the subject) on the curriculum. By contrast, the law of property is regarded as fundamental to a law degree.

Defining the Person in Law

Although legal personality as it applies to humans tends no longer to be the subject of sustained theoretical analysis,[7] lawyers are constantly obliged to employ the term and therefore have necessarily produced working definitions of the concept. It is possible to identify two broad understandings of legal personality: the one offered by positivists; the other by natural lawyers. The classic positivist account of the legal person comes from Hans Kelsen. 'That the human being is a legal subject (subject of rights and obligations)', to Kelsen, 'means nothing else...but that human behaviour is the content of legal obligations and rights - nothing else than that a human being is a person or has personality'. According to Kelsen,

A legal person is the unity of a complex of legal obligations and rights. Since these obligations and rights are constituted by legal norms (more correctly: *are* these legal norms), the problem of "person" is in the last analysis the problem of the unity of a complex of norms ... The so-called physical person, then, is not a human being, but the personified unity of the legal norms that obligate or authorise one and the same human being. It is not a natural reality but a social construction, created by the science of law — an auxiliary concept in the presentation of legally relevant facts. In this sense a physical person is a juristic person.[8]

Thus Kelsen maintains a general insistence that the legal person does not reside outside the law, is never antecedent to and independent of law, but is always a creature of law. There is no 'additional entity', he maintains, beyond this complex of legal norms.[9] Kelsen's analysis of personality therefore bears a strong resemblance to his analysis of property (expounded in the last chapter).

The central proposition of positivism is that the legal person is a purely formal legal concept — a fiction, a device, a construct, an invention. Legal personality comprises the variable legal rights and duties that are, or can be, exercised within purely legal relations. This view is nicely expressed by Bryant Smith who asserts that 'without the relations ... there is no more left than the smile of the Cheshire Cat after the cat had disappeared'.[10] Or to the positivist Albert Kocourek, writing of Anglo-American law,

Legal personality is the sum total of the legal relations of a person. A person, therefore, in the law is a mere ideal or conceptual point of reference ... The person...is an irreducible juristic subsistent. It comes into existence and goes out of existence. During existence it has only one quality — the capacity of attracting legal relations ... In a word, a person has a capacity for rights and ligations. The legal relations which the person attracts are the person's personality. While the idea of person is irreducible and ultimate, the idea of personality is subject to expansion and contraction.[11]

From this it follows, as Dias puts it, that 'There is no "essence" underlying the various uses of "person"... Neither the linguistic nor legal usages of "person" are logical'.[12] Consequently, legal rights possessed and exercised within legal relations depend on specific legal purposes that vary according to the particular legal concerns of the parties and their particular circumstances. The legal person is fully a creature of law and, within law, legal rights and duties vary according to legal relation.

In the positivist account, personality is a highly flexible concept with no fixed content. To Richard Tur, an avowed Kelsenian, the legal person is 'wholly formal ... an empty slot'.[13] This slot 'can be filled by anything that can have rights or duties.'[14] To Salmond, 'Legal persons, being the *arbitrary* creations of the law, may be of as many kinds as the law pleases' (emphasis added).[15] For some purposes, an entity may have no or little ability to function in law, but for other purposes may be said to be in rude good health. Thus a person with an intellectual disability or mental disease may not be able to enter into an enforceable contract (if she is unable to appreciate its terms),[16] but she may, with the aid of another, be able to sue for damages suffered as a consequence of a civil wrong. According to Salmond, 'So far as legal theory is concerned, a person is any being whom the law regards as capable of rights or duties. Any being that is so capable is a person, whether a human being or not, and no being that is not so capable is a person, even though he be a man'.[17] Richard Tur explains that even the thinnest set of rights will constitute a legal person, because personhood is 'a matter of degree' and can be highly variable between persons.

> The law will ascribe legal personality to two entities even where they bear different clusters of rights and duties. So, legal personality is a cluster concept, where in some cases a different cluster of rights and duties is present, and in other cases a different cluster of rights is present, perhaps overlapping somewhat with the first ... it is conceivable that two entities, both of which are legal persons, might have no rights and duties in common at all.[18]

There is therefore, in this view, no necessary relation between any given set of human characteristics (say, the ability to reason and reflect) and legal personality. Moreover there is no minimal threshold level of intelligence required to constitute a person. Once a legal right is in evidence, so is a person. Modern legal personality lacks a persistent character over time and place; even its beginnings and cessations are not easy to recognise. Rather, legal personality is better regarded as groupings of rights and duties whose content depends on such factors as age, sex and mental ability (all regarded as natural categories), as well as legal purpose and jurisdiction. Positivists such as Tur invoke these different manifestations of personhood in law to demonstrate what they regard as the essentially arbitrary technical nature of the legal device of the person.

The other interpretation of the person is to be found among natural lawyers. In this account, there is a natural human subject, with an intrinsic character, for whom rights and obligations are natural and inevitable. We have them because of our human natures, because of what and who we are. Legal rights map on to this natural subject. Or, put another way, legal rights are natural to human beings; they are a legal expression of natural attributes of a subject that has its own inherent nature. As Philippe Ducor expresses the natural lawyer's view of the person, '[t]he human being is the paradigmatic subject of rights'.[19]

For human rights lawyers, this mapping of legal rights onto an antecedent human subject is axiomatic.[20] Thus it is said that rights 'inhere in the natural condition of being human'.[21] For some, this subject of legal rights is simply 'the human being'. For others, this subject is the 'normal' human being. The very idea of a human right connotes a natural human being that forms the basis of the right. The classic work on legal persons, which is wedded to a naturalistic view of the concept, is that of John Chipman Gray. In *The Nature and Sources of the Law*, Gray contends that the will is the defining characteristic of the natural person and that the will finds its expression in law in the idea of the legal person. The paradigmatic legal person is the so-called 'normal' person — the adult of sound mind — who possesses a 'natural will' and so can personally assert his legal rights without recourse to a next friend or guardian.[22] In short, Gray conflates the legal person with his particular understanding of a normal natural human being. In his view of the person, the expression of the will appears to be the essence of being human and therefore also the essence of being a legal person. When this normal human being is asserting his legal rights as a legal person, it seems that there is no legal fiction involved in his legal personality. It is only when a will is attributed artificially to a child or 'idiot', for legal purposes, that legal personality entails a fiction.[23]

Although legal personality is remarkably undertheorised as a legal concept, when it is defined (and usually in a fairly cursory way), it is usually according to positivism, rather than natural law. It is regarded as a technical legal device for organising and grouping clusters of legal rights and duties. Chipman Gray and his idea of a 'normal' natural person, who forms the template for the legal person, would no doubt be regarded as naïve, as lacking legal scientific rigour in his treatment of the subject.

And yet there is an important sense in which Gray was right to think that a so-called 'normal' person subtends the legal person. For, as we will insist in this book, a particular conception of human nature is generally presupposed by the prevailing legal concept of the person, even though it usually goes unremarked precisely because it is so powerfully naturalised. Our purpose is to denaturalise this human being implied by the legal concept of person and, in a more positivist spirit, to suggest that this person behind the legal person is itself a construct of law. In other words, we not only regard the legal person as a formal legal fiction,[24] but we think also that there is a tacit view of the person that underwrites the official fiction, and that it too is a legal invention, one which is of course strongly influenced by broader social and cultural assumptions about the nature of being human.

Although we will emphasise the constructed nature of the person behind the legal person, we are at odds with the positivists who are also constructivists, but who would treat legal personality as a creation of law that has no necessary connection with social or moral facts. (Recall that Salmond described legal persons as 'the *arbitrary* creations of the law'.) For we will argue that the concept of legal personality fairly systematically helps to support a quite particular interpretation of the person, and one which has an intimate connection with its companion concept, property. We suggest that the modern legal concept of the person presupposes certain property relations, both within and outwith the person. The person behind the legal person may at various times be regarded as either or both the subject and the object of property rights; as self-owner and as the property of others. This is a controversial proposition to advance because, in the modern legal understanding of persons and property, the two concepts are supposed to be mutually exclusive. As we observed in Chapter One, to be a person is, in the orthodox view, precisely not to be property; and that which is property is, by definition, not a person. We will question both of these statements in the course of this chapter and this book.

In order to make sense of the modern understanding of the legal person, and his relation to property, it is necessary to give a brief account of the legal history of the concept. We will discover that legal personality has grown up alongside the concept of property, that the interdependence of the two concepts was once openly acknowledged, and that although the two concepts are now supposed to be utterly distinct, in truth they have retained a vital kinship.

From Mask to Character: A Short Legal History of the Person

A history of personality may be traced through its shifting etymology. 'The earliest traceable meaning of *persona*', according to Duff, 'is a mask, such as Greek and Roman actors regularly wore on the stage'.[25] As Keeton explains: 'Originally it meant simply a mask. Later it denotes the part played by a man in life, and still later, the man who plays it. ... Last of all, the term comes to denote a being capable of sustaining legal rights and duties'.[26] John Austin describes the linguistic process in terms of a series of metaphorical shifts.

> It signified originally, a mask worn by a player, to mark the character
> he bore in the piece: and is transferred by a metaphor to the character
> itself. By a further metaphor it is transferred from dramatic character
> to legal condition. For men as subjects of law are distinguished by
> conditions, just as players by the characters they present.[27]

In his influential study of the category of the person, anthropologist Marcel Mauss also documents its transformation in meaning: from that of a mask or 'superimposed image', to 'the individual, with his nature laid bare and every mask torn away' and finally to the autonomous 'psychological being' who is characterised by his 'self-knowledge' and self-consciousness and who thus acquires moral status. While a sense of artificiality is integral to the first meaning of person, with its idea of a 'role-player' or 'man clad in a condition' (personage), as we move towards the modern meaning we acquire a sense of a sovereign, reflective subject, a being with his own self-determining personality, not one imposed by others.[28]

The Roman Man Clad in a Condition

It is conventional to trace the first legal usage of the concept of person back to ancient Rome. Although Roman Law provides the foundations of modern civil law, as opposed to common law, in the common law countries such as England and Australia we are nevertheless indebted to the Romans for their organisation of law and for many of their legal concepts. The high point of legal writing was the great compilation and codification of law by the Emperor Justinian published between 533 and 534 and now known as *The Institutes of Justinian*.[29] Much of this work was drawn directly from *The Institutes of Gaius* and in fact used the original wording.

It is in the Roman codification of law that we first find elaborated the concept of the person as a legal category and we also find the concept of person distinguished from other legal categories, especially the concept of property. The Romans drew a basic distinction between *ius publicum* and *ius privatum*. Public law pertained to the relationship between the individual and the state and included what we now call criminal law and constitutional law, ecclesiastical law and administrative law. Private law pertained to the relationship between individuals and included family law, the law of obligations, succession and property. The law of persons fell within private law. Within their private law, the Romans (both Justinian and his predecessor Gaius) created a tripartite division of law into persons, things and actions. Or as Thomas has expressed it, the law considered 'the persons involved, the subject matters in issue and the remedies available'.[30] The law of persons was 'a catalogue of the classes of person capable of being affected by Roman Law and how they enter and leave their categories; the law of things [was] a list of rights and duties that such persons may have, their creation and extinction; and the law of actions [was] the various legal processes and where they apply'.[31]

The Romans, however, did not use the term 'person' in its modern legal sense, that is, to denote the basic legal entity, whether it is a human being or an association. For the Romans, the term 'person' meant a natural person, rather than the bearer of legal rights and duties, and thus slaves were classified under the law of persons, despite their lack of legal competence in most respects. Another important difference between the Roman and modern view of the person is in relation to so-called artificial persons. The Romans recognised abstract entities as the bearers of rights — such as the Roman State itself — but they did not call this entity a person, as we do today. Or as Thomas observes, 'Roman law also knew and recognized non-human subjects of rights and duties ... [but] these were not considered *personae*'.[32] That is, corporations could be legal subjects but they were not regarded as *personae* and hence were not dealt with in the law of persons. It is modern law that has not only accorded corporations juristic personality but has also deemed them to be persons at law. The modern idea of a legal person is therefore more inclusive than the Ancient one: not only are all human beings now regarded as legal persons, but so too are some non-natural or incorporeal entities.

It is therefore not the Roman term 'person' that best corresponds with our modern concept of legal personality - because the Roman 'person' was anybody, free person or slave, and slaves were not recognised as the bearers of legal rights. According to Thomas,

> In Roman terminology, the two terms which most nearly correspond with the modern concept of personality are *status* and *caput*. Essentially *status* signified the legal condition of a person — as free man, freedman etc — and *caput*, literally a head, the sum of rights duties, powers etc vested in him by virtue of that condition; hence the conception that any change of *status* was *capitus deminutio*.[33]

In Roman law, the person who possessed the most complete set of legal rights was the free Roman male citizen who was at the head of a family: the *paterfamilias*. According to Thomas,

> The ideal person of Roman law would have been the person of full *caput*, ie the freeborn citizen ... of full age and sound mind who had in public law ... the right to vote in the assembly elections and also, at any rate in the Republic, to stand for office ... and in private law, *connubium*, the right to contract a Roman civil law marriage which would in turn confer the power to have *potestas* over any issue thereof and *commercium*, the right to participate in transactions of the *ius civile*.[34]

As we saw in the last chapter, it was the *paterfamilias*, the head of the family, who exercised *patria potestas*, or paternal power over the rest of the family. The *paterfamilias* controlled not only the individual family members but also their property. Indeed it may be said that the real source of power of the *paterfamilias* was the property of the family which he owned absolutely and which has been described 'in a general sense [as] a natural extension of [his] liberty and personality'.[35] By contrast, those *in potestas* had no proprietary rights and, at least in early Roman law, were effectively themselves a form of property. This meant that the *paterfamilias* was able to sell his children into slavery.

Slaves occupied a position in Roman law that has no direct equivalent in modern Western law in that they were explicitly regarded as both persons and property. As Rattigan observes, 'the Roman law while recognising a slave as a natural being, and therefore one who had to be considered in a general classification of persons, regarded him as utterly devoid of legal existence ... he only acquired a civil status on the day of his manumission'.[36] Thus the Romans distinguished between civil and natural persons: slaves were the latter but not the former. Their civil status was as 'mere things'; their natural status was as persons. And yet the slave was not regarded entirely as 'an impersonal object or thing',[37] for she could be left a legacy, while a horse could not.

In Roman law, women were not regarded as property, and so were clearly distinguishable from slaves. And yet in most respects they occupied a position inferior to men. As we have seen, it was the *paterfamilias*, not the *mater*, who controlled the family property, and who therefore represented the citizen of full status. It was his personality that found fulfilment in the exercise of his proprietary rights. In Roman law, women were an explicitly subordinate class, placed under perpetual tutelage.[38]

So to return to our etymology of the term 'person', in Roman law we may observe the operation of the early meaning of the term. The adult male Roman citizen was very much man clad in a condition. He obtained his character by dint of his socially-assigned familial role as head of a family and as man of property.

The Medieval Estate of Man

In this brief legal history of the person, we now undertake a major shift, from Roman law, to the early common law of England, though we may observe interesting links between the two bodies of law. As Goodrich has remarked,

> the centralization of the legal system which occurred soon after the Norman conquest was very much an exercise in developing and systematizing native law according to the precepts and principles of Roman law. The first centralized courts were royal courts and the first judges were royally appointed from amongst the clergy and legally trained in canon law and Roman law.[39]

The influence of Roman jurisprudence is also plain to see in the document on English law prepared by Glanville in 1187, described as 'the first systematic Treatise on English Law',[40] and also in the more thorough and detailed exposition of English law of 1256 by Bracton, entitled *On the Laws and Customs of England.*[41] Bracton had studied Italian jurisprudence and drew from it the idea of a law book as well as its arrangement.[42] Thus he adopted the Roman division of law — into persons, things and actions. However Bracton demoted the law of persons in his account of the common law, paying vastly more attention to the law of things or estates. In view of the English preoccupation with the ownership and disposal of property, this is not surprising. As Graveson remarks in his legal history of status, 'After the Norman Conquest the law of estates and land tenure became the greatest and most uniform part of English law'.[43]

The law of estates, however, had a very direct bearing on the law of persons. 'For what a man had', according to Graveson, 'largely determined what he was. His status as a legal person depended on his legal estate and tenure in English land. If he held land in free tenure he was, at least until the thirteenth century, usually a free man, and similarly he was personally unfree if his holding was by villein tenure'.[44] Relationship to land was therefore vital to personal condition. In fact Graveson suggests that the interaction between property and personality was so close that 'it is extremely hard to tell whether personal status determined tenure or vice versa'.[45]

Confusion over Latin terminology helped to strengthen the relation between personal status and property. The one word *status* was employed in the records to convey two meanings: one relating to property; the other to personal status. Bracton was apparently alert to this ambiguity and yet also used the term in both its senses. Graveson informs us that

> though he generally used the term in the sense of a legally imposed condition, he occasionally employed status in its proprietary meaning, as when he wrote that the status of an infant in property must not be changed during his minority, and even seems to have given a wider meaning, that of the totality of a person's rights, personal and proprietary, to the term.[46]

The close connection between personal status and property in the early common law was also evidenced by the political idea of the 'estates of men'. As Graveson explains, the idea was that 'every man was supposed to hold an interest in land corresponding to his "estate" in a political sense. The aggregation of "the estates of men" constituted the state, the totality of individual proprietary estates together with the collective organisation upon them'.[47] And it was not just the status of tenants which was determined by relation to land: 'until the latter part of the eighteenth century ... a person with a superior relational status was considered as having a proprietary interest in the maintenance of that status'.[48]

Feudal society and the early common law were therefore both explicitly hierarchical. As with Roman law, the major distinctions were between the free and the unfree (villeins) and between men and women. Although the common law never subscribed to full slavery, in the Roman sense, the villein was still considered to be 'unfree'. Villeins could own property, but their rights were tenuous in that the landlord could always seize the property of a villein. This led to the popular saying 'that villeins owned only what they had in their bellies'.[49] The villein was also subject to the physical discipline of his lord: 'the villein could not run away from his tenement ... [and] escape could be prevented by force'.[50]

To the legal historian J H Baker, however, it is the law of marriage which represents 'the most pervasive aspect of the English law of persons, not only because of its effect on ... the legal capacities of the married woman, but also because the inheritance of property was always predicated on relationships brought about by marriage'.[51] In other words, the superior legal status of husbands and the associated rules governing the husband's property and its inheritance were really at the heart of the English common law. The law of couverture meant that upon marriage the legal personality of the woman was dissolved into the personality of the husband who became her guardian and assumed control of her freehold land, 'absolute power over her personal chattels',[52] and free access to her person.[53] The two became one flesh in law, but the flesh was his, not hers. Or as Graveson explains, the relationship was 'was one of profit to the guardian'.[54]

The doctrine of couverture was to endure until well after the modernisation of social roles. As William Blackstone described the doctrine as it obtained late in the eighteenth century,

> By marriage, the husband and wife are one person in law: that is, the very being or legal existence of the woman is suspended during the marriage, or at least is incorporated and consolidated into that of the

husband: under whose wing, protection, and cover, she performs everything; and is therefore called in our law-french a feme-covert ... is said to be ... under the protection and influence of her husband, her baron or lord; and her condition during her marriage is called coverture.[55]

The Emergence of Modern Legal Personality and the Possessive Individual

The final part of this schematic legal history of the person is about the emergence of the modern legal subject. The shift from feudal to modern social and legal relations, and to our modern conception of the legal individual, has been described most famously by Henry Maine:

> The movement of the progressive societies has been uniform in one respect. Through all its course it has been distinguished by the gradual dissolution of family dependency, and the growth of individual obligation in its place. The individual is steadily substituted for the family, as the unit of which civil laws take account.[56]

The shift from medieval status society to modern society based on contract entailed, to a large extent, a freeing up of relations, legally, economically and socially. It entailed a new emphasis on the rights of the individual over their persons and their property. It stressed freedom of contract and freedom from non-contractual obligations to others. It was a shift from the family to the individual as legal unit: a shift from customary relations based on one's specific location within a family, and then within a community, to more impersonal relations based on contractual relation which was, ideally, a product of one's free choice. Or as Maine said, it was a shift 'from status to contract'.

In the medieval England documented by Glanville and Bracton, relationships were largely static and based on custom. As PS Atiyah observed in his history of contract, 'A man had his place and role in a communal society; he inherited, usually, his father's trade or craft or status'.[57] That is, the accident of one's birth largely determined one's future place in society: the past determined the present. People's lot in life was therefore largely predetermined for them; it was not a matter of individual choice. 'Men were not, nor were they thought to be, free to do what they chose'.[58] Both the person and property of medieval man was tied up in feudal rights and feudal obligations.

By the middle of the eighteenth century, however, 'the older feudal relationship had been obsolete for many years even before the abolition of feudal dues in 1660'.[59] The unpropertied man who lived off his labour no longer did so out of a feudal relationship and feudal obligation, but rather he sold his labour impersonally in a free market economy. That is, 'labour became increasingly a market commodity'.[60] What now characterised the new economic relations, therefore, were not the personal obligations of the feudal structure but rather the contractual obligations of the market, which did not depend on social or customary relationship between the parties.

Political theories developed in the previous century by Hobbes and Locke (discussed in the previous chapter) lent support to this new contractual view of social relations. In these imaginary accounts of the formation of modern political society, people came together not by custom or tradition or nature but by a free agreement or contract between persons to form a society under government. The great legal document of the eighteenth century, which captured much of this new liberal spirit of individualism, is that of Sir William Blackstone. In his *Commentaries on the Laws of England*, Blackstone undertook the heroic task of summarising the entire common law as it stood late in the eighteenth century. As Bracton had endeavoured to bring together the laws of his times, so too did Blackstone, some 500 years later. Also like Bracton, Blackstone used the Roman division of law into persons, things and actions.

For Blackstone, 'the principal aim of society is to protect individuals in the enjoyment of those absolute rights'.[61] Blackstone thus declared his commitment to the individual as the basic unit of society.

> The absolute rights of man, considered as a free agent, endowed with discernment to know good from evil, and with power of choosing those measures which appear to him to be the most desirable, are usually summed up in one general appellation, and denominated the natural liberty of mankind. This natural liberty consists properly in a power of acting as he thinks fit, without any restraint or control.[62]

Blackstone endorsed the ideas of the social contractarians, Hobbes and Locke, who believed that civil society was best regarded as a social contract between its citizens and the sovereign to hand over to the state the right of each person to use force against the next person, in exchange for a guarantee of peace and security.

Blackstone declared that the individual possessed a number of absolute rights 'which appertain to every Englishman',[63] which the law must preserve. The first absolute right of the person was the right of personal security, the second was the right to personal liberty and the third was the right of property, the *dominium* discussed in the previous chapter 'which consists in the free use, enjoyment, and disposal of all his acquisitions, without any control or diminution, save only by the laws of the land'.[64] Blackstone thus described and endorsed the new market society in which the basic unit was the individual and relations between individuals were defined contractually as those of exchange, and basically the exchange of property. To Blackstone, 'The public is now considered as an individual, treating with an individual for exchange. All that the legislature does is to oblige the owner to alienate his possessions for a reasonable price, which the legislature indulges in with caution'.[65]

The society described by Blackstone was a product of individual choice, not an organic or customary communal grouping. As Atiyah explains, 'In short, what was new in contractual theory was ... the idea that the relationship was created by, and depended on, the free choice of the individuals involved in it'.[66] And thus the political and legal character who emerges within this new conception of social relations is quintessentially an individual whose life is self-governed, not governed by others. He is also, importantly, a proprietor in that it is the acquisition of, and secure control over, property which provides the very *raison d'etre* of the new contractual society. He is also thought to be a type of proprietor of his very self, an idea to which we will return shortly. Or as McPherson describes this quintessentially liberal view of the nature of the person and their relations,

> Society becomes a lot of free individuals related to each other as proprietors of their own capacities and of what they have acquired by their exercise. Society consists of relations of exchange between proprietors. Political society becomes a calculated device for the protection of this property and for the maintenance of an orderly relation of exchange.[67]

Atiyah's analysis of modern social and legal relations emphasises their individualistic and voluntary nature, rather than their basis in socially-assigned status. However there was an important sense in which status was retained after the modernisation of political and legal relations, and this was in the form of the family. Atiyah himself writing late in the twentieth century both assumes the disabilities of women as members of families and makes little of it; the index to his book contains no reference to women. But as Blackstone made plain, the family was to remain a place of explicit social ordering, with (in the eighteenth and nineteenth century) the master retaining authority over servant, and (more enduringly) the husband retaining control of his wife. And it was the husband acting for himself as well as for the inferior members of his household who represented the public individual or the basic legal unit. The new ethic of individualism was not intended to apply to life within the family, which in many ways remained feudal, if not Roman, in its social ordering.

Atiyah is curiously silent on the disabilities suffered by married women though he is eloquent on the problems of those without property. He observes that the new emphasis on equal freedom to deal with property was something designed for property owners, who were in fact a very small segment of English society in the eighteenth century: the property right might be an equal one but the actual possession of property was not. Blackstone, however, was clear about the retention of status in other more explicit ways. Chapter 14 of the *Commentaries* deals with the relation between master and servant. Blackstone asserts that 'pure and proper slavery does not, nay cannot, subsist in England; such I mean, whereby an absolute and unlimited power is given to the master over the life and fortune of the slave'.[68] However the master was accorded certain rights over the servant, which suggested a form of relationship akin to ownership. 'A master may by law correct his apprentice for negligence or other misbehaviour, so it be done with moderation ... But if any servant ... assault his master or dame, he shall suffer one year's imprisonment, and other corporeal punishment'.[69] In Chapter 15, Blackstone deals with relations between husbands and wives and especially the doctrine of couverture, which, as we have seen, entailed the legal fiction that husband and wife are one person. Consequently, the husband could not enter into contracts with his wife, for this would be to grant her a separate legal existence.

The Modern Legal Subject as Proprietor

Notwithstanding the tenacity of status forms within the family (a subject to which we will return), the legal individual who notionally emerges with the modernisation of legal relations is a being who can now give full unfettered expression to his subjective personality. Etymologically, we have made the final move, from *persona* to subjective personality. The individual is freed from his legal condition, and at last he is allowed to discover his own nature and to be himself. But, paradoxically, we are also told what this nature will be. Man's true unfettered nature is that of a self-owner, an individual who exercises exclusive control over his person and his property. This is the character ascribed to the person freed from status. Freedom to be oneself is freedom to be a 'possessive individual', as McPherson has dubbed him.[70]

The concept of the person as self-proprietor has a secure place within our modern liberal political theory and liberal jurisprudence. It has become a convenient way of highlighting the freedoms enjoyed by the modern individual, a sort of legal shorthand, a rhetorical device, which serves to accentuate the fullness of the rights enjoyed by persons in relation to themselves and to others. To be a free and complete individual, as Katherine O'Donovan observes, 'one must be an appropriator, defined by what one owns, including oneself'.[71] To John Frow the very 'form of the person' in Western liberal legal thought is one of 'self-possession'.[72] Thus the relationship between personality and property has been retained, but in a new form.

Despite the liberal rhetoric of universal self-ownership, the self-possessing individual is not anyone or everyone. Indeed a major purpose of the ensuing chapters is to show precisely how this concept of the self-proprietor continues to be deployed in law in a highly discriminating fashion. But for the moment, it is possible to make the point briefly, noting a few examples of the conferral and denial of this privileged status. For one thing, a possessive individual is clearly not a wife for, right up until the end of the twentieth century, the wife has not been able to complain of spousal rape. (We return to the modern legal personality of women in the next chapter.) He is not a child, because children retain many of the characteristics of the early forms of status. He is not a pregnant woman because the laws of abortion govern her and surely these are incompatible with self-ownership. Nor does he suffer an intellectual disability or a disease that diminishes his legal abilities to act as a proprietor. The old statuses are still in evidence, but now they are regarded as limitations imposed by nature, not by law. They are natural not legal statuses.

In later chapters we will consider the various ways in which law diminishes the property rights over self of various sections of the population, while sustaining a rhetoric of universal self-ownership. But for now we can simply conclude, with some confidence, that the idea of the self-owner has become central to modern legal and political thought. This conclusion carries important implications for jurisprudential understandings of the person, for if the individual is to be regarded as a free volitional subject, who comes before the law with his nature already formed, then it is vital that he not be regarded as a creation or construction of law. In other words the person must be seen to come before the law as already himself.

The idea of the naturally-sovereign possessive individual does not pose a problem for natural lawyers, for they have tended to assert that our law is a response to the pre-legal humanity of the subject: that law responds to the nature of man. However the positivist view of the legal person, which prevails in contemporary legal accounts of the person, surely represents a direct denial of the person as pre-legal proprietor. In the positivist view, the legal person is a legal creation with variable content: the law makes the legal person; the law does not passively respond to that which already exists. Certainly an antecedent subject does not determine it. So how can it be said that the legal person has a character, as proprietor, when positivists insist that he is simply a passive creation of legal processes? How can he have a nature when he is only a legal contrivance?

The reason why a particular and yet naturalised understanding of the person before the law — the person as proprietor — has endured in the face of positivism is that positivists have tended to cease their theorising at the very point at which it becomes most interesting and so have simply not engaged with the question of the form of law's personification. By persisting with the view that the legal person is just a formal concept, an empty slot, positivists have demonstrated a wilful blindness to the legal subject and his character and have helped to discourage constructive dialogue among legal theorists about the nature of law's personification. The poverty of theory on personality may therefore at least in part be explained by the positivist insistence that all we have in the person is a politically-neutral, but practically-enabling, legal device. For if the legal person is only a legal artefact, devised for purely legal purposes, then he cannot also have his own nature, so there is no need to analyse critically his personality, as we are choosing to do here. Indeed, there is no sense in it.[73]

This positivist construction of the person serves also to remove the analysis of the legal person from its socio-political context. Though legal personality was once explicitly a mode of imposing a particular social hierarchy, and in our view retains this function, the positivist assertion that personality is now purely a technical enabling device contains the implicit message that the law of persons no longer serves to impose a social or political order. The great books of social classification and social hierarchy — Justinian, Bracton and Blackstone — are now thought to be of purely historical interest.

By setting such narrow limits to their theory, the positivists have foreclosed much of the debate about personality and its important relation to property. Indeed the paucity of modern theory of legal persons, especially when compared with the companion literature on property, may be regarded as testimony to the successes of positivism in extinguishing both the philosophy and the politics of personality in law.

Notes

1   The term 'legal person' and 'legal personality' will be used interchangeably as it is common to do in legal writing.

2   One does not have to be a human being to be a legal person. The most prominent example of a non-human legal person is the corporation, which, interestingly, is both person and property. However our concern in this volume is with rights as they are awarded or denied to human beings, not artificial entities.

3   See eg Peter Singer *Animal Liberation: A New Ethics for Our Treatment of Animals* (London: Jonathon Cape, 1976). Some limited success in the endeavour to protect the interests of the Great Apes has been achieved in New Zealand with the passage of the *Animal Welfare Act* 1999 which places certain restrictions on the use of non-human hominids in research. It does not however grant the Great Apes enforceable rights.

4   James T McHugh 'What is the Difference Between a "Person" and a "Human Being" within the Law?' (1992) 54 *Review of Politics* 445, 446.

5   The twenties produced Alexander Kokourek's account of the person, *Jural Relations* (Indianapolis: Bobbs-Merrill, 2nd ed, 1928). In 1931 Charlton

Kemp Allen published *Legal Duties and Other Essays in Jurisprudence* (Aalen: Scientia) and in 1938 Alexander Nekam published *The Personality of the Legal Entity* (Cambridge, Mass.: Harvard University Press) which remains the most sustained critical analysis of the subject this century.

6   Richard Tur 'The "Person" in Law' in Arthur Peacocke and Grant Gillett (eds) *Persons and Personality: A Contemporary Inquiry* (Oxford: Basil Blackwell, 1987), 123.

7   Corporate lawyers remain interested in legal personality as it applies to corporations and so the modern literature on personality is mainly about the so-called artificial entity of the corporation.

8   Hans Kelsen *Pure Theory of Law* (Berkeley: University of California Press, 1967), 173–174.

9   Hans Kelsen *General Theory of Law and State* (New York: Russell and Russell, 1945), 93.

10   Bryant Smith 'Legal Personality' (1928) 37 *Yale Law Journal* 283, 294.

11   Albert Kocourek *Jural Relations,* 292.

12   Reginald WM Dias *Jurisprudence* 5th ed (London: Butterworths, 1985), 270.

13   Ibid.

14   Tur 'The "Person" in Law', 121–2.

15   John W Salmond *Salmond on Jurisprudence* 12th ed (London: Sweet and Maxwell, 1960), 306.

16   The ability of persons with an intellectual disability to make a contract depends on whether they understand the nature of each specific contract: *Gibbons* v *Wright* (1954) 91 CLR 423.   Intellectual disability also raises issues of undue influence and unconscionability.

17   Salmond *Salmond on Jurisprudence,* 298.

18   Tur 'The "Person" in Law', 122.

19   Phillipe Ducor 'The Legal Status of Human Materials' (1996) 44 *Drake Law Review* 195, 200.

20   David Kinley (ed) *Human Rights in Australian Law: Principles, Practice and Potential* (Sydney: Federation, 1988), 4.

21   Ibid, 5.

22   John Chipman Gray *The Nature and Sources of the Law* (New York: Macmillan, 2nd ed, 1921), 28.

23   Ibid, 30.

24 See Lon Fuller *Legal Fictions* (Stanford University Press, 1967) especially at 19 for his commentary on the legal fiction of the person.

25 Patrick W Duff *Personality in Roman Private Law* (Cambridge University Press, 1938), 3.

26 George W Keeton *The Elementary Principles of Jurisprudence* (London: Sir Isaac Pitman and Sons, 1930), 117.

27 John Austin *Lectures on Jurisprudence* (London: John Murray, 1886), 164.

28 Marcel Mauss (WD Halls trans) 'A category of the human mind: the notion of person; the notion of self' in Michael Carrithers, Steven Collins and Steven Lukes (eds) *The Category of the Person: Anthropology, Philosophy, History* (Cambridge University Press, 1985), 15.

29 JAC Thomas, *The Institutes of Justinian* (Amsterdam: North Holland Publishing Co, 1975).

30 JAC Thomas *Textbook of Roman Law* (Amsterdam: North Holland, 1976), 66.

31 Ibid, 66.

32 Ibid, 135.

33 Ibid, 387.

34 Ibid, 387–388.

35 Donald R Kelley *The Human Measure: Social Thought in the Western Legal Tradition* (Harvard University Press, 1990), 51.

36 WH Rattigan *Roman Law of Persons* (London: Wildy and Sons, 1873), 3.

37 Ibid, 5.

38 Ibid, 8.

39 Peter Goodrich *Reading the Law: A Critical Introduction to Legal Method and Technique* (Oxford: Basil Blackwell, 1986), 68.

40 Frederic W Maitland and Francis C Montague *A Sketch of English Legal History* (New York and London: G P Putnam and Sons, 1915), 43.

41 Henry de Bracton *On the Laws and Customs of England* Samuel Thorne (trans) (Cambridge: Belknap Press, 1968, first published c1250).

42 Maitland and Montague *A Sketch of English Legal History*, 44.

43 RH Graveson *Status in the Common Law* (London: Athlone Press, 1953), 7.

44 Ibid, 7.

45 Ibid, 9.

46 Ibid, 8.

47 Ibid, 10.

48   Ibid, 13.

49   JH Baker *An Introduction to English Legal History* (London: Butterworths, 1990), 533–4.

50   Ibid.

51   Ibid, 545.

52   Graveson *Status in the Common Law,* 21.

53   She could not complain of spousal rape.

54   Graveson *Status in the Common Law,* 21.

55   William Blackstone *Commentaries on the Laws of England, Volume 1: Of the Rights of Persons* (University of Chicago Press, 1979, reprint of 1st ed 1765), 430.

56   Henry Maine *Ancient Law: Its Connection with the Early History of Society and its Relation to Modern Ideas* (London: John Murray, 1930), 180.

57   Patrick Atiyah *The Rise and Fall of Freedom of Contract* (Oxford: Clarendon, 1979), 60.

58   Ibid, 62.

59   Ibid, 25.

60   Ibid.

61   Blackstone *Commentaries on the Laws of England Vol 1: Of the Rights of Persons* 120.

62   Ibid, 121.

63   Ibid, 136.

64   Ibid, 134.

65   Ibid, 135.

66   Atiyah *The Rise and Fall of Freedom of Contract* 41.

67   CB McPherson *The Political Theory of Possessive Individualism* (Oxford: Clarendon Press, 1964), 3.

68   Blackstone *Commentaries on the Laws of England Vol 1: Of the Rights of Persons,* 411.

69   Ibid, 416.

70   McPherson *The Political Theory of Possessive Individualism.*

71   Katherine O'Donovan 'With Sense, Consent, or Just a Con? Legal Subjects in the Discourses of Autonomy' in Ngaire Naffine and Rosemary J Owens (eds) *Sexing the Subject of Law* (Sydney: Law Book Co, 1998), 46.

72   John Frow 'Elvis' Fame: The Commodity Form and the Form of the Person' (1995) 7 *Cardozo Studies in Law and Literature* 131, 149.

73   Hans Kelsen is an honourable exception here in that he has recognised the ideological function performed by the liberal idea that certain fundamental concepts, such as the German 'subjective right', are external to law. The ideological function is to convey the impression that the individual is in certain fundamental ways secure from legal intervention. See Hans Kelsen *An Introduction to the Problems of Legal Theory* (Oxford: Clarendon, 1992), 40.

4 Sex, Reproduction and the Self-Proprietor

In the last chapter we documented the emergence of the modern legal being: the rational, self-determining, autonomous and, perhaps most significantly, self-owning person. We reflected also on the reasons why positivists have failed to recognise this character: in particular their wilful insistence that the legal person is a purely formal concept. The task of this chapter is to amplify our reply to the positivists by providing a fuller account of the legal person as self-proprietor. We will also consider how well this being serves the population at large. We have seen that this individual is now meant to be all-embracing: he is now universal 'man'. Ostensibly, we are all liberal legal individuals now, autonomous and self-possessing. Our purpose is to indicate some important ways in which this is not the case. We will suggest that the quite particular defining characteristics of the legal person serve to exclude large parts of the population from a full and rich legal life. More specifically, this chapter will suggest that the sexual and the reproductive life of the self-proprietor necessarily characterises him as a certain type of man.

Characterising the Self Owner: Mind/Body Dualism

Who Owns What?

Our analysis of the character of the legal person begins with a closer scrutiny of the structure of self-ownership. What can it mean to say that we own ourselves? Who can be said to own whom or what, and indeed is this an appropriate question to ask? How can it make sense to describe a single entity or being — the human being — as both the subject and the object of property rights? How can the one entity be two?

John Frow has commented on the 'curious reflexivity' of the idea of self-possession in which 'the subject form is split between that which owns and that which is owned'.[1]   But he takes the analysis of the subject and object of property in the person no further: he does not examine precisely *who* owns what or whom. The problem one soon faces with the endeavour to make sense of the writing on self-ownership is that, initially, it is not at all clear who is this mysterious owner. Indeed GA Cohen has denied the need to find such a being, suggesting that this is to misunderstand the concept. In his view '[t]he term "self" in the name of the thesis of self-ownership has a purely reflexive significance. It signifies that what owns and what is owned are one and the same, namely, the whole person'.[2]

Further reflection on some of the different formulations of the concept, however, suggests that self-ownership is usually not intended to denote the entire person reflexively owning the entire person, as Cohen believes it does. Rather there is presumed to be an internal division of the person, two different and distinct parts which represent the owner and the owned. Richard Arneson, for example, expounds the Lockean concept of self-ownership thus: 'Owning himself, each person is free to do with his body whatever he chooses so long as he does not cause or threaten any harm to non-consenting others'.[3]   The subject 'he' of this sentence, the subject of property, is evidently something other than the material being — the body. The body is that which is owned by this nonmaterial subject. In his account of self-ownership, John Christman observes that 'insofar as my body moves or acts, *I* should be the one who has the ultimate say over what it does and where it goes'.[4]   Again a distinction is drawn between the governor of the body and the body itself. In Christman's account, the body is reduced to an 'it' — a thing (the very move that worried Kant).

In his critical account of the idea of self-ownership, JW Harris seems also to equate the idea of self-ownership with body-ownership, necessarily implying a divided self, with the body as the object of property, and something other than the body as the subject of property in self. His concluding remark that 'nobody owns my body, not even me'[5] (ultimately he repudiates the idea of legally-manifested self-ownership)[6] instates an incorporeal 'me' as the potential ethereal owner, and the mundane body as the object of ownership.[7]   What emerges from a close reading of the literature on self-ownership (both for and against it) is an internal structure in which the incarnate mind is divided from the carnal body. Or as Margaret Davies has observed, 'the view of true subjectivity as self-control, self-possession or self-mastery...relies on a dichotomization of our selves into subject and object [or]...into mind and body'.[8] In short, it relies on a form of Cartesian dualism. For Descartes, physical and mental things were utterly distinctive, they were made of quite different stuff, and it followed that the most fundamental division of the human being was between that part of us which thinks (*res cogitans*), and our material beings (*res extens*) that is, the body.[9]

The fiction underlying the work of writers such as Arneson, Christman and Harris is that mind can be separated from flesh. The essential person is identified with what is thought to be the freedom and intentions of the mind, not with the supposedly natural creature of the flesh. The important thing for self-ownership is that the subject 'I' — the person as mind — should retain control of its object body; no-one else should exercise this self-possession or self-control. The divided self must operate in this manner if personhood is to be retained.

The property relation of mind to body may be seen to operate in at least two senses. Relying on the etymology of the word, we can see that the body is being thought of as 'proper to' or belonging to its subject mind. It is a defining attribute of the subject self (defined as mind), a limiting condition which individualises and distinguishes person from person. This is my body, not your body; it is proper to (and so defines) me not you. The body is not the subject person — because that is the mind — but rather it is an object that belongs to that subject. The body is therefore alienated and fetishised. The body is not literally exterior to the person, in the manner of other objects of property (the other sense of property), and yet it is regarded as a form of external housing for the immaterial mind. It is baser, it is mundane, it is inferior, and it is natural. And yet it is a necessary condition of the person.

A second sense in which it might be said that mind owns body is that identified by CB McPherson. As we saw in the last chapter, in our politico-legal tradition we are quintessentially 'possessive individuals' and this would seem to suggest that the true subject self is the rational mind, the superior part of the person, which possesses, and so should take charge of, an object body as well as external objects. If the mind fails to do so, the person is lost. That is to say, McPherson's possessive individual seems to invoke a form of self-ownership conceived of as body-ownership. It demands self-control and the ability to repel the encroachments of others. The body is a thing of nature, of the passions, to be controlled and possessed and used by the rational subject mind to the exclusion of all others. Self-ownership, and hence autonomy, is lost when the flesh is no longer subject to one's own control or is surrendered to another.

As the theorists of property-for-personhood have made plain (Margaret Jane Radin especially,[10] but also Charles Reich[11]), in our liberal legal tradition, our encounter with the other entails a setting down of property boundaries between the other and ourselves. Our property right in ourselves, conceived of as mind controlling body, and our property right in our other possessions ensures that the other by law must keep off and keep out. Thus is personhood preserved. Relations occurring at a distance therefore secure self-ownership within the civil sphere.[12] In our liberal model of the possessive individual, incorporeal minds only must meet, not bodies, with the potential of bodily objectification and so loss of property in self.

The expectation of our law is that it should regulate and facilitate this meeting of minds in civil society, while setting narrow, limiting conditions on the interaction of physical beings. And all this necessarily presupposes a division between mind and body, already conceived of in the pre-social person. In civil relations which preserve property in self, the social encounter is one of establishing boundaries and borders which limit and exclude you and so allow me to retain my essential control of myself. In this understanding of social relations, people relate to one another as 'bounded selves', to borrow a term coined by Jennifer Nedelsky.[13] In this meeting of minds, there is retained a clear differentiation of self-interested wills.

In many respects, modern law operates with this model of public life as a meeting of minds, not of bodies. The starting assumption of criminal law is that it is unlawful for one person intentionally to touch another without their consent; this is, in essence, the basic crime and tort of assault. As Lord Justice Goff declared in *Collins v Wilcock*, 'the fundamental principle, plain and incontestable, is that every person's body is inviolate. It has long been established that any touching of another person, however slight, may amount to a battery'.[14]

In the common law tradition, this view may be traced to William Blackstone who asserted the absolute right to 'personal security' which 'consists in a person's legal and uninterrupted enjoyment of his life, his limbs, his body'.[15] Blackstone believed that a person's integrity depended on a legally-enforceable right to police the boundaries of the body. Full personhood was equated with the effective exercise of something akin to a property right in one's body.

In the civil jurisdiction, the propertied view of persons is evident in the legal conception of the work contract. At first blush, the idea that one can sell one's physical or mental labour to another seems to undermine the concept of the person as proprietor of self, as mind possessed of a body from which all others are excluded. However, mind/body dualism is so fundamental to our understanding of persons in our culture and in our law that we are receptive to the remarkable proposition that a person can go to work for another without their body being wrested from their control. Mind is said to remain in possession of the body because it has agreed (with another mind) to the body labouring for another.[16]

The Self-owner as Sexual Being

We have suggested that the structure of self-ownership entails a relation between a subject mind and an object body, with mind possessing body. This is why it is important to sustain the fiction that persons are not divested of this bodily property in their civil relations, when they work for another. But can the fiction of self-possession be sustained in the most intimate bodily acts of all — the acts of sex? How can civil subjects retain their subjecthood and yet, as a matter of course, make their bodies available to others? The argument that will be developed below is that the very structure of heterosexual sex in marriage (the sex which is presupposed and sanctioned in our law), mirrors the subject-to-object relation of self-ownership, thus ensuring that the subject within sexual relations, who we argue is the man, retains property in self while the woman is cast as his object.[17]

The means by which this possessive form of sexuality is countenanced in a liberal culture ostensibly committed to the more egalitarian social forms of contract, forms which are intended to secure universal property-in-self, is simply to deny the social and conventional nature of sex. Sexual relations are considered to be unlike contractual relations, which are worked out afresh each time according to the intentions of the parties. Rather sexual relations are believed to have a naturally inegalitarian and constant form, a form dictated by nature not society. The fiction is that sex occurs outside the conventions of society — that social meanings are, like clothing, stripped away in the act of sex, to the point that the sex act is just raw nature.[18] The 'natural' heterosexual form of sex is one which allows man to retain property in his own body, while appropriating the body of a woman. Clearly this is no accident, but rather it is integral to the story of the social contract which is a liberation tale of men.[19]

It is because legally-sanctioned sex enables a man to take possession of a woman, but not himself to be taken into her possession, that sexual relations between man and woman in marriage have not been regarded as a breach of the man's bodily boundaries, or as a threat to his property in himself. It follows that man does not go home at night and become unmanned (dispossessed) by physical intimacy with a woman. Nor must he reclaim himself next morning, recover his property-in-self as he goes off to work. For in the act of sex, man's natural role preserves his social role; the one is congruent with the other. Man therefore has sex with a woman without any loss of self-possession.

All of this was once explicit in the common law. Today it is part of the subtext of modern legal doctrine and therefore less apparent. The classic statement about the nature of lawful and appropriate intimacy is that of Blackstone writing about the relation between husband and wife. He declared that '[b]y marriage, the husband and wife are one person in law'.[20] To Blackstone, the wife was an attribute or property of the husband. In his account of the nature of marital relations, Lord Hale also suggested that the wife was an object of sexual property, a physical being over which the husband exercised exclusive rights of use and possession. Hence, in the view of Hale, the husband could not be charged with the rape of his wife.[21] In this common law understanding of relations between husband and wife, the wife by consenting to marriage gave her perpetual consent to sex with her husband, but he did not give himself to her; there was no loss of sovereignty for him.[22]

The modern law of marriage remains the law of approved sex. It spells out the form that sex must take if it is to receive the law's positive sanction, as opposed to mere tolerance.[23] As the Australian High Court recently observed, 'the institution of marriage and the status of husband and wife are inseparable from the connubial rights and obligations which are the incidents of the institution and which give content to the status'.[24] The form of marriage has changed little. It remains as Lord Penzance described it in 1866 in *Hyde v Hyde and Woodmansee*, as 'the voluntary union for life of one man and one woman, to the exclusion of all others'.[25] Thus the core property right of exclusion is absolutely central to the concept of marriage.[26]

As well as the right of exclusion, the proprietary rights of use and possession imbue the legal understanding of marital sex. Connubial or conjugal rights are essentially sexual rights. They are rights to sexual intercourse 'at all reasonable times and subject to fit health' and they are rights which are said to form 'a condition going to the very root of the contract [of marriage]'.[27] In *R v L*, the Australian High Court was at pains to stress the mutuality of conjugal rights.[28] The Court suggested that sexual rights ran in both directions, that there was mutual possession and hence sexual equality. Although it is true that wives have long been able to assert a legal right to sex with their husbands (so in a strict sense the High Court is correct), this proprietary style of sex right, this exclusive right of sexual use, has been at base a male right.

The law of consortium, the law conferring *inter alia* a right to affection and companionship and providing a remedy for its loss, has generally been understood as a husband's right to the affections of his wife, not a female right to male affection. As the Australian Family Court once observed, 'the principle at the basis of the relations between husband and wife is that a husband is entitled to enjoy the society and consortium of his wife'.[29] In 1929, the High Court of Australia made clear that consortium was not a mutual right.[30] So too did the House of Lords in 1952.[31] Though most of the Law Lords considered the husband's right of consortium to be an anomaly, they felt it was so well entrenched that it should be abolished by Parliament (as it later was),[32] not by the courts. The basis of the right, according to Lord Goddard, was the proprietary interest that a husband had in his wife.[33] Lord Morton of Henryton agreed, and noted that, as wives have never had a proprietary interest in their husbands, there was no justification for the extension of the right of consortium to wives.[34]

Moving from the law of approved sex to the law of prohibited sex, that is moving from civil marital law to criminal sex law, we can learn still more about the possessive sexual relations assumed between the sexes. There is little controversy in the proposition that rape laws were originally devised as a means of preserving the sort of male property interests in women which were the concern of the law of consortium — hence the right of the husband to the body of his wife, whatever her view of the matter.[35] In England, the crime of rape remains sex-specific: it is still cast as an exclusively male criminal activity directed at a woman or a man.[36] If a woman is involved, she is necessarily the one who is taken by the man. The crime of rape may therefore be regarded as the law of unacceptable sexual possession of a woman by a man. The sexuality presupposed by English rape laws entails a unidirectional proposal of a man to have sexual intercourse with a woman. The act is lawful when the woman accepts, or submits to, his proposal; it is rape when the woman refuses to be had. In jurisdictions which have rendered the crime gender-neutral, such as those of Australia, the sexual form has remained the same.[37] If considerable persuasion is exercised to achieve this sexual possession, but no direct force is applied or threatened, then the sexual act may still be interpreted as voluntary and normal, as no more than vigorous seduction.[38] For normal sex is consistent with an active, appropriating male sexuality and a complementary passive and surrendering female sexuality. This remains the romantic norm.[39]

The English laws of incest reflect also this possessive understanding of sex. Thus it is an offence 'for a man *to have* sexual intercourse with a woman whom he knows to be his grand-daughter [etc]' and 'for a woman ... *to permit* a man whom she knows to be her grandfather [etc] ... to have sexual intercourse with her by consent'. The background understanding of conventional sexuality is of men *having* sex with women and of women *being had*.[40] He retains property in himself, while she surrenders herself to him.

So entrenched is the male possessive sexuality of sex law that it is exceedingly difficult to imagine, just as a thought experiment, what it would be like if women were to be viewed as sexual proprietors. Certainly gender-neutral sex laws have not achieved this. Our thought experiment requires a good deal more than the simple insertion of gender-neutral language into rape and other sex law. The act of sex surely has to be imagined quite differently. How might rape laws, for example, be redrafted so as explicitly to recognise women as possessive sexual individuals. A crude reversal of the sexual form implicit in the law gives us some idea of the predatory female. Thus it might be an offence for a woman to sexually enclose or engulf the penis of a man with her vagina, without first obtaining his consent or permission. Although the gender-neutral laws of some Australian jurisdictions in fact provide for the rape of a man by a woman, they do not employ language such as this, which explicitly depicts the woman as the sexual aggressor who *possesses* or *takes* or *has* the male. The idea of a woman having carnal knowledge of a man is still alien to legal thinking, though it has been contemplated in social theory. According to Sharon Marcus we can imagine heterosexuality differently.

> In the place of a tremulous female body ... as an immobilized cavity,
> we can begin to imagine the female body as subject to change, as a
> potential object of fear and agent of violence. Conversely, we do not
> have to imagine the penis as an indestructible weapon ... we can take
> the temporality of male sexuality into consideration and bear in mind
> the fragility of erections and the vulnerability of male genitalia.[41]

We are not suggesting that this crude reversal represents a desirable reform
to the law. Rather, the point of our thought experiment of the possessive
sexual female is to demonstrate the extent to which a view of the
possessive male still informs current legal thinking about the nature of sex
between the sexes, despite the liberal claim of universal self-ownership.

The Reproductive Woman as Self-Proprietor

In the last section we considered the operation of the concept of the self-
proprietor within the context of possessive heterosexuality. We saw that in
our current legal understandings of sexuality, it is the heterosexual male
who is necessarily the sexual proprietor, not the female; inversion of this
relation seems to make little sense. Possessive individualism therefore
does not have universal application, as it is supposed to, in modern liberal
legal theory. As currently understood, possessive individualism does not
allow both the man and the woman to retain their ownership of self in the
heterosexual act of sex. The shift to contract and the emergence of the
autonomous individual, described by Maine, is therefore incomplete when
it comes to the sexual woman, for it is men as sexual beings who still do
the owning in the act of intercourse and women who are still thought to be
owned.

A second way of demonstrating the illiberal nature of the legal
concept of self-owner is to consider its application to the pregnant woman.
Indeed as bearers of human beings, there is a strong case for putting
women and reproduction at the centre of legal thinking about personality.
But does it make sense to think of the pregnant woman as an owner of her
self? Does the law allow for this? And if so, what are the implications for
the foetus? Can both woman and foetus be possessive individuals? If the
woman is regarded as a possessive individual, is not the foetus reduced to a

species of property? And reciprocally, if the foetus is granted personality, does not the woman become a form of housing for the foetus?

Legal and moral debates about the status of the pregnant woman and the foetus demonstrate precisely this tension in legal thinking. With the liberal legal individual characterised as a self-proprietor, it seems that women must be afforded full control of their bodies if they are to be recognised as autonomous legal individuals and this must remain the case, whether or not the foetus is at risk. As the English Court of Appeal recently insisted in *St George's Healthcare NHS Trust*, the pregnant woman 'is entitled not to be forced to submit to any invasion of her body against her will, whether her own life or that of the unborn child depends on it. Her right is not reduced or diminished merely because her decision to exercise it may appear morally repugnant'.[42]

Thus the pregnant woman has been declared to be a fully autonomous person. But does this mean that the foetus has neither personality nor protected interests and is simply to be regarded as a part of the woman — in a sense, her property — if she is taken to be a possessive individual? Both judges and legislators have been unwilling to sustain the logic of self-ownership with a late-term foetus. This has generated conspicuous unease among the legal community about the rights of the pregnant woman. For it is not lost on them that if the woman cannot control her body, she is necessarily diminished as a legal person, as proprietor of self. Heroic efforts have been made to resolve this tension, but with limited success.

The Pregnant Woman as Self-Proprietor

The starting presumption of any legal analysis of the status of the pregnant woman in law is that she is indeed a fully autonomous legal person, a possessive individual. As Celia Wells and Derek Morgan have observed, 'The law treats the pregnant woman as if she were not pregnant'.[43] Thus it is usually observed that in most respects at common law, the foetus is not a legal person, and does not have enforceable rights until born and separated from its mother. The pregnant woman and foetus are one legal person and that is the woman. Law thus imposes a unity on the woman asserting that only she is present in law. The foetus is an attribute of her, not a separate entity. One of the most cited authoritative legal statements on the status of the foetus is to be found in the English case of *Paton v Trustees of British Pregnancy Advisory Services*, where it was said that

> The foetus cannot, in English law ... have any right of its own at least
> until it is born and has a separate existence from its mother. That
> permeates the whole of the civil law of this country ... and is indeed
> the basis of the decisions in those countries where law is founded on
> the common law, that is to say, America, Canada, Australia, and, I
> have no doubt, in others.[44]

The Australian Family Court has also confirmed that a 'foetus has no legal
personality and cannot have a right of its own until it is born and has a
separate existence from its mother'.[45] This was a dispute between a married
couple in which the husband sought an injunction to prevent the wife from
undergoing an abortion. Justice Lindenmayer refused the injunction,
observing that the grant of such an order would oblige the woman to carry
the foetus to full term and that 'the fact that the foetus must grow within
the wife's body, not the husband's cannot ... be overlooked'.[46]

Because the foetus lacks legal personality, it cannot be the victim of
an offence against the person, such as assault or homicide.[47] For a homicide
charge to be successful, the baby must be born alive and then die of
injuries sustained *in utero*.[48] Although this is also true for the purposes of a
tortious action in negligence, an action may nevertheless be brought by the
child after it is born (and so acquires personality) in relation to injuries
caused *in utero*.[49] Not only may the action be brought by the child against a
third party, but against the mother herself.[50]

Nevertheless the formal legal recognition of only the pregnant
woman's personality, with the foetus deemed to be part of her, accords
with the conventional legal approach to personification which presupposes
a unitary subject who is clearly separated from other legal subjects and
who is in full possession of their own person and so can assert its rights
against other persons. As Bennett observes, '[r]ights discourse presupposes
a minimal degree of bodily autonomy by the actors claiming their rights. It
assumes one's existence as an individual physically separate from others'.[51]
With differentiation and self-ownership the hallmark of personality, the
idea of a legal person within another legal person is necessarily incoherent
in law. It also poses a profound threat to the autonomy of the pregnant
woman, as Justice Lindenmayer observed. The legal person is by definition
autonomous, self-governing, not heteronomous, not governed by another.
For the woman to be subordinated to the personhood of the foetus would,

in this logic, be to reduce her to a type of foetal incubator or what Purdy has called a 'fetal container'.[52]

Thus, within the current conceptual framework of legal personification, with its unitary autonomous subject,[53] either the woman or the foetus must apparently be reduced to the status of attribute or thing, for the one or the other to be a person. Such is the moral and legal dilemma. Its effect has been to polarise much of the political debate about the status of the foetus, with one group arguing that the foetus should be regarded as a full person, even from conception (this is the conservative position advocated, for example, by the Roman Catholic Church in relation to abortion) and the other group insisting that 'the foetus is part of the woman' (many feminists put this position and so argue that the woman should therefore have exclusive control of herself).[54]   Or as one feminist has put it, 'there is room for only one person with full and equal rights inside a single human skin'.[55]

The Pregnant Woman as Property?

Although the foetus has been most consistently conceptualised as non-person, as a physical feature of the person which is the woman, there are both American and English precedents for subordinating the woman's autonomy to the perceived interests of the foetus *in situ* in instances where her refusal of medical treatment or her drug use has placed the foetus at risk.[56] This has been done either by an explicit recognition of the separate and competing interests of the foetus or by a declaration that the pregnant woman who refuses medical intervention is legally incompetent to do so and therefore her wishes can be overridden. There have also been judicial endeavours to retain a sense of the woman as autonomous legal subject, while recognising that the foetus is something other than a mere part of the woman, that it has a special and protected status, though it does not possess separate rights or separate personality.

What these legal controversies about the autonomy of pregnant women have singly failed to do is explicitly to call into question the adequacy of the self-proprietor model of legal personality. At no time has there been any suggestion that the possessive individual fails in his ability to describe the populace at large. Indeed the most recent cases from England, while formally affirming the rights of pregnant women to refuse medical treatment, simultaneously assert that the starting point of any legal analysis must be the separate, bounded (implicitly non-pregnant), autonomous, legal subject.[57]

In the 1980s, several American State Courts expressed the view that the autonomy interests of the pregnant woman could be subordinated to the interests of her foetus. For example in 1981, in *Jefferson v Griffin Spalding County Hospital Authority*, the Georgia Supreme Court ordered the performance of a caesarean section, declaring that the state had a compelling interest in the welfare of the 'child', which it was thought was almost certain to die without medical intervention. (Despite the court order, and believing intervention to be unnecessary, the woman went into hiding and successfully gave birth without intervention.) In 1986, the Superior Court of the District of Columbia in *In Re Madyun* invoked its *parens patriae* jurisdiction (which protects the welfare of children) to order a caesarean section despite a refusal of treatment on religious grounds. However, a year later the same court strongly asserted the right of the pregnant woman to refuse treatment.[58] But this was only after the woman in question had had her wishes overridden by a judicial order, had undergone a forced caesarean section and after both mother and baby had died. (The woman had advanced leukemia.)

English courts, by contrast, have been more consistent in their expressions of support for the autonomy of the pregnant woman. And yet the practical outcomes of much of the case law necessarily raise doubts about the seriousness of judicial intentions to respect the self-ownership of women when pregnant. In 1992, in *Re T (Adult: refusal of medical treatment)*,[59] the English Court of Appeal confirmed a court order overriding a pregnant woman's refusal of treatment on religious grounds, declaring her to be suffering from duress (applied by her mother). While Lord Donaldson affirmed that 'an adult patient who, like Miss T, suffers from no mental incapacity has an absolute right to choose whether to consent to medical treatment, to refuse it or to choose one rather than another of the treatments being offered', he noted that this may not be the case where the choice may lead to the death of a 'viable foetus'.[60] 'On the facts', according to Lord Donaldson,

> the doctors had been justified in disregarding T's instructions and in administering a blood transfusion to her as a matter of necessity as the evidence showed that T had not been fit to make a genuine decision because of her medical condition and that she had been

subject to the undue influence of her mother, which vitiated her
decision to refuse a blood transfusion.[61]

Even more remarkable is the decision of the English High Court, a
year later, to overrule a pregnant woman's refusal of treatment on religious
grounds (she and her husband were both born-again Christians) in the
absence of evidence of either incompetence or undue influence. In *Re S*,
Sir Stephen Brown P. authorised a caesarean section to be performed,
stating that this was 'the only means of saving her life, and also I
emphasise the life of the unborn child'.[62] Although this decision has since
been doubted by the English Court of Appeal,[63] we should perhaps examine
the practice rather than the rhetoric of the courts. This would cause us to
observe, as Kennedy does, 'the growing line of first instance authority'
justifying the overriding of a pregnant woman's refusal of treatment.[64] Or
as Sara Fovargue and Jose Miola have expressed the implications of the
English cases, 'pregnant women have become a new category of
incompetent adults'.[65]

The case in which *S* was doubted, and patient autonomy strongly
reasserted, concerned a pregnant nurse who had a terror of needles and
who as a consequence refused medical intervention that entailed the use of
needles. In *Re MB*,[66] notwithstanding the Court of Appeal's strong
pronouncements to the effect that competent pregnant women have the
same rights as other competent patients, the Court nevertheless insisted that
in the case before them, the woman was at the time of the relevant decision
temporarily incompetent and so her wishes could lawfully be overridden.
In the view of Ian Kennedy, 'the Court's apparently unequivocal
commitment to autonomy is not, in fact, total. Paternalism, whereby the
final decision is taken for the woman rather than by her, is the trumping
principle'.[67] Fovargue and Miola suggest that after *MB*, 'any pregnant
woman who informs the doctors of her fear of medical procedures, needles
etc, runs the risk of being deemed "temporarily incompetent" and thus
incapable of consenting to, or refusing to consent to, medical
intervention'.[68]

In 1998 the English Court of Appeal (in *St George's Trust*)
disapproved a judicial declaration dispensing with the woman's consent to
a Caesarean section.[69] In this case the pregnant woman insisted that she
wanted the birth to proceed naturally, even though this threatened both her
life and the life of the foetus. Although she refused treatment both verbally
and in writing in the most articulate fashion, she was deemed incompetent

and judicial permission was given for the operation. The Court of Appeal both asserted the autonomy of the pregnant woman and roundly condemned the decision to override the woman's refusal, but it must be said that this was only after the operation had been performed. Thus the Court declared that

> Although human ... an unborn child is not a separate person from its mother. Its need for medical attention does not prevail over her rights ... The declaration in this case involved the removal of the baby from within the body of the mother under physical compulsion. Unless lawfully justified this constituted an infringement of the mother's autonomy.[70]

St George's Trust may therefore be thought to stand for the present right of the competent pregnant woman in England to make her own medical decisions, whatever the consequences for her foetus. Indeed this is how it has been interpreted by Andrew Grubb, who has stated in his commentary on the case that 'A more conclusive defeat for the defendants in S would be hard to imagine. The Court of Appeal ... left no one in any doubt that S had a cast-iron claim in trespass for damages'.[71]

However this does not disturb the line of authority which suggests that a pregnant woman's competence is in jeopardy if she expresses too much fear of the proposed procedure. Moreover, Judge LJ in *St George's Trust* added a further important qualification to the autonomy of the pregnant woman. 'It does not follow without any further analysis', he said, 'that this entitles her to put at risk the healthy viable foetus which she is carrying'.[72] The theory (if not the practice) of female self-ownership is thus preserved, but within limits. To Fovargue and Miola, '[this] assertion of the autonomy of a pregnant woman has a hollow ring to it'.[73]

The Australian position has yet to be settled: to date no Australian court has been required to consider a pregnant woman's refusal of medical intervention. However it seems likely that Australian courts will continue to respect the wishes of the pregnant woman.[74] The existing case law suggests that the Australian courts do not regard the foetus as having separate and independent legal rights. Legal rights and personhood only occur after the child has been born alive. As Helen Reed explains, no criminal law statute in Australia provides that it is an offence for a pregnant woman to deny medical treatment where to do so would endanger the life of her [foetus]. Nor do any of the various emergency treatment statutes which authorise the performance of emergency medical treatment on children without parental consent provide a definition for 'child' which would include a foetus.[75]

According to Reed, 'the trend of authority indicates that the pregnant woman's rights will have priority'.[76] As a consequence, we may assume that the pregnant woman's refusal of treatment will be respected in Australia (should she be deemed competent to make such a decision), which means that the foetus is still construed as an attribute of, or part of, her person, not as a separate legal entity. And so notionally, when faced with the threat of medical intervention she does not want, the pregnant woman retains her property in self.

While this conceptualisation of the foetus as a property of the woman carries the important benefit of preserving the legal independence of the pregnant woman, at least when her decisions are deemed to be competent and free from duress, it clearly causes considerable unease both in legal and feminist circles. Recent comments by the English Court of Appeal and House of Lords reveal the discomfort felt at the reduction of the foetus to body part. Forced into a binary decision — the foetus is either person (which would seem to turn the woman into Purdy's 'container') or a feature of the woman (giving the foetus much the same status as a liver or a kidney) — the courts have opted for the latter but then sought to qualify their decision in a manner which has had no legal effect because it is unintelligible in law.

In *St George's Trust*, for example, the Court of Appeal said that 'Whatever else it may be a 36 week foetus is not nothing: if viable it is not lifeless and it is certainly human'.[77] In *Attorney-General's Reference (No 3 of 1994)*[78] the House of Lords was obliged to consider the legal status of the foetus after a pregnant woman's former lover had stabbed her in the abdomen with the intention of doing harm to both her and the foetus and the baby subsequently died as a consequence. The Lords maintained that the relationship between what it termed 'the mother and her unborn child' was 'one of bond, not of identity. The mother and the foetus were two distinct organisms living symbiotically, not a single organism with two aspects. The mother's leg was part of the mother; the foetus was not'.[79] This was an explicit rejection of the view of the foetus offered by the Court below. The Court of Appeal had asserted that '[i]n the eyes of the law the foetus is taken to be part of the mother until it has an existence independent of the mother. Thus an intention to cause serious bodily injury to the foetus is an intention to cause serious bodily injury to a part of the mother just as an intention to injure her arm or leg would be so viewed'.[80] But according to Lord Mustill, the Court of Appeal was wrong to see the foetus as part of the mother because the woman and foetus were genetically different. Lord Hope was of a similar view: 'the foetus cannot be regarded as an integral part of the mother in the sense indicated by the Court of Appeal, notwithstanding its dependence upon the mother for its survival and birth'.[81]

Pregnancy and the Possessive Individual

Notwithstanding the misgivings of the House of Lords, the prevailing legal view of the foetus seems to be that it is best regarded as a part of the woman and that it has no separate personality. This indeed is the only way that the foetus can be viewed if women are to be afforded the legal status of self-proprietor, as that concept is currently understood. This is not to say that this is an appropriate characterisation of either the pregnant woman or the foetus. As John Seymour has observed, 'in reality, (potential) parents, doctors and others do not behave as if the mother is merely growing a vegetable'.[82] Seymour is clearly dissatisfied with the current legal characterisation of the foetus. The self-proprietor model of the person leaves the courts in a bind, apparently unable to find a satisfactory conceptual home for the foetus.

As it stands, the body-part model of the foetus means that deliberate attacks on a pregnant woman specifically designed to injure the foetus do not generate offences against the person involving the foetus specifically as the victim, because the foetus is a part of a person, not a person itself. But as Seymour is also well aware, to treat the foetus otherwise while we retain our current legal understanding of the person in law is necessarily to make of the woman herself a 'container' or 'incubator'. At present our choices are tightly constrained. Either the woman or the foetus is the person.

Feminists such as Catharine MacKinnon have also commented on the unreality of the prevailing legal understanding of the foetus and challenged us to see it differently. According to MacKinnon,

> Physically, no part takes as much and contributes as little. The fetus does not exist to serve the woman as her body parts do. The relationship is more the other way around; on the biological level, the fetus is more like a parasite than a part. ... She is whole with it or without it ... Fetal dependence upon the pregnant woman does not make the fetus a part of her any more than fully dependent adults are parts of those on whom they are dependent. The foetus is a unique kind of whole ... Whatever credibility the body part analogy has evaporates at the moment of viability ... No other body part gets up and walks away on its own eventually.[83]

Our purpose here, however, is not to undertake the considerable task of legal reconceptualisation of woman and foetus.[84] Our more modest purpose is to show that the ability of the prevailing legal model of the person as self-proprietor to accommodate the facts of pregnancy is a powerful test of its adequacy and its universality. And we have found clearly that the possessive legal individual is rendered incoherent by the cultural and biological facts of reproduction.

What is then perhaps most remarkable about the scale of the existential legal problems posed by the pregnant woman and her foetus is that they have failed even to dent legal thinking about the person as possessive individual. It is remarkable because every human being starts their existence within a woman and yet this fact appears to have little bearing on legal understandings of the person. Thus it is still utterly commonplace in Anglo-Australian-American case law to commence any discussion about the autonomy rights of the person with a 'motherhood' statement about the physical integrity and separateness of persons and their right not to have their personal territory transgressed. The response of law to the legal dilemmas posed by the pregnant woman and foetus has not been to reconceptualise its subject. The standard model of the person remains firmly the non-pregnant and indeed impregnable person, the self-proprietor who possesses clear territorial boundaries[85] and pregnant women remain legal curiosities who must somehow be made to fit the model.

Notes

1   John Frow 'Elvis' Fame: The Commodity Form and the Form of the Person' (1995) 7 *Cardozo Studies in Law and Literature* 131, 155.

2   GA Cohen 'Self-Ownership, World-Ownership and Equality' in Frank S Lucash (ed) *Justice and Equality Here and Now* (Ithaca: Cornell University Press, 1986), 108, 110.

3   Richard Arneson 'Lockean Self-Ownership: Towards a Demolition' (1991) 39 *Political Studies* 36.

4   John Christman 'Self-Ownership, Equality and the Structure of Property Rights' (1991) 19 *Political Theory* 28, 39.

5   JW Harris 'Who Owns My Body?' (1996) 16 *Oxford Journal of Legal Studies* 55, 84.

6   There is indeed a considerable debate among the theorists of self-ownership about whether the concept is useful or even meaningful. Neither Arneson nor Ryan find it a particularly helpful means of characterising the autonomous person. To Arneson it is vague. Arneson 'Lockean Self-Ownership', 54. To Ryan the concept of self-ownership simply does not extend our understanding of human autonomy. Alan Ryan 'Self-Ownership, Autonomy and Property Rights' (1994) 11 *Social Philosophy and Policy* 241, 241–242.

7   One could point to still further examples of this dualism within the literature on self-ownership. Thus Alan Ryan (who suggests that it is 'naive' to ask the question 'who is the owner and who is the owned?') proceeds on the unanalysed assumption that there is a distinction between 'ourselves and our bodies' and makes clear that the body is that which is manipulated by the higher non-material self. Ryan 'Self-Ownership, Autonomy and Property Rights', 254–255.

8   Margaret Davies 'Feminist Appropriations: Law, Property and Personality' (1994) 3 *Social and Legal Studies* 365, 380.

9   René Descartes *Meditations on First Philosophy* (Indianapolis: Bobbs-Merrill, 1960).

10 Margaret Radin 'Property and Personhood' (1982) 34 *Stanford Law Review* 957 and Margaret Radin *Reinterpreting Property* (University of Chicago Press, 1993).

11 Charles Reich 'The New Property' (1964) 73 *Yale Law Journal* 733; and Charles Reich 'The Individual Sector' (1991) 100 *Yale Law Journal* 1409.

12   For an analysis of the impersonal nature of civil relations see Katherine O'Donovan *Sexual Divisions in Law* (London: Weidenfeld and Nicholson, 1985).

13   Jennifer Nedelsky 'Law, Boundaries and The Bounded Self' in Robert Post (ed) *Law and the Order of Culture* (University of California Press, 1991).

14   [1984] 3 All ER 374, 378.

15   William Blackstone *Commentaries on the Laws of England, Volume 1: Of the Rights of Persons* (University of Chicago Press, 1979, reprint of 1st ed 1765), 125.

16   See Rosemary J Owens 'Working in the Sex Market' in Ngaire Naffine and Rosemary J Owens (eds) *Sexing the Subject of Law* (North Ryde: LBC and London: Sweet and Maxwell, 1997), 119 for a fuller discussion of the way law sustains this illusion.

17   The central case of sex, the sex which is institutionalised and which remains the sex at the heart of the legally-defined family, is sex between a man and a woman. In England, consenting sex between men is lawful if performed in certain circumstances (in private, between no more than two adult males). *Sexual Offences Act* 1967 (UK) s1. In Australia, there are not even these limiting conditions on male homosexual sex. However our point, which we will develop below, is that this is still not thought to be the natural and desirable form of sex. Sex between persons of the same sex is tolerated rather than positively affirmed.

18   But as the cultural critic, Angela Carter, has argued cogently, the truth is that: 'We do not go to bed in simple pairs; even if we choose not to refer to them, we still drag there with us the cultural impedimenta of our social class, our parents' lives, our bank balances, our sexual and emotional expectations, our whole biographies'. Angela Carter *The Sadeian Woman: An Exercise in Cultural History* (London: Virago, 1979), 9.

19   As Carole Pateman maintains, the story of contract is a story of men acquiring sex-rights over women. Carole Pateman *The Sexual Contract* (Cambridge: Polity, 1988).

20   William Blackstone *Commentaries on the Laws of England, Volume 1: Of the Rights of Persons* 430.

21   Matthew Hale, *The History of the Pleas of the Crown Volume I* (London: Professional, 1971, reprint of 1736 ed), 515.

22   The husband's immunity from rape prosecution endured late into the twentieth century, until *RvR* [1991] 4 All ER 481 and *RvL* (1991) 174 CLR 379.

23   The considerable economic and social benefits which flow from the ability of sexual partners to fit themselves to the marital form of sex have caused many members of the gay community to argue for the recognition of same-sex marriage. Other gay activists positively reject the idea of same-sex marriage precisely because of its record of sexism and exclusion.

24   *RvL* (1991) 174 CLR 379, at 397–398.

25   *Hyde v Hyde and Woodmansee* (1866) LR 1 P&D 130, 133.

26   The property concept of exclusion running through the Western view of the heterosexual couple has been analysed by Margaret Davies in 'The Heterosexual Economy' (1985) 5 *Australian Feminist Law Journal* 27.

27   *Lush on the Law of Husband and Wife* (1933) 33 quoted in *RvL* (1991) 174 CLR 379, 395.

28   Ibid, 398.

29   *Lotz v Bullock* (1912) St R Qd 36, 48 per Chubb J.

30   *Wright v Cedzich* (1929) 43 CLR 493.

31   *Best v Samuel Fox & Co Ltd* [1952] 2 All ER 394.

32   *Administration of Justice Act* 1982 (UK) s2.

33   [1952] 2 All ER 394, 398.

34   Ibid, 400.

35   Australia, Model Criminal Code Officers Committee, *Model Criminal Code Chapter 5, Sexual Offences Against the Person: Discussion Paper* (Canberra: The Committee, 1996) Introduction.

36   *Sexual Offences Act* 1956 (UK) s1 as amended by the *Criminal Justice and Public Order Act* 1994 (UK) s142.

37   A more detailed discussion of the possessive sexuality still implicit in Australia's gender-neutral rape laws is to be found in Ngaire Naffine 'Possession: Erotic Love in the Law of Rape' (1994) 57 *Modern Law Review* 10; and 'Windows on the Legal Mind: Evocations of Rape in Legal Writing' (1992) 18 *Melbourne University Law Review* 741.

38   The concept of consent in Australian rape law is subjected to critical scrutiny in Vicki Waye 'Rape and the Unconscionable Bargain' (1992) 16 *Criminal Law Journal* 94.

39   In Australia, this possessive form of sexuality was recently sanctioned by a current member of the South Australian Supreme Court. During a rape trial Bollen J approved the 'no rougher than usual handling' of a husband by a wife, in order to persuade her to have sex. See *Case Stated by DPP (No 1 of 1993)* (1993) 66 A Crim R 259.

40   *Sexual Offences Act* 1956 (UK) s10. For a brief analysis of the possessive language employed by English incest laws see Nicola Lacey, Celia Wells and Dirk Meure, *Reconstructing Criminal Law: Critical Perspectives on Crime and the Criminal Process* (London: Weidenfeld and Nicholson, 1990), 355.

41   Sharon Marcus 'Fighting Bodies Fighting Words: A Theory and Politics of Rape Prevention' in Judith Butler and J W Scott (eds) *Feminists Theorize the Political* (New York: Routledge, 1992), 400.

42   *St Georges Health Trust v S.* [1998] 3 WLR 936, 957.

43   Celia Wells and Derek Morgan 'Whose Foetus is it?' (1991) 18(4) *Journal of Law and Society* 431, 431.

44   [1978] 2 All R 987, 989.

45   *In the Marriage of F* (1989) 13 Fam LR 189 per Lindenmayer J. The Australian High Court has similarly stated that 'a foetus has no right of its own until it is born and has a separate existence from its mother'. AG *(QD) (Ex rel Kerr) v T* (1983) 57 ALJR 285, 286 per Gibbs CJ.

46   (1989) FLC 92–031, 77,437–77,438.

47   A few American jurisdictions have extended, by statute, the definition of homicide to include the killing of the foetus. See John Seymour *Childbirth and the Law* (Oxford University Press, 2000), 141.

48   Thus in *R v Hutty* [1953] VLR 338 it was asserted that 'Murder can only be committed on a person who is in being, and legally a person is not a being until he or she is fully born in a living state. A baby is fully and completely born when it is completely delivered from the body of its mother and it has a separate and independent existence in the sense that it does not derive its power of living from its mother': per Barry J, 339. This position has been recently confirmed by the House of Lords (in *Attorney-General's Reference (No 3 of 1994).* See also Jane E S Fortin 'Legal Protection for the Unborn Child' (1988) 51 *Modern Law Review* 54.

49   *Watt v Rama* [1972] VR 353 (in which the pregnant woman was in a motoring accident and injured by the negligence of the defendant) is the leading Australian case. See also *X and Y (By Her Tutor X) v Pal* (1991) 23 NSWLR 26 (in which an obstetrician and gynaecologist failed to perform a syphilis test on a pregnant woman).

50   See *Lynch v Lynch* (1991) 25 NSWLR 411 (CA) in which the mother who caused injuries to her foetus by her negligent driving was held to owe a duty of care to the foetus.

51   Belinda Bennett 'Pregnant Women and the Duty to Rescue: A Feminist Response to the Fetal Rights Debate' (1991) *Law in Context* 70, 86.

52   See Laura Purdy 'Are Pregnant Women Fetal Containers?' (1990) 4 *Bioethics* 273.

53   Although it is not the purpose of this paper to canvass other models, it has been suggested that the pregnant woman and her foetus could be treated as 'two indivisibly linked entities', rather than as 'one entity' or as separate, and potentially conflicting, entities. See John Seymour 'A Pregnant Woman's Decision to Decline Treatment: How Should the Law Respond?' (1994) 2 *Journal of Law and Medicine* 27, 27.

54   Isabel Karpin 'Foetalmania: Foetal Legal Identity and the Three Headed Monster' (1994) 5(1) *Polemic* 10, 12.

55   MA Warren 'The Moral Significance of Birth' (1990) 4 *Hypatia* 46 quoted in Wells and Morgan 'Whose Foetus is it?', 431.

56   See especially *Jefferson v Griffin Spalding County Hospital Authority* (1981) 247 Ga 86, 274 SE 2d 457 (Supreme Ct of Georgia) and *In re Madyun* (DC Super. Ct. July 26 1986) 114 Daily Wash. L.Rptr. 2233. The American decisions are discussed in Belinda Bennett *Law and Medicine* (North Ryde: LBC, 1997), 127–131. But note that more recently (in 1994) the Appellate Court of Illinois (*In Re Baby Boy Doe* 632 NE 2d 326) refused to compel a woman to undergo caesarean section asserting that 'the rights of the foetus should not be balanced against the rights of the mother', 333.

57   See for example the strong endorsement of the right to refuse contact issued by LJ Schloss in *Re MB (Medical Treatment)* [1997] 2 FLR 426 (and the ultimate declaration by the court that this particular pregnant woman lacked competence).

58   *In Re AC* 533 A 2d 611 (1987).

59   [1992] 4 All ER 649.

60   Ibid, 653.

61   Ibid, 653.

62   *Re S* [1992] 4 All ER 671, 672.

63   *Re MB (Medical Treatment)* [1997] 2 FLR 426.

64   Ian Kennedy 'Commentary on Re MB' (1997) 8 *Medical Law Review* 317, 319.

65   Sara Fovargue and Jose Miola 'Policing Pregnancy: Implications of the Attorney-General's Reference (No 3 of 1994) (1998) 6 *Medical Law Review* 265, 281.

66   *Re MB (Medical Treatment)* [1997] 2 FLR 426.

67   Kennedy 'Commentary on Re MB', 323.

68   Fovargue and Miola 'Policing Pregnancy', 283.

69   *St George's Healthcare NHS Trust v S* [1998] 3 WLR 936.

70   Ibid, 692 per Judge LJ.

71   Andrew Grubb, 'Commentary on St George's Healthcare NHS Trust v S' (1998) 6 *Medical Law Review* 356, 363.

72   *St George's Healthcare NHS Trust v S* [1998] 3 WLR 936, 951-952 per Judge LJ.

73   Fovargue and Miola 'Policing Pregnancy', 286.

74   See Seymour, 'A Pregnant Woman's Decision to Decline Treatment', 27 and Seymour *Childbirth and the Law*. Helen Reed also expresses this opinion: 'A Pregnant Woman's Rights Versus a Fetus's Rights: What is the Australian Position?' (1996) 4 *Journal of Law and Medicine* 165, 175.

75   Reed 'A Pregnant Woman's Rights Versus a Fetus's Rights', 172–173.

76   Ibid, 175.

77   *St George's Healthcare NHS Trust v S* [1998] 3 WLR 936, 952.

78   *Attorney General's Reference (No 3 of 1994)* [1998] AC 245.

79   Ibid, 255.

80   [1996] 2 WLR 412, 422.

81   [1998] AC 245, 267.

82   John Seymour 'Commentary: Unborn Child (Pre-Natal Injury): Homicide and Abortion, Attorney-General's Reference (No 3 of 1994)' (1995) 3(3) *Medical Law Review* 299, 306.

83   Catharine MacKinnon 'Reflections on Sex Equality under Law, (1991) 100 *Yale Law Journal* 1281, 1316.

84   An excellent sustained analysis of this relationship is to be found in Seymour *Childbirth and the Law*. See also Isabel Karpin 'Reimagining Maternal Selfhood: Transgressing Body Boundaries and the Law' (1994) 2 *Australian Feminist Law Journal* 36 and Jennifer Nedelsky, 'Property in Potential Life? A Relational Approach to Choosing Legal Categories' (1993) 6 *Canadian Journal of Law and Jurisprudence* 343.

85   Critical discussions of the 'bounded self' are also to be found in Jennifer Nedelsy 'Law, Boundaries and the Bounded Self' and Ngaire Naffine 'The Body Bag' in Ngaire Naffine and Rosemary J Owens eds *Sexing the Subject of Law* (North Ryde: LBC and London: Sweet and Maxwell 1997), 79.

5 Personality and Property at the End of Life: The Will and the Corpse

By now we have learned several important things about the relation between personality and property. One is that our jurisprudential understanding of the person is that of a proprietor of self and of the external world. In modern Western law, to own is to be. We are quintessentially possessive individuals. It is therefore wrong to say that personality and property are mutually exclusive legal concepts, though this is legal orthodoxy. Rather, the idea of property permeates our idea of personality: ownership is at the heart of legal being.

We have discovered also that possessive individualism in law, though still robust in contemporary legal thinking, fails to supply a sensible, credible understanding of our embodied selves. For one thing, it is only through a gross distortion of the workings of heterosexuality that possessive individualism is sustained within the laws of sex. Even then possessive individualism is not given the universal application that our liberal law demands. That is to say, it is men who are still expected to possess women in the act of sex (regardless of the physical facts) and so women have yet to ascend to the status of possessive individuals in lawful sex.

We have further reflected on the ways that women are diminished as self-proprietors not only in the act of sex with men, but also if they become pregnant. Again, a law that is notionally committed to the idea that we are all now (self) possessive individuals has been found to deal poorly with the facts of female embodiment. The modern legal person as proprietor must be able to possess and make decisions about the fate of their most important possession — their body. And yet repeatedly this fundamental right to decide what is to happen with one's physical person has been denied the pregnant woman.

In this chapter we will discover that possessive individualism poses further, related problems at the end of biological and legal life. It clouds our legal understanding of the body at death, to the point that we are not at all sure how to characterise the corpse in law. Is it owner or owned? Is it person or property? The available conceptual vocabulary does not seem up to the task of making legal sense of the dead body.

The pervasive legal idea that we are most-characteristically proprietors generates another problem in relation to the proprietorial will of the person. The problem is how to kill off the proprietor: how to stop him or her exerting control after death. Because the will of the person as proprietor can be documented, and so does not depend on continuing corporeal life, lawyers have had to find ways of limiting the effects of the possessive individual beyond the grave.

Legal Status at the End of Life

In the last chapter we further observed that a form of Cartesian dualism[1] imbues legal understandings of the sexual person and that it is also implicit in the legal view of the reproductive person. This is true as well at the end of life. That is to say, the lawyer tends to divide the dead person in two: into body and mind. At death, there is the person as a material thing: a set of physical remains calling for lawful disposal in a proper manner. Then there is the person as a set of legal intentions regarding the disposition of property, expressed by a person of sound mind and set down in a legal document called the will. This is in fact how law analyses the deceased — bisecting the person, and then according one part far greater priority than the other. In the mind of the person, in the sovereign rational will of the proprietor at death, law continues to find personality in the deceased, and so extends legal existence beyond death. However lawyers find virtually nothing in the way of personality in the corpse and indeed do tend to treat 'it' as a species of property.

Legal Personality as Expressed in the Will

The question 'When does a legal person die?', or to put it in a more lawyerly way, 'When does legal personality cease?', is susceptible of no clear answer, partly because legal personality is not a static monolithic thing with a persistent character over time and place whose cessation is easily recognisable. As we saw in Chapter Three, legal personality is better regarded as a cluster of legal capacities and incapacities and attendant rights and duties, which greatly varies according to such factors as age, sex, legal purpose and jurisdiction. However the most commonly stated view is that biological (though still legally defined) death[2] marks the end of the legal person. Thus in a recent text on succession it is observed that 'English law proceeds upon the basis that the deceased as a legal person does not survive his physical death'.[3] Paton's *Jurisprudence* is cited as authority for the proposition that 'Most modern legal systems lay down the rule that, in cases where legal personality is granted to human beings, personality begins at birth and ends with death'.[4]

According to Simes, 'In the Anglo-American system of law, the dead have neither rights nor duties ... We may appoint a guardian *ad litem* to protect the expectant interests of the unborn. There is no guardian *ad litem* for the deceased because he has no interest'.[5] However Simes then concedes that 'though death eliminates a man from the legal congeries of rights and duties, this does not mean that his control, as a fact, over the devolution of his property has ceased. A legal person he may not be; but the law still permits his dead hand to control'.[6]

More recently, Richard Tur has suggested, however, that the definition of the end of a legal life is not as sharply-defined as Simes would have it.

> We do not even have ... any clear idea of when a legal person comes into being or when he ceases to exist. ... Nor should we regard physical death as marking the termination of legal life, if for no other reason than the existence of a legal will, through which the physically dead person seeks to control the disposition of his property.[7]

The law of testation in fact has been accorded a central place in English law. As we saw in Chapter Two, when we briefly sketched the history of property, the right to dispose of property has long been regarded as essential to the legal freedom of the individual. This suggests that the operation of the legal will should, as Richard Tur intimates, be regarded as a vital sign of continuing legal life after biological death.[8] The law of bequest has been described as standing alongside the law of contract as the 'two great institutions without which modern society can scarcely be supposed of holding together'.[9] To the eighteenth-century jurist, William Blackstone, wills were 'necessary for the peace of society'[10] and testamentary freedom was a 'principle of liberty'.[11] Blackstone also believed, more controversially, that private property rights were 'sacred and inviolable' and 'probably founded in nature'.[12]

The great utilitarian thinker, and debunker of the common law, Jeremy Bentham, expounded similar views on the utility of testamentary disposition; he took as given his postmortem legal powers to control and dispose of his property.[13] For Bentham, his will as a proprietor of his external possessions, and even of his physical remains, necessarily transcended his biological death. Bentham explicitly proclaimed and justified the purposes and effects of testamentary freedom. He (rightly) assumed and asserted his legal effectiveness as a proprietor, even beyond his own biological life, because he believed so firmly in both the validity and utility of the power of bequest.[14] Bentham regarded his right to dispose of his property as fundamental to his ability to control and prescribe the behaviour of the next generation (though he was himself without issue). It was a natural extension of his paternal authority.[15] In his *Principles of the Civil Code*, Bentham thus asserted that:

> The power of making a will .... may ... be considered as an instrument of authority, confided to individuals, for the encouragement of virtue and the repression of vice in the bosom of families. ... The interest of each member of the family is, that the conduct of each should be conformable to virtue, that is to say, to general utility. ... In this respect, every proprietor may obtain the confidence of the law. Clothed with the power of making a will ... he may be considered as a magistrate set over the little kingdom which is called a family, to preserve it in good order. ... The power of making a will ... is a means of governing, under the character of *master*, not for the good of those who obey, as in the preceding article, but for the good of those who command. The power of the present generation is thus extended over a portion of the future, and the wealth of each proprietor is in some respect doubled. By means of an assignment upon a time when he shall be no more, he procures a multitude of advantages beyond what he actually possesses. By continuing beyond the term of their minority, the submission of

children, the indemnity for parental cares is increased; an assurance is given to the parent against ingratitude; and though it would be more pleasant to think that such precautions were superfluous, yet, if we reflect upon the infirmities of old age, it will be perceived, that it is necessary to leave all these factitious attractions to serve as their counterpoise. In the rapid decline of life, it is proper to husband every resource; and it is not without advantage, that interest is made to act as the monitor of duty.[16]

For Bentham, then, the will was a form of paternal command, ensuring the continuing submission of children.[17] Quite explicitly, 'The power of the present generation [was thus] extended over a portion of the future'. A man's will ensured the subsistence of his legal personality, asserting his proprietorial authority after his death. Bentham was writing at a time when women were divested of most of their property rights upon marriage and so he was therefore writing, quite literally, of paternal authority. At common law, marriage meant that a woman's property vested in her husband.[18] Married women also lacked contractual capacity.[19] It was not until the Married Women's Property Acts, some 150 years later, that women were granted the power to own separate property.[20] In asserting his rights to have his intentions honoured after death, however, Bentham was also insisting, as does law, that his legal effect should not stop at his death, for that would be to undermine his paternal authority.

It has been said that testamentary freedom 'crystallised eighteenth century liberal thinking in relation to property' and was seen as 'a means of self-fulfilment'.[21] As Cockburn CJ observed in the 1870 case of *Banks v Goodfellow*: 'The law of every civilised people concedes to the owner of property the right of determining by his last will, either in whole or in part, to whom the effects which he leaves behind him shall pass'.[22]

The continuity of the legal person after death is further evidenced by the rule against perpetuities which prevents remoteness of vesting of property beyond a life in being and 21 years. That a legal need was seen thus to rein in the legal person, to prevent his controlling the proprietary interests of endless generations that succeeded him, reveals the troubling durability of the legal person. In English law, postmortem property rights have been accorded such significance that they have posed a threat to the free economy. As Gray and Symes explain, 'the unhindered exercise of dispositive power by one generation may curtail or even destroy the dispositive power of succeeding generations'.[23] The perceived legal problem has *not* been how to give expression to the wishes of the dead, a thing assumed, but how to limit their continuing effects.[24] Our argument therefore is that the power of bequest is not only an important element in the bundle of proprietary rights (although it does not always exist in a property relation)[25] but that it is defining of legal personality because property is so important to personality. Blackstone realised this; so did Bentham; and the view persists into the present day.   Indeed, as we maintain throughout this book, ownership of self and the external world remains an essential characteristic of the legal person.

One further reason for saying that legal personality transcends biological death, through the vehicle of the will, is that there has been a long and powerful association between legal personality and the governing rational will, as opposed to the mortal or finite body. By this we mean that in our Western legal tradition, personhood has been regarded as a status based on abstract reason: on the rational disembodied will.[26] A quick and simple example of this legal way of viewing the person is to be found in the idea of the meeting of minds which marks the point of formation of a legal contract. Our legal personhood derives from our ability for rational reflection and deliberated action; our ability to think, to direct our will and so to enter into binding legal relations. As Roscoe Pound observed in his sustained jurisprudential analysis of legal personality, 'the ultimate basis of securing the protected interest [of a legal person] may be said to be the will of the holder of the right'.[27] This will has in turn been characterised as non-material.[28]

The priority that has been given in law to the abstract will as evocative of legal personality therefore strengthens further the argument that, to the extent that a person's will can find legal expression, then so their legal life can be said to persist. Law's reliance on the idea of the person as will endows the legal person with a timeless quality, because the will does not depend on a living human being to give voice to it. A separate document can also do the job.

The Legal Status of the Body after Death

We have suggested that the legal document of the will is a clear expression of continuing personhood. Is this also true of the physical remains of the person? Do lawyers continue to find legal existence in the cadaver and if not, is the body therefore reduced to property? That is, does the body at death assume the legal status of merely a thing for use?[29]

If we return to the reflections of Bentham on death, we would certainly gain the impression that the body at death is stripped of personality and is effectively a form of property. For while Bentham took as given that he should be able to exert his legal will and so extend himself into the next generation, he regarded himself as quite finished at death in a physical sense. Bentham is dryly pragmatic about the remains of his body. They should be treated with neither respect nor reverence, for they were only things for use. Bentham had no patience with what he regarded as the prevailing mystical nonsense about the spiritual significance of his physical remains. He had this to say about cadavers: 'Generally in the present state of things', he claimed, 'our dead relations are a source of evil — and not of good; the fault is not theirs but ours'.[30]

Manifestly with tongue in cheek, though with an underlying seriousness of purpose, Bentham explains his attitude to the bodies of the recently departed:

> They are nuisances — and we make them so: they generate infectious disease; they send forth the monster Typhus, to destroy; — we may prevent this. Why do we not prevent it?
>
> They levy on us needless contributions: undertaker, lawyer, priest — all join in the depredation. To the relatively opulent, pride, vanity, and ostentation, present a compensation: but in the case of the poor, often are the savings of a family thrown into the grave, — relations left destitute, creditors defrauded.
>
> So much for the evil done — and now for the good prevented: of the dead a certain number might have served the living; knight's service, no — what end of utility is in that? but surgeon's service, yes! — and the utility is immense.
>
> Immense as it is, far wider is the field of possible usefulness. As in the progress of time, instruction has been given to make 'every man his own broker', or 'every man his own lawyer': so now may every man be his own statue. Every man is his best biographer. This is a truth, whose recognition has been followed by volumes of most delightful instruction. Auto-Icon — is a word I have created. It is self-explanatory.

> Two objects have been proposed: 1. a transitory, which I shall call
> anatomical, or dissectional: 2. a permanent, — say a conservative, or
> statuary.[31]

And Bentham insisted that he be made a prime example of his own
utilitarian thinking. His will dictated that he be made the subject of an
anatomical dissection and then his skeleton employed as the frame of an
image of himself, a self-statue or 'auto-icon'. Both requests were honoured
on his death.

By mandating that his body be treated with such apparent
insensitivity, Bentham was deliberately setting out to shock. His stated
utilitarian purpose was to ensure the availability of corpses for dissection
by the anatomists and thus to assist medical education which was being
hindered by a shortage of cadavers.[32] Bentham wished to challenge the
dominant contemporary view that the whole corpse was essential for
resurrection and that what was commonly regarded as mutilation of the
corpse by the anatomists would therefore threaten the immortality of the
soul.[33] Bentham's gesture preceded by a matter of months, and indeed
assisted, the passage of the *Anatomy Act*. This Act ensured the availability
of corpses for dissection, both by creating a legal procedure for the
donation of corpses to the anatomy schools by the charitably-inclined and
by giving to the doctors unclaimed corpses from the workhouse.[34]

Despite Bentham's bold insistence that his future corpse was
property, something he as the apparent owner could dispose of at will, and
by will, the law at the time was far from clear on this, and to this day the
law of the corpse remains in a state of uncertainty. As we will discover,
there has been considerable judicial reluctance to characterise the corpse as
property. At the same time, the common law has maintained a fairly
consistent position on the non-personality of the corpse.

A Brief Legal History of the Corpse

The idea that the corpse was not a person, was no-one, was expressed most
clearly in one of the earliest English cases on the status of the corpse. In
Haynes's Case, decided in 1614, one William Haynes was found to have
dug up several graves, taking the winding sheets in which the bodies were
wrapped and re-burying the bodies. It was held 'that the property of the

sheets remain in the owners, that is, in him who had property therein, when the dead body was wrapped therewith; for the dead body is not capable of it. ... a dead body being *but a lump of earth hath no capacity:* also, it is no gift to the person, but bestowed on the body for the reverence towards it, to express the hope of resurrection'.[35] Thus it was early asserted that the dead body could not own property as the corpse was not a person: it was 'but a lump of earth'.

It is in *Haynes's Case,* however, that we can also identify the beginnings of the conceptual uncertainly about the positive legal status of the corpse. For although the corpse was called 'earth', it was not to be subject to the laws of property in the same manner as real earth. In his discussion of this case, some thirty years on, Sir Edward Coke reflected on his role in the decision, confirming that at the time

> we all resolved that the property of the sheets was in the Executors, Administrators or other owner of them, for the dead body is not capable of any property, and the property of the sheets must be in some body: and according to this resolution, he was indicted of felony at the next Assises, but the Jury found it but petty larceny, for which he was whipped, as he well deserved.[36]

In short, the corpse lacked one of the main indicia of legal personhood, the capacity to own property.

But Coke observed also that the corpse 'itself' was not to be regarded as property, and so enunciated explicitly the no-property-in-a-corpse rule. 'The burial of the Cadaver (that is, *caro data vermibus*)' he said, 'is *nullius in bonis*, and belongs to Ecclesiastical cognisance'.[37] To Coke, the corpse was neither person nor property. But having stripped the corpse of both of its two potential legal characters, Coke failed to indicate how it was positively to be viewed in law. He failed to give it a positive presence.

In 1736, Sir Matthew Hale confirmed that the corpse was incapable of owning its winding-sheet, observing that 'if *A.* put a winding-sheet upon the dead body of *B.* and after his burial a thief digs up the carcase and steals the sheet, he may be indicted for felony *de bonis and catallis A.* because it transferd no property to a dead man'.[38] The corpse was not enough of a person to own property. Then, in 1783, William Blackstone reiterated that the corpse itself was not to be regarded as property: it was neither owner nor owned.

> But though the heir has a property in the monuments and escutcheons of his ancestors, yet he has none in their bodies or ashes; nor can he bring any civil action against such as indecently least, if not impiously, violate or disturb their remains, when dead and buried. The parson indeed, who has the freehold of the soil, may bring an action in trespass against such as dig and disturb it: and, if any one in taking up a dead body steals the shroud or other apparel, it will be felony; for the property thereof remains in the executor, or whoever was at the charge of the funeral.[39]

And elsewhere he maintained that

> stealing the corpse itself, which has no owner, (though a matter of great indecency) is no felony, unless some of the gravecloths be stolen with it. Very different from the law of the Franks, which seems to have respected both [stealing of shroud and corpse] as equal offences; when it directed that a person, who had dug a corpse out of the ground in order to strip it, should be banished from society, and no one suffered to relieve his wants, till the relations of the deceased consented to his readmission.[40]

As Blackstone remarked, the Franks dealt firmly with the 'thief' of the corpse, banishing him from society; the English, however, left him unpunished.

The Body Snatchers

The legal status of the corpse was to become a more pressing concern, as corpses assumed commercial value and so became vulnerable to the body snatchers. The reason for the commercialisation of corpses was the rising demand of anatomists for cadavers for educational dissection. Over the course of the eighteenth century, there was a dramatic increase in the number of medical students in Britain. The first private medical schools also emerged.[41] As Clare Gittings observes, 'By the eighteenth century it had become generally accepted that a training in medicine should include a detailed study of anatomy'.[42] However the provision of corpses for medical schools was woefully inadequate. There was no convention of leaving one's body to medicine and in fact the Christian preference for a decent burial countenanced against it. In Scotland, the anatomists had access to 'the body of one executed criminal each year for anatomical dissection'.[43] In England, the doctors were granted around ten corpses of executed criminals per annum.[44]

Moreover the no-property rule meant that it was impossible to buy a corpse with the law's sanction. The same rule, however, also meant that the corpse could not be stolen and so those who disinterred the dead, and 'sold' them to the doctors could not be charged with the felony of larceny. By the end of the eighteenth century, body snatching was considered a serious social problem: 'no corpse was safe from disturbance, no matter how eminent the deceased'.[45] The legal dilemma posed by the activities of the resurrection men was highlighted by the 1788 case of *R* v *Lynn*[46] in which a corpse had been removed from the grave for the purpose of dissection. The court affirmed that:

> The crime imputed to the defendant [was] not made penal by any statute: the only Act of Parliament which has any relation to this subject, is that ... which makes it felony to steal dead bodies for the purposes of witchcraft. ... And the silence of Hale, Hawkins, and Stamford, upon this subject is a very strong argument to shew that there is not any such offence cognizable in Criminal Courts.[47]

There was an action at common law for defacing the monument but not for taking the corpse. 'And all the writers on this subject have considered the injury which is done to the executors of the deceased by taking the shroud, and the trespass in digging the soil; taking it for granted that the act of carrying away a dead body is not criminal'.[48] The court's solution in *Lynn* was to treat the taking of the body as an offence of indecency. It declared the action to be 'highly indecent, and *contra bonos mores*'; at the bare idea alone of which nature revolted'.[49] The fact that the removal of the body was for the purposes of dissection made the offence no less serious.

This was insufficient as a deterrent to the body snatchers and so, in response to public criticism, the English Parliament appointed a Select Committee in 1828 'to report on the degree of social need to obtain bodies for anatomic examination'.[50] Evidence was given by resurrectionists which revealed the scale of the problem. One reported 'that he and his gang had dug up and sold 1,211 adults and 179 smalls (children) in London in the five years 1809 to 1813'.[51] Although the Committee presented its report to Parliament in June 1828, Parliament failed to act until the spur provided by the trial of Bishop, Williams and May, who had murdered a woman and two boys for the purpose of selling their bodies to teachers of anatomy.[52]

The resulting statute provided a specific statutory solution for the doctors' problem of obtaining cadavers and the public nuisance of body snatching. The Anatomy Act 1832

> introduced the principle of licensing. ... Strict rules were imposed upon anatomy schools, including the licensing of both instructors and students of anatomy. ... A simple procedure was created whereby any person or his relatives could direct that his dead body be handed over for anatomic examination. Unclaimed bodies could also be handed over for the same purpose by those in lawful possession of them.[53]

It also abolished the Murder Act which had provided the doctors with their meagre allowance of corpses. The Anatomy Act has been described as 'a simple and completely effective piece of legislation that at one stroke destroyed the trade of the body snatchers'.[54] What it failed to do, however, was to clarify the legal character of the corpse. It left the no-property rule undisturbed, but did not invest the corpse with a positive legal status.

The 'Right' of Burial: Possession and Disposal of the Corpse

Notwithstanding the interventions of Parliament through the Anatomy Act, confusion about the legal status of the corpse persisted. As cases continued to arise concerning who could and who should bury the dead, judges continued to be confounded by the legal character of the corpse. In 1840, in *R v Stewart*,[55] a dispute arose when a woman died in hospital and her husband was too poor to pay for the burial. The hospital sought a writ to have the overseers of the poor of the parish pay for the burial. The court held that: 'Every person dying in this country ... has *a right to Christian burial*; and that implies the right to be carried from the place where his body lies to the parish cemetery' and, quoting another case, 'That bodies should be carried in a state of naked exposure to the grave, would be a real offence to the living, as well as an apparent indignity to the dead'.[56] The court had no doubt 'that the common law casts on someone the duty of carrying to the grave, decently covered, the dead body of any person dying in such a state of indigence as to leave no funds for that purpose. The feelings and the interests of the living require this, and create the duty'.[57] Who bears this duty? In a case such as this, where the next of kin was too poor to bury the body, 'the individual under whose roof a poor person dies is bound to carry the body decently covered to the place of burial'.[58]

In *Stewart*, the court spoke of 'a right of burial', and so appeared to personify the corpse (for only persons can have rights). However this case appears exceptional, the more common view being that the corpse did not have 'rights'. As Potter J observed in the 1872 American decision of *Pierce v Proprietors of Swan Point Cemetery*, 'strictly speaking, according to the strict rules of the old common law, a dead man cannot be said to have rights. Yet it is common to so speak, and the very fact of the common use of such language, and of its being used in such cases ... justifies us in speaking of it as a right in a certain qualified sense, and a right which ought to be protected'.[59] A few years later, the English case of *R v Price* also questioned the accuracy of referring to 'the "rights" of a dead body' in *R v Stewart*, saying this was 'obviously a popular form of expression — a corpse not being capable of rights'.[60]

Over the course of the nineteenth century, the courts continued to negotiate the practical difficulties of, in the first instance, finding someone to bury the dead and then ensuring that the dead were not disturbed once burial had been achieved. The legal problem they had to overcome was that the corpse was *nullius in bonis* (and so was not protected by the law of property) and yet possessed no rights of its own to burial or to remain undisturbed in the grave.[61] In 1857 in *R v Sharpe*[62] the court resorted to the tort of trespass (to a burial ground) when confronted with a man who had disinterred his mother so that she could be buried in a churchyard with his father. The Court insisted that the 'wrongful removal of a corpse' was not excused by the son's filial devotion. 'Neither does our law recognize the right of any one child to the corpse of its parent, as claimed by the defendant. Our law recognizes no property in a corpse ... and there is no authority for saying that [filial] relationship will justify the taking of a corpse away from the grave where it had been buried'.[63]

The American judiciary was less insistent on the no-property rule. In the 1872 decision of *Pierce v Proprietors of Swan Point Cemetery*,[64] dealing with similar facts to *Sharpe*, Potter J acknowledged a '*quasi* property' interest in a dead body. The person having charge of the buried corpse had a right to act to protect it, and held it on a sort of trust for all of those who had an interest in it.

The English courts, however, held firm to the no-property rule. In 1882 in *Williams v Williams*[65] the deceased had stated in his will that he wished his friend Eliza Williams to cremate his body and place his ashes in a Wedgewood vase he supplied for the purpose. The executors ignored this and had the body buried. Ms Williams organised for the disinterment and cremation of the corpse, and then sued the executors for the expenses. The court followed *Sharpe*, saying 'It is quite clearly the law of this country that there can be no property in the dead body of a human being'.[66] This notwithstanding, the court also declared that, 'prima facie the executors are entitled to the possession [of the corpse] and are responsible for the burial of a dead body'.[67] This supposedly non-proprietorial right of the executors to possession of the corpse, and the incidental duty to dispose of it, has continued to be affirmed until the present day.[68]

The questionable logic of the rule that an executor may possess but never own the corpse, and yet has a duty to dispose of it, is not difficult to discern. In the view of one commentator:

> Quite how to reconcile these propositions has remained something of a mystery. In part it has been fudged in that the relatives appear to be only one of a number of groups of persons on whom the duty to dispose is placed. ... In asserting, however, that they may claim the body, English law to that extent recognises a right to the body, if only to carry out the duty to dispose. ... But this cannot be a property right, there being no property in a corpse. At this point English law appears to give up and hope for the best.[69]

More Property than Person?

Despite the reiteration of the no-property rule since the time of Coke, the legal language used to describe the corpse has been drawn consistently from the vocabulary of property law. In particular, the right 'to possess' the unburied corpse, a right which is normally regarded as an incident of property, has been one repeatedly recognised, and American courts have also been willing to concede a quasi-property right in buried corpses.[70] Despite some early references to 'the right' of burial, there is little sense in the case law of the person remaining a person after death. Not only does death mark the moment at which a human being formally ceases to be a person for most legal purposes, but death also marks the moment at which the human form becomes explicitly objectified in law — when the human non-being becomes something to be possessed and disposed of: 'but a lump of earth'.

The most explicit recognition of the 'propertied' view of the corpse is to be found in the leading Australian High Court case *Doodeward v Spence*,[71] decided in 1908. Here the Court was given an unusually free hand to theorise the status of the corpse because of the special nature of the body in question: the corpse was a two-headed baby, and so never quite a person in the eyes of some of the judges. The facts were unusual. The doctor of a woman who had given birth to the still-born baby (40 years earlier) 'took the body away with him, preserved it with spirits in a bottle, and kept it in his surgery as a curiosity'[72] and it was sold at his death. The father of the plaintiff bought the 'bottle and the contents' and the plaintiff displayed it for profit. It was confiscated by the police and the plaintiff sued successfully for conversion and detinue of his 'property'.

One of the two majority judgments was given by Griffith CJ who declared that although the 'unburied corpse awaiting burial is *nullius in rebus*', that does not stop it 'becoming the subject of ownership'.[73] Indeed, '[a]fter burial a corpse forms part of the land in which it is buried, and the right of possession goes with the land'.[74] Here we see a virtual paraphrasing of the early view expressed in *Haynes* that the corpse is 'but a lump of earth'. The very fact that a corpse can be in 'lawful possession', said Griffith CJ, 'connotes a right to invoke the law for its protection'.[75] He maintained also, in a manner reminiscent of Locke, that 'a human body ... is capable by law of becoming the subject of property. ... when a person has by the lawful exercise of work or skill so dealt with a human body or part of a human body in his lawful possession that it has acquired some attributes differentiating it from a mere corpse awaiting burial'.[76] He was however unwilling to express any opinion 'on the question whether a still-born child falls within the authorities relating to human corpses'.[77]

The other majority judge, Barton J, did not regard this 'aberration of nature'[78] as a human corpse and so was able to find for the plaintiff, while casting not 'the slightest doubt upon the general rule that an unburied corpse is not the subject of property, or upon the legal authorities which require the proper and decent disposal of the dead'.[79]

A recent decision of the English Court of Appeal, Criminal Division, has confirmed that parts of a corpse are capable of being property for the purposes of a charge of theft 'if they had acquired different attributes by virtue of the application of skill, such as dissection and preservation techniques'.[80] Thus an artist who had been permitted access to preserved anatomical specimens at the Royal College of Surgeons, who made off with some 35 to 40 body parts, was liable to prosecution under the *Theft Act* 1968.

Over the past several decades, the no-property rule has been rejuvenated by the new medical technologies, the development of transplant surgery and the consequent injection of value in the corpse and its parts.[81] Again the activities of the doctors can be seen to be driving the demand for bodies and their parts, investing the corpse with potential commercial value and so stimulating concerns about the legal nature of both the living and the dead body. This has generated an extensive and rapidly expanding literature on whether the body and its parts should be regarded as property.[82] Although space does not allow for a close consideration of this scholarship, it is pertinent to note that these contemporary debates again disclose a mixed attitude to the body as proprietary interest. On the one hand, the dominant view seems to be that it would be inappropriate to regard the body as property and, to this end, many legislatures around the world have banned the sale of body parts.[83] On the other hand, the legal language employed to describe the body and its reusable parts has borrowed heavily from the vocabulary of property. As Mykitiuk has observed, 'A review of the scholarly legal literature on this subject will find that the vast majority of articles are concerned with issues of ownership, possessory interests, who shares in the profits, supply and demand, exchange transactions and markets'.[84]

Whereas the early legal commentaries and cases had little to say about the reasons for the no-property rule, often simply asserting it to be the case (and usually citing Coke as authority for the rule), there is now a more open ethical debate about the reasons for such a rule. They include the legacy of slavery and a concern that formal property rights in the body would sanction the commodification of human beings. It is also suggested that if parts of the body were to be regarded as proprietary interests, those who are least advantaged would be subjected to almost irresistible economic pressures to sell their parts and perhaps even sacrifice their life and so experience the most gross form of human exploitation.[85]

What is lacking from the modern debate about the legal status of both the corpse and the living body is any sense of 'its' personhood — the sense of a live body with rights or any sense of the rights of the dead. Nor is there a sense of an integrated embodied person whose materiality is part of their essential personhood, and whose body is therefore not objectified but is simply self.

Conclusion

Coming into being and ceasing to be provide important tests of the adequacy of law's concept of the person to the processes of human life. As we have seen in this and the last chapter, at the limits of life, the law has encountered persistent difficulties in making sense of its subject. Fearful of dehumanising and commodifying people, jurists have resisted the idea that there are any stages of the human life cycle in which people are property and yet its limited conceptions have necessarily imposed this understanding. As the person ceases to be, she tends to transform into property, except to the extent that she can assert her abstract, rational proprietary interests. And before personhood is acquired, there is a strong legal tendency to construe the entity coming into being as mere body part. As we saw in the last chapter, the pregnant woman perhaps proves the most rigorous test of the adequacy of law's idea of a bounded unitary sovereign person who is always a self-proprietor and never herself a form of property. Her legal incoherence signals the failure of law to make sense of human transition and the many states of being human. But so too does law's failure to make sense of our mortality.

Notes

1   René Descartes *Meditations on First Philosophy* (Indianapolis: Bobbs-Merril, 1960), 73–122.

2   That is, brain death.   See for example the South Australian *Death (Definition) Act* 1983 which defines death as either 'irreversible cessation of all function of the brain of the person' or 'irreversible cessation of circulation of blood in the body of the person'. But even biological death is an unclear concept because the dying of a person occurs at so many stages, from the death of all consciousness to cellular death.

3   Olive Wood and GL Certoma Hutley, *Woodman and Wood: Succession: Commentary and Materials* (Sydney: Law Book Co, 4th ed, 1990), 309.

4   Ibid. As we discovered in the last chapter, however, this is perhaps an over-simplification of the legal view of the birth of the legal person in that the English courts continue to express concerns about the welfare of the 'viable foetus' and have been unwilling to consign it to legal nothingness.

5   Lewis Simes *Public Policy and the Dead Hand* (University of Michigan Law School, 1955), 1.

6   Ibid.

7   Richard Tur 'The "Person" in Law' in Arthur Peacocke and Grant Gillett (eds) *Persons and Personality: A Contemporary Inquiry* (Oxford: Basil Blackwell, 1987), 123.

8   As Atherton and Vines observe: 'The ability of the testator to leave his or her property by will to whomever pleased him or her (the testator's testamentary freedom) was the dominant doctrine in the common law world for about 200 years before the twentieth century. The emphasis on the right to do what one liked with one's property reflected the succession theory of the time — the importance of the individual, the emphasis on free will, the importance of contract and the rise of capitalism'. Rosalind Atherton and Prue Vines *Australian Succession Law* (Sydney: Butterworths, 1996), 34.

9   Henry Maine *Ancient Law* (London: John Murray, 1930), 222–223.

10   William Blackstone *Commentaries on the Laws of England, Volume II: Of the Rights of Things* (University of Chicago Press, 1979, reprint of 1st ed 1765–69), 489.

11   William Blackstone *Commentaries on the Laws of England, Volume I: Of the Rights of Persons* (University of Chicago Press, 1979, reprint of 1st ed 1765), 438.

12   Ibid, 134–135.

13   These writings are discussed below in the body of the chapter.

14   He was not alone in this. John Locke regarded the power of bequest as part of paternal authority: John Locke *Two Treatises of Government* Peter Laslett (ed) 2nd ed (Cambridge University Press, 1967, first published 1690) *Second Treatise*. Although John Stuart Mill had utilitarian reservations about inherited wealth, he maintained nevertheless that '[e]ach person should have power to dispose by will of his or her whole property': *Principles of Political Economy* 8th ed (London: Longmans, 1878), 281.

15   Bentham himself benefited from an inheritance from his father. For a brief but elegant biography of Bentham see John Dinwiddy *Bentham* (Oxford University Press, 1989).

16   Jeremy Bentham 'Principles of the Civil Code' in John Bowring (ed) *The Works of Jeremy Bentham, Volume I* (Edinburgh: William Tait, 1843), 337.

17   John Locke used similar reasoning to defend the will. He maintained that 'God Planted in Men a strong desire ... of propagating their Kind and continuing themselves in their Posterity'. (Locke *Two Treatises of Government, First Treatise,* 206–207) and that men have a power 'to bestow their Estates on those, who please them best' (*Second Treatise,* 315).

18   Donna Dickenson *Property, Women and Politics: Subjects or Objects?* (Cambridge: Polity Press, 1997) especially chapter 3.

19   Kevin E Lindgren, John W Carter and David J Harland *Contract Law in Australia* (Sydney: Butterworths, 1986), 288–289.

20   The original *Married Women's Property Acts* were passed in 1870 (UK), 1870 (Vic), 1883 (SA), 1884 (Tas), 1886 (NSW), 1890 (Qld) and 1892 (WA).

21   Rosalind Atherton 'Expectation Without Right: Testamentary Freedom and the Position of Women in 19th Century New South Wales' (1988) 11 *University of New South Wales Law Journal* 133, 134.

22   (1870) 5 LR QB 549, 563 quoted in Atherton 'Expectation Without Right'.

23   KJ Gray and PD Symes *Real Property and Real People: Principles of Land Law* (London: Butterworths, 1981), 189.

24   George Haskins '"Inconvenience" and the Rule for Perpetuities' (1983) 48 *Missouri Law Review* 451.

25   John Stuart Mill described 'the right of bequest or gift after death' as forming 'part of the idea of private property' *Principles of Political Economy* 273.

26   Theorised most extensively by Immanuel Kant.

27   Roscoe Pound *Jurisprudence Volume IV* (St Paul: West Publishing, 1959), 196. Pound also observes that, historically, the will has been been regarded as 'the essence of legal personality': *Jurisprudence* 194.

28   There is an extensive feminist and political literature on the abstract, disembodied nature of the legal person. See for example Katherine O'Donovan *Sexual Divisions in Law* (London: Weidenfeld and Nicholson, 1985) and Ngaire Naffine *Law and the Sexes: Explorations in Feminist Jurisprudence* (Sydney: Allen and Unwin, 1990).

29   For a fuller analysis of the legal status of the corpse see Ngaire Naffine 'But a Lump of Earth? The Legal Status of the Corpse' in Desmond Manderson (ed) *Courting Death: The Law of Mortality* (London: Pluto Press, 1999), 95.

30   This short valedictory 'fragment' of writing by Bentham, his self-described 'last work', is extracted and analysed in CK Ogden *Jeremy Bentham 1832– 2032: Being the Bentham Centenary Lecture, delivered in University College, London, on June 6th, 1932* (London: Kegan Paul, 1932) Appendix 12, 119.

31   Ibid.

32   For a fuller description of the body shortage in the eighteenth and nineteenth centuries see Ruth Richardson *Death, Dissection and the Destitute* (London: Routledge, Kegan Paul, 1987).

33   See Clare Gittings *Death, Burial and the Individual in Early Modern England* (London: Croom Helm, 1984); P Linebaugh 'The Tyburn Riot Against the Surgeons' in Douglas Hay et al (eds) *Albion's Fatal Tree: Crime and Society in Eighteenth-Century England* (London: Lane, 1975), 65; RC Finucane 'Sacred Corpse, Profane Carrion: Social Ideals and Death Rituals in the Later Middle Ages' in Joachim Whaley (ed) *Mirrors of Mortality: Studies in the Social History of Death* (New York: St Martin's, 1981), 40; and Caroline Walker Bynam *The Resurrection of the Body in Western Christianity, 200–1336* (Columbia University Press, 1995).

34   In *Death, Dissection and the Destitute*, Ruth Richardson presents a blistering criticism of this legislation and also of Bentham and his role in assisting its passage.

35   (1614) 77 ER 1389, 1389 (emphasis added).

36   Edward Coke *Institutes of the Laws of England Part III* (London: Thames Baset, 1680), 110.

37   Ibid, 203.

38   Matthew Hale *History of the Pleas of the Crown Volume I* (London: Professional, 1971, reprint of 1736 ed), 515.

39   Blackstone *Commentaries on the Laws of England Volume II: Of the Rights of Things* (University of Chicago Press, 1979, reprint of the 1st ed 1765–69), 429.

40   William Blackstone *Commentaries on the Laws of England, Volume IV: Of Public Wrongs* (University of Chicago Press, 1979, reprint of the 1st ed 1765–69), 236.

41   Russell Scott *The Body as Property* (London: Allen Lane, 1981), 5.

42   Gittings *Death, Burial and the Individual,* 74.

43   Scott *The Body as Property,* 5.

44   Gittings *Death, Burial and the Individual,* 74.

45   Scott *The Body as Property,* 6.

46   (1788) 100 ER 394.

47   Ibid.

48   Ibid, 395.

49   Ibid.

50   Scott *The Body as Property,* 8.

51   Ibid.

52   Ibid, 11.

53   Ibid.

54   Ibid, 12.

55   (1840) 113 ER 1007 (emphasis added).

56   Ibid, 1009 (emphasis added).

57   Ibid.

58   Ibid.

59   14 Am Rep 667, 678 (1872).

60   *R v Price* (1884) 12 QBD 247, 253.

61   As the court observed in *Williams v Williams,* 'although there is no property in a dead body ... [the] executors have a right to the custody and possession of his body (although they have no property in it) until it is properly buried. It follows that a man cannot by will dispose of his dead body. If there be no property in a dead body it is impossible that by will or any other instrument the body can be disposed of': (1882) 20 Ch D 659, 665.

62   (1857) 26 LJMC 47.

63   Ibid, 48.

64   14 Am Rep 667 (1872).

65   (1882) 20 Ch D 659.

66   Ibid, 663.

67   Ibid, 664.

68   Thus in the 1992 Australian decision of *Calma v Sesar* (1992) 106 FLR 446, in which a mother and father were in dispute over where their son should be buried, the Supreme Court of the Northern Territory declared that the parents had an equal right and duty to dispose of the body.

However, the court stated that: 'It is clear that there is no property in a human corpse held for the purposes of burial. What the law recognises as incident to the duty to dispose of the body is the right to the possession of the body until it is disposed of' (450). Similarly in the 1996 English decision of *Dobson v North Tyneside Health Authority* [1996] 4 All ER 474, which involved a dispute over the destruction of a brain, the court held that: 'Although there was no property in a corpse, unless it had undergone a process or other application of human skill, such as stuffing or embalming, the executors ... charged by law with the duty of interring the body had a right to its custody and possession until it was buried' (474).

69   Ian Kennedy 'Negligence: Interference with Right to Possession of a Body: Mackey v US' (1995) 3 *Medical Law Review* 233. Note that Australian courts have recently affirmed the American view. Thus in the 1997 New South Wales Supreme Court decision of *Smith v Tamworth City Council* (1997 41 NSWLR 680) the Court approved of the statement in the US case of *Polhemus v Daly* 296 SW 442, 444 (1927) that 'while there is no right of private property in a dead body in the ordinary sense of the word, it is regarded as property so far as to entitle the next of kin to legal protection from unnecessary disturbance and violation or invasion of its place of burial'. The court held that this states the law of New South Wales. In 1999, the South Australian Supreme Court expressed a similar view of the corpse in *Jones v Dodd* (1999) SASC 125.

70   For American cases on buried corpses, see Paul Matthews 'Whose Body? People as Property' *Current Legal Problems* (1993) 201–202.

71   (1908) 6 CLR 406.

72   Ibid, 410–411.

73   Ibid, 411.

74   Ibid, 412.

75   Ibid.

76   Ibid, 414.

77   Ibid, 415.

78   Ibid, 416.

79   Ibid, 417.

80   *R v Kelly* [1998] 3 All ER 741.

81   See discussion in Rosalind Atherton 'Claims on the Deceased: The Corpse as property' (2000) (8)1 *Journal of Law and Medicine* 361.

82   See for example Lori Andrews 'My Body My Property'(1986) 16(5) *Hastings Center Report* 28; Roy Hardiman 'Toward the Right of

Commerciality: Recognising Property Rights in the Commercial Value of Human Tissue' (1986) 34 *UCLA Law Review* 207; Michelle Bourianoff Bray 'Personalizing Personalty: Toward a Property Right in Human Bodies' (1990) 69 *Texas Law Review* 209; Courtney Campbell 'Body, Self, and the Property Paradigm' (1992) 22(5) *Hastings Center Report* 34; Roger Magnusson 'The Recognition of Proprietary Rights in Human Tissue in Common Law Jurisdictions' (1992) 18 *Melbourne University Law Review* 601; Stephen Munzer 'Kant and Property Rights in Body Parts' (1993) 6 *Canadian Journal of Law and Jurisprudence* 319; Brian Hannemann 'Body Parts and Property Rights: A New Commodity for the 1990s' (1993) 22 *Southwestern University Law Review* 399; Paul Matthews 'The Man of Property' (1995) 3 *Medical Law Review* 251; Danielle Wagner 'Property Rights in the Human Body: The Commercialisation of Organ Transplantation and Biotechnology' (1995) 33 *Duquesne Law Review* 931.

83   In South Australia, there is a prohibition on trading in tissue contained within the *Transplantation and Anatomy Act* 1983. Section 35 says that 'a contract or arrangement under which a person agrees, for valuable consideration ... to the sale or supply of tissue from his body or from the body of another person, whether before or after his death ... is void.'

84   Roxanne Mykitiuk 'Fragmenting the Body' (1994) 2 *Australian Feminist Law Journal* 77.

85   See discussion in Scott, *The Body as Property*, especially 183, and articles listed in note 82.

6 Intellectual Property in the Person

In the previous two chapters we considered the nature of the person–property distinction in some cases where full legal personality is not completely assured. In Chapter Four, we saw that the notion of the self-owning individual has not been readily applied to women. In particular, when women are considered by law as participants in heterosexual sex or as pregnant, they are not regarded as self-proprietors and autonomous, but may be subject to the control of another. The model legal person is not pregnant. In Chapter Five, we examined another instance of an entity which is regarded as having both (limited) attributes of legal personality and some of the attributes of property — the dead. Once a person has died, their documented will is recognised, but their bodily remains are necessarily subject to the control of others, who may even have a limited and exclusive right to determine matters relating to burial. It is in these marginal cases that the dichotomy between person and property is most in tension. Where the physical 'person' under consideration departs from the standard model envisaged by the law, it is not always clear how the person is to be treated. Cases overriding the will of a pregnant woman, while asserting strongly her moral autonomy, indicate very clearly the uncertainties of the legal approach to personhood.

In this and the next chapter, we discuss the problem of self-ownership as it relates to attributes of the physical self which can be rendered as abstract objects. In this chapter, we will consider the law relating to control and ownership of the image or 'persona' in media such as photographs, pictures, or other reproductions of personal attributes. In Chapter Seven we analyse some of the issues raised by patenting of genetic patterns. Genetic sequences, while derived from a physical body, are reduced to codes or information: it is not the ownership of the actual body which is at stake, but rather the control of information derived from the body.

It has been recognised in Canada, as well as in parts of the United States, that a person has a proprietary interest in their 'persona',[1] whether that persona has been commercially marketed or not. This is one of the most explicit examples of recognition of a form of self-ownership by the law. Ownership of the persona is enshrined in what has been termed a 'right of publicity'. Cases involving a variety of celebrities, such as Elvis Presley, Bette Midler, Jackie Onassis and Martin Luther King,[2] have been central in developing this form of self-ownership. The courts in Australia have been much more reluctant to recognise a proprietary interest in the persona, although in cases dealing with 'character merchandising' it has arguably been recognised that a person has an interest in the realisation of the *commercial* value of their persona. Such results do not amount to *de jure* recognition of property in the image, but they do achieve some of the same practical results as such recognition. English courts have been even more cautious about extending proprietary rights to those whose images have a commercial value.[3] In previous chapters we have noted that any explicit acknowledgement of self-ownership has brought with it a fear of commodification of persons. Such a fear may explain the reluctance of the English and Australian courts to adopt the North American approach.

The question of whether we can own our 'persona' generates further interesting questions about the property-person relationship. Exactly what can be said to be 'owned' here, and what is the content of such ownership rights? Is the persona as image, or other distinct attribute, separable from the physical person? Should persona in certain cases be recognised as part of the intellectual commons 'owned' by all humanity? What does 'ownership' mean in this context, and how has the liberal discourse of self-ownership been deployed? In keeping with the argument of the book to date, this chapter aims to consider the ways in which the liberal idea of self-possession is reflected in law concerning ownership of the persona. As we will see, the delineation between 'property' and 'person' in this context involves a delicate balancing of the private interest to control uses of one's own image and the public interest in gaining access to images of famous persons. We will also consider more broadly some of the philosophical dimensions of this particular problem.

Persona — Commodifying the Mask

> So that a *Person*, is the same as an *Actor* is, both on the Stage and in
> common conversation; and to *Personate*, is to *Act*, or *Represent*
> himselfe, or an other; and he that acteth another, is said to beare his
> Person, or act in his name[4]

Because intellectual property concerns abstract objects rather than physical
things, the object of intellectual property in a person is not the body but
rather abstractions of the self which are intrinsically repeatable.[5] As we
noted in Chapter Four, the very concept of self-ownership divides the self
into two, normally a mind and a body. Ownership of the 'persona' makes
this division explicit, except here the 'object' which is owned by the self is
not the body itself, but rather representations of the body. Such
representations are not unique, as is the physical body, but can be
reproduced repeatedly, for instance, as a photograph in a magazine.

Intellectual property is a species of property in intangibles.
Importantly, there is no single category of 'intellectual property', but rather
a range of different types of intellectual property, such as patents,
copyright, and designs.[6] These forms of intellectual property are like other
forms of property in that they protect the right of the owner to exclude
others from the use and enjoyment of the abstract object. They are also
different in other respects. For instance, a patent in most cases lasts only
twenty years, while in most cases copyright lasts for fifty years after the
death of the author, composer or artist.[7] By contrast to the case of property
in a personal chattel, which continues for as long as the chattel itself exists,
property in an invention simply expires with the passing of time.[8] Some
areas of law which are sometimes included within the category of
'intellectual property' do not fit into a traditional notion of property: for
instance, the requirements of the tort of passing off, which has been used
in Australia to protect persona, are not satisfied by showing a mere taking
or appropriation, but rest upon the existence of some form of deception.
The category of intellectual property, therefore, illustrates the
'disaggregation' of the notion of property which we discussed in Chapter
Two.

Unlike property in physical things, intellectual property protects
'things' which are infinitely reproducible, and which obtain their
commercial value largely through the policing and protection afforded by

law. The phrase 'Sydney 2000' has no natural scarcity and could potentially be used in a variety of commercial and non-commercial contexts. The phrase has a social value because of its association with a particular event, but its commercial value arises from the legal restrictions placed upon its use,[9] not from any intrinsic scarcity. Similarly, in order for a patent application to be granted, full specifications, including the industrial use of the invention, must be placed on a public record. The invention is therefore available to all as an object of knowledge. But the patent protects the commercial exploitation of the invention, and therefore draws an 'area of non-interference' around the abstract object. Thus, paradoxically, intellectual property protects as property (and therefore as identifiable, unique, attaching to a particular person) something which is intrinsically not unique, and which exists on a continuum with the intellectual 'commons' of language, science, and artistic convention. There is no inherent separability of an object of intellectual property from our abstract life — any separation and attribution of proprietary rights is purely a conventional, or legal, act.

To some extent intellectual property laws also allow a person to control her image and other personal attributes. In the United States and Canada, the interest a person has in their 'persona' is recognised as a proprietary interest. Both of these jurisdictions recognise a right of publicity, which is derived from the right of privacy[10] — derived, that is, from the (quasi-proprietary) right of a person to exclude others from interference in their lives.[11] As the court in one of the (numerous) cases involving Elvis Presley defined it, the 'right of publicity' means

> the right of an individual, especially a public figure or a celebrity, to control the commercial value and exploitation of his name and picture or likeness and to prevent others from unfairly appropriating this value for their commercial benefit.[12]

As a property right, rather than a personal right, the right of publicity has been recognised in most jurisdictions of the United States to be fully transferable *inter vivos*. In some jurisdictions, the right of publicity also survives the person's death.[13] It becomes fully 'other' to the person, fully objectified, thereby illustrating the division of self-as-subject and self-as-object which we considered in Chapters Four and Five. In Australia and the United Kingdom, no such right of publicity is explicitly recognised, and, as we will discuss in some detail, protection of one's image is effected through the tort of passing off and through use of the *Trade Practices Act 1974* (Cth), which prohibits 'misleading and deceptive conduct'. Transgressions of Australian law do not arise merely with the unauthorised use of an image, but require some deception that the plaintiff is somehow associated with the business of the defendant.

As we saw in earlier chapters, however, the legal concepts of both the person and property are immensely flexible, and rely not on a natural or inherent content, but rather on a bundle of conceptually-separable characteristics. It is therefore arguable that the co-existence of several of the rights in the proprietary bundle, such as excludability and alienability, indicate a strong quasi-proprietary connection between a person and their image in some circumstances. We may also observe that the *rhetoric* of self-ownership features strongly in legal and commercial discourse in this area. Indeed, it is commonplace for a person to license or lease their image, in the sense of granting rights of commercial exploitation to another party.

The objects of intellectual property are abstract rather than physical. As a result, such objects can be intimately connected to a person's abstract 'identity' without being attached to the body itself. An image of the person, or their genetic pattern, is derived from the physical characteristics of the person, but because of their abstract quality can also be easily separated from the body, without necessarily altering that body. Consequently, it might be easy to view the abstract attributes of the person as objects of property. Because of the intrinsic separability of abstract elements of the self from the actual person, it could be argued that the treatment of such abstractions as property is neither an infringement of the principle of self-possession or a form of commodification of the person. It is easy to distinguish our self from our image, as subject distinguished from object. The simple act of looking in a mirror produces an abstract self which is not our (physical) self. Indeed, most forms of intellectual property assume the fungibility of the object, and accordingly grant economic rights which may be commercially alienated.

However, there may be objections to this reduction of our image to property. In some cultures a taking of the image (or a sampling of the blood) may be regarded as a taking of the person's spirit or of a community's heritage. Such a strong connection of the person to their image is not explicitly a feature of the common law, where images of people are often regarded as part of commonly-available streetscapes, and where some people go to extraordinary lengths to have their image widely disseminated. It seems nonetheless probable that the concept of self-ownership does extend, socially if not legally, to the 'persona', such that a person might feel violated if their image (or, as we will see in Chapter Seven, their genetic sequences) are used without their prior authorisation.

One example of an intellectual property right which strongly associates the person with their product is the emerging category of 'moral rights'. Fungibility, or full alienability, is a characteristic of most forms of intellectual property. In addition to (and separate from) the normal range of marketable intellectual property rights, civil law jurisdictions have also historically recognised certain 'moral rights' held by a creator. Such rights are also being recognised by statute in common law jurisdictions, in order to bring the laws of copyright into line with the requirements of the Berne Convention.[14]

The moral right is a personal right, much like the right to physical integrity, and normally consists of the right of an author to be identified as the author of a work (right of attribution or 'paternity') and to object to a derogatory use of the work (right of integrity).[15] Moral rights are held by natural persons only, not by corporations, and cannot usually be alienated or waived. These rights are said to recognise the fact that the author's work is 'an emanation or extension of his or her personality and inseparably linked to that person's honour and reputation'.[16] An injury to the work is therefore an injury to the person. Here we see the concept of the self-possessed individual extending well beyond the physical body to any creative works produced by a person. Although 'moral rights' are conventionally included within the category of 'intellectual property', they are unlike many forms of property which are assignable. With a moral right the work is regarded as a 'property' of a person in the sense of being their own personal attribute. Nothing the creator does can sever their connection to their work.

Moral rights provide an interesting case of legal recognition of the extension of the personality into the world. In this section of the book, however, we are more concerned with attributes of the person's *physical* self which can be rendered as abstract objects, in particular the genetic pattern and the image. Several questions therefore remain fundamental. What is the relationship of the human being to attributes which are not 'created' as separate objects but may be bound up with the identity of the person to an even greater extent than any creative output? If property and personality are constructed as mutually exclusive, so that the person cannot be property, where is the line to be drawn when the personality *is* the 'property'?

Philosophising Intellectual Property

There are two dimensions of the philosophy of intellectual property which we need to understand before we move on to the question of intellectual property in the person. One concerns the basic conceptual character of intellectual property *as* a form of property. The other concerns the ways in which the standard accounts of property, especially those attaching property to the person, are translated into the context of intellectual property. Here we are not interested in whether intellectual property can be justified according to any of the traditional justificatory theories of property. Rather, we wish to indicate the ways in which the language of self-proprietorship, embedded in these theories of justification, is reflected in intellectual property theory. John Locke's labour justification for property, which we briefly outlined in Chapter One, is used extensively in relation to intellectual property, and we will focus here on this justification in our discussion of the philosophy of intellectual property.[17]

Objects Uniquely Repeatable

In order to think about self-ownership in the context of intellectual property, we must depart from, and extend, our previous discussion in several ways. We have already observed that intellectual property concerns abstract objects, rather than physical objects. Typically, intellectual property refers not to the book, but to the copyright in the book, not to the compact disc, but to the right to reproduce the material on the disc, not to the machine but to the patent allowing sole right to benefit commercially from an invention, not to the physical person, but to the right to abstract and reproduce some aspect of the person. As property, intellectual objects are unlike most of the objects of non-intellectual property insofar as they are repeatable or reproducible, not unique or naturally scarce. Although there is no intellectual property in mere ideas, only in the *expression* of ideas, intellectual property necessarily relates to 'ideational' objects.[18] Any scarcity of intellectual property, and the value which flows from scarcity, is a product of legal restrictions placed upon the exploitation of such objects — that is, restrictions which take the object out of what has been termed the 'intellectual commons' and place it firmly within the realm of private ownership.[19]

Of course, as we indicated in Chapter Two, *all* objects of property are in some sense constructed and therefore have an abstract dimension. In order to become legally regarded as propertisable, the thing must first be individualised as an object and then regarded as capable of appropriation. The 'property' is always a fiction, and the excludability which it enforces is also always a legal construct. Similarly, as we saw in Chapter Three, the social person and the legal person are the product of social and legal processes of construction. Aspects of the physical person which we have considered, such as the foetus and the corpse, are themselves the products of socio-legal discourses concerning the beginning and ends of human personality. For example, the pregnant woman could be regarded as a model for a socio-legal concept of personality, but she is not. As we saw in Chapter Four, pregnancy is regarded as a marginal condition, one which is a deviation from the norm of the territorially-bounded impregnable adult. The conventional nature of these constructions is generally masked by the assumption that they describe the natural order in which persons *are* autonomous and pregnancy *is* a deviation.

One way of explaining the distinction between intellectual property and physical property is to say that intellectual property concerns not so much the abstract or physical nature of the object in itself, but rather the abstract or physical *aspect* of the object which the property regime in question seeks to control. Under the regime of personal physical property one person owns the compact disc, but the production company or the recording artist owns the copyright. One person owns a physical copy of a book, while the publisher has the right to produce further copies.

Sherman and Bently identify two conceptual conditions of intellectual property: identifiability of the 'object', and a capacity to reproduce it. As they point out, intellectual property has a paradoxical structure: to be characterised as 'property', it must be capable of being particularised and identified within fairly certain limits; at the same time it must be capable of being repeated or reproduced endlessly.

we see that the law is faced with the problem that, on the one hand, the intangible must be, at least potentially, reproducible and susceptible to repetition; at the same time, one of the primary tasks facing intellectual property law is the need to identify the scope and nature of the intangible property — a qualitative task which highlights the individual nature of the intangible.[20]

In order for intellectual objects to become the objects of property, therefore, they must be equated to other, more concrete, forms of property, by being particularised, privatised, or contained. It is necessary to be able to 'identify the property, to trace the protected subject matter as it is translated into new formats'.[21] If a person wishes to claim that another has infringed their intellectual property, they must be able to illustrate the identity of the original intellectual property with the allegedly illegal reproduction. In the case of a bootleg copy of a compact disc, proving such identity might seem relatively straightforward. But how can a distinction be drawn between a musical 'quotation' and a copy? What happens to 'identity' when an artistic source is transformed into a newly-created object?[22] At what point is a lookalike, or *pastiche*, sufficiently different from the persona of a celebrity?

At the same time, the mere existence of 'new formats' indicates a qualitative difference between intellectual property and types of property which are not intrinsically repeatable. Intellectual property would be meaningless without repeatability of an 'identity', yet every new instance is arguably different from the original idea. The process of establishing identity must therefore be a matter of convention or boundary-setting, justified by legal and social understandings. It is not a matter for rational truth-finding of 'natural' or absolute identity. In other words, the perception that several instances are different manifestations of the same thing, or referable to a single original, is a judgement determined by convention, and not by *a priori* reason.

The conventional nature of identity is well illustrated by an analysis of the idea of misappropriation of personae. The criteria of identifiability and repeatability might seem relatively simple to satisfy in most cases. Reproductions of a person's unique image are normally easily identifiable as representations of a particular body. An unambiguous photograph of a celebrity which is used, without permission, in an advertising campaign, will constitute an unlawful appropriation under the United States law mentioned above. However, the clear cases belie many conceptual difficulties with the condition of uniqueness or particularity. How suggestive of a person's identity does a representation need to be in order for it to be treated as an unfair appropriation? Consider the Midler case. Ford was found to have misappropriated Bette Midler's identity by using a sound-alike singer on a commercial without showing her image.[23] The judge left no question as to the ownership of such a distinctive quality:

> A voice is as distinctive and personal as a face. The human voice is one of the most palpable ways that identity is manifested. We are all aware that a friend is at once known by a few words on the phone. At a philosophical level it has been observed that with the sound of a voice 'the other stands before me'... A fortiori, these observations hold true of singing, especially singing by a singer of renown. The singer manifests herself in the song. To impersonate her voice is to pirate her identity.[24]

Bette Midler's voice may well be distinctive, and highly suggestive of her persona, but what of her fashion sense, or her hairstyle, or her turn of phrase?[25] Why is a voice quality, in fact a voice which can be imitated, not in the intellectual commons, while other distinctive qualities may be? Where is the line to be drawn between common attributes and personal characteristics?

Or consider the Onassis case. Is a person to be prohibited from commercially exploiting their image just because by mere accident they happen to look (or sound) just like some celebrity? Why should Barbara Reynolds have been prevented from exploiting her image just because she happened to look like Jackie Onassis?[26] Can one person monopolise an image just because they became famous first? Or should the latecomer merely be prohibited from taking on the identifiable characteristics (such as the hairstyle or make-up) of the celebrity and from using their image commercially, but otherwise free to devise and conduct transactions in an image of their own making?[27] The process of defining and limiting personae is conceptually very difficult, especially if we regard the person as a construct of a multitude of publicly-accessible components. Certainly these components of identity all come together in one unique form, but at the same time they are never re-presented in their entirety, meaning that appropriation of 'identity' is only ever appropriation of a part.

Such high-profile celebrity cases raise a further question which is at the heart of the application of intellectual property law to images: on what basis should we distinguish between objects that are subject to intellectual property and objects that are part of the so-called intellectual commons? Almost anything that can be objectified can be conceptualised as private property, but the concept of the intellectual commons, like that of the physical commons, is an attempt to reserve some objects to common access and use.

To Peter Drahos the 'intellectual commons' encapsulates the idea of an 'objective world of knowledge' from which people are not barred from gaining access by conventional (primarily legal), technological, or physical means.[28] In his view, the 'objective world of knowledge' does not refer to a world of objective knowledge, but rather to a world of humanly-constructed abstract objects which, like language, exist independently of any individual desires. Once a work of art has been created, it becomes part of an intellectual or abstract world of knowledge, and is no longer part of the artist's interior world. It can therefore be easily transferred to the commercial world as a fungible object. As Roland Barthes said several decades ago, when a narrative begins, 'the voice loses its origin, the author enters into his own death, writing begins'.[29] The textual object, in other words, becomes ontologically separate from the author. It is a commodity capable of being alienated in a commercial marketplace. (At the same time, as we saw above, the separate recognition of 'moral rights' suggests that in some respects the work is inalienably connected to the creator.) Under current legal arrangements, a work of art will initially be an object of intellectual property and under the proprietorship of an author or their assignee, but once its copyright protection has lapsed, it generally becomes an object in the intellectual commons.

Drahos also notes, however, that the concept of the intellectual commons is like the 'territorial' and 'group-specific' notion of common land in English law, in that it *need not* refer to a world of *universally-*accessible abstract objects.[30] We could note, for instance, that particular aspects of indigenous knowledge are neither private property nor universally accessible. Nor is such knowledge even accessible to all members of a particular indigenous community. The difficulty which Western legal minds have in conceptualising and protecting such knowledge arises from the more simple dichotomy which we tend to employ — something is either property or not property (and therefore accessible to all).

The delineation of intellectual property from the intellectual commons raises significant political issues. Intellectual property is supposed to reward, and therefore encourage, investment in individual creativity and inventiveness,[31] while protection of the intellectual commons is said to ensure that human knowledge and culture are reserved for common use and the enhancement of our existences within a community. What sort of limitations ought to be placed upon the use of an individual's image, especially if she has become a 'historical figure'?[32] Should history be limited? As David Wall illustrates in relation to the recreation of Elvis Presley after his death, intellectual property regimes operate at some level to impose restrictions on cultural production.[33] However, there is far more at stake than simply deciding on policy grounds, or according to a cost-benefit analysis, whether an intellectual resource ought to be capable of being owned. As the case of indigenous knowledge illustrates, the very mechanism of intellectual property brings with it certain cultural presuppositions about individual creativity which are very difficult to dislodge. Even within the liberal West, the forms of creativity which are normally rewarded are those associated with what Shelley Wright calls the 'solitary male genius' operating in the public artistic or inventive marketplace.[34]

Self-Constructing Labour

We saw in Chapter One that one of the predominant philosophical justifications for the institution of private property is the ability of individuals to transform nature, or to mix their labour with natural resources which are otherwise owned in common.[35] According to John Locke, the act of appropriation which grounds ownership is an act of labour, and labour is a capacity naturally owned or possessed by the person.[36] It is natural self-ownership which, for Locke, justifies property: because we own our labour, when we mix it with the resources of the external world, we effectively appropriate those resources. Traditionally, this line of thinking has been strong in debates over the justifications for intellectual property. The person is seen to have a justifiable interest in the products of their *mental* labour.[37]

It is impossible to consider in detail here the application of Locke's thought to intellectual property.[38] However, it can easily be seen that aspects of the Lockean analysis might be more appropriate as a foundation for intellectual property (which protects immediate acts of creativity) than they are for more tangible forms of property (which are generally less directly produced by their owner). In an economic context where the means of production are privately owned, wealth which is reducible to tangible property rarely has any connection to the actual labour of the owner, whereas intellectual property frequently, and seemingly 'naturally', attaches to an individual creator, writer, artist, designer, or inventor (or, in many cases, their employer, with whom the creator has a contractual relationship). It seems self-evident that the individual creator should have the first moral, and therefore legal, right, provided that she can meaningfully be said to have created the object, and not merely to have discovered it. As we will see in Chapter Seven, the distinction between discovery and invention is crucial to patent law.[39] Of course our sense that it is appropriate to attach the moral or natural right of ownership to the creator is entirely a product of Western individualism. The author has not always held such a privileged position, even in the West.[40] Individualism has certainly played a large part in the development of modern notions of rewarding and properly recognising individual creativity.[41]

We may, however, encounter more doubt about the application of the labour justification for property when we turn to the issue of the persona. Is the persona really a product of labour, or is it more like our genetic characteristics which are just there as part of our physical self?[42] Or is the persona a co-operative venture, produced by social demands, our own choices and labour, and our pre-given characteristics? We will return to these questions shortly.

Locke's two qualifications on the right to appropriate are, on the face of it, easier to satisfy in relation to intellectual property than for (at least some types of) tangible property. The first qualification on the right to appropriate is that the appropriator should leave as much and as good for others.[43] While this is almost impossible to satisfy for a tangible commodity with any value, it may not apply at all to intellectual property because the forms of abstract objects are infinite.[44] The intellectual commons will not be exhausted by exploitation in the same way as arable land, or mineral resources, and it is therefore possible to claim that, as long as the protection granted by law is specific rather than general, one leaves 'as much and as good' for other creators of abstract objects. A monopoly may be granted over a particular literary work, or invention, but that does not exclude others from creating new literary works or different inventions. As far as the persona is concerned, the condition is quite easy to satisfy. There are few contexts in which exploitation of persona could possibly result in a diminution of opportunity for another to exploit their own persona. An identical twin, or a very close look-alike, might lose their opportunity to exploit their image because someone has done it first, but such situations must surely be rare.

Locke's second qualification is that a thing can be appropriated from the commons '[a]s much as any one can make use of to any advantage of life before it spoils'.[45]   The significance of the spoilage condition is diminished in Locke's scheme as soon as a money economy takes over.[46] But while it may still be immoral and unjustifiable to withhold food or some other perishable good, abstract objects cannot in the same way be said to be subject to spoilage. They may go out of date or be transcended by new objects, but if one has a stock of ideas and only uses one or two of them, would this constitute waste?[47]

The idea that labour justifies ownership raises some interesting questions about self-ownership, some of which have already been considered in previous chapters. In Chapter One we discussed *Moore's Case*[48] in which a person unwittingly providing raw material in the form of a tissue sample that some scientists fashioned into a useful and valuable commodity. Because the scientists applied their skill and labour to the material (and Moore was nothing but a passive patient) they were able to defend a claim of conversion made by Moore, even though the product would have been impossible without his contribution.[49] As Boyle points out, 'while discussing genetic information, the court views Mr Moore as a "naturally occurring raw material", a public domain to be mined by inventive geniuses'. At the same time, in his capacity as a patient or consumer, he is 'a sovereign individual with an unchallengeable entitlement to the facts necessary to make informed decisions'.[50] Therefore, as Boyle so aptly puts it, 'Mr Moore is the author of his own destiny, but not of his spleen'.[51] We will return to Moore's Case in Chapter Seven, as it also raises the issue of whether a cell-line produced in a laboratory is the same as, or different from, the originating human cells.

Star Qualities

> be not afraid of greatness. Some are born great, some achieve greatness, and some have greatness thrust upon 'em.[52]

In Chapter Four we asked what it means to say that we own ourselves. As we saw, the notion of self-ownership is normally taken to imply a split in the person: the person as subject (or mind) owns the person as object (or body). Less conventionally, self-ownership is taken to indicate mere identity, so that the person is regarded simply as a single integrated being.[53] In accordance with this less conventional understanding of self-ownership, the image and the person *might* be regarded as inseparable, like the person and their body. If treated as unlawful, an appropriation of an image regarded in this light would be tantamount to a trespass to the self-possessed person — an offence against the person, rather than a wrong done to property. However, images are more susceptible to separation from the person than are body parts. The dominant understanding of self-ownership (as involving a mind and a material object) therefore applies well in this context. While the law may have difficulty saying that something which is essential to a person's existence (such as her heart) may be 'owned', self-ownership (or even control by another) is far easier to justify when an alienation of the personal attribute does not threaten bodily integrity.

As we noted above, *Moore's Case* illustrates the difficulty of asserting ownership of the body, especially where the raw material has been altered by another's labour. But while it may be difficult to assert that a person has created the basic material out of which her own body is constructed, we may by contrast assume a highly creative role in relation to our image or appearance. A person's image or *persona* (truly a mask) is frequently a highly-constructed public face or even a fictional character,[54] and may even stand in relation to the person as an artificial object — something which is deliberately constructed and assumed for certain occasions such as public appearances. Our genetic structure, which is beyond our control, may indeed provide the 'raw material' for our appearance, but we have a fair degree of control over how we present ourselves. Moreover, the labour of constructing the image is not necessarily that of the image-bearer alone. Richard Dyer illustrates this point in his extensive writings on the process of construction of film stars:

the person is a body, a psychology, a set of skills that have to be mined and worked up into a star image. This work, of fashioning the star out of the raw material of the person, varies in the degree to which it respects what artists sometimes refer to as the inherent qualities of the material; make-up, coiffure, clothing, dieting and body-building can all make more or less of the body features they start with, and personality is no less malleable, skills no less learnable. The people who do this include the star him/herself as well as the make-up artists, hairdressers, dress designers, dieticians, body-building coaches, acting, dancing and other teachers, publicists, pin-up photographers, gossip columnists, and so on.[55]

Dyer's description of the production of the star evokes the Lockean distinction between raw material and product of labour. It also draws our attention to the number of labourers involved in fashioning an image-product. Of course, the construction of a personal image is not confined to celebrities, but is an ordinary human activity. Whether we are born great, achieve greatness, or have it thrust upon us (or indeed whether we are not in the least famous), we by and large have some control over our appearance. There may be large variations in the degree of effort, time, and expense which goes into image construction, but for most people it is a controlled and therefore created aspect of their identity.

Not only is the personal image the product of a multitude of individual labourers, it is also a response to social norms, expectations, codes and stereotypes.[56] And perhaps most importantly, the commercial *value* of any persona is a function of the notoriety of the image-product. Only when the media and the public take notice and attach significance to a personal image can it enter fully into the marketplace. Although the labour involved in creating a persona may be reducible, in part, to the labour of the particular celebrity (or to labour contracted by the celebrity), the 'celebrity' status, and hence the greater part of the commercial value of a persona, is attributable to the public domain.[57]

In one case concerning the image of Elvis Presley, a US court expressed reservations about extending a right of publicity to a celebrity's estate in part because of the level of public and media participation in the creation of the celebrity.[58] Although this case was overturned on appeal, in England the Court of Appeal has refused to grant a general protection to

Elvis as a trademark.[59] Jennifer Davis comments that 'the judgement appears to recognise a public sphere in which meaning is socially created and to which the public should have access' and that 'it is the public which has endowed [Elvis] ... with the celebrity which makes memorabilia carrying his name so popular'.[60] It may also be argued that it was Presley, his publicists, and his producers who 'created' Elvis-the-image: the public sphere does little but provide the common cultural material from which the image is fashioned, and the demand through which the constructed image becomes a celebrity and therefore valuable.

Film theorists have devised several methods of classifying the various dimensions of the celebrity's self (such as private person, character, and public persona) which we need not discuss in detail here. The important point is that, in many cases, the 'persona' or 'image' is created or produced as an object conceptually separable from its author/subject.[61] Given this division of the celebrity into (original) subject and (produced) object, it may appear to be a relatively simple matter to make the conceptual transformation from person to property: being object, the image is no longer person but rather a species of art, and may therefore be grasped as an object of property. Non-consensual appropriation of the image would not be tantamount to appropriation of the person, but rather merely a trespass to their property. Nor would alienation of the image, for instance to a marketing company, involve alienation of the self. In other words, the prohibition of slavery is not violated, and it becomes acceptable for images to be fully exploited commercially.

The dimension of self-ownership which is expressed through intellectual ownership of the persona therefore poses some interesting dilemmas for classical liberal justifications of property. The conceptual conditions for classifying an interest in an image as intellectual property — identifiability and repeatability — are reasonably well satisfied. Although the Lockean justification for recognising property as derived from labour is possibly more applicable here than in relation to other forms of property, it may be difficult in some cases to attribute the role of 'creator' to any one person. Moreover, in creating an image, one cannot help but leave as much and as good for others, for there is an endless supply of potential images, even if the popular ones are only variations on a limited number of themes or stereotypes. Finally, the separability of subject from product (which is the condition of any type of self-ownership where the object is alienable and marketable and not merely an inseparable dimension of the self-possessed person) is far easier to conceptualise where the self is not necessarily physically attached to the object, as Mr Moore was to his spleen.

The concept of self-ownership may thus appear to be less problematic in relation to images than to body parts, which can never fully be separated from the person without diminishing it physically. And yet, ownership of one's image has not been explicitly recognised to any great degree by the law in Australia and the United Kingdom. By contrast, in the United States, ownership of the image (or the right to publicity) is now well recognised in a number of states. In the next section we will consider the law of ownership of the image, concentrating on Australian law which, we will argue, does reflect a concept of self-ownership, despite its refusal to acknowledge such ownership as a basis for a broad legal entitlement.

The Law of the Image-Product

In Australia, the issue of unauthorised use of a person's 'persona' has traditionally been dealt with by the laws of passing off and 'misleading and deceptive conduct'.[62] The 'image' has not strictly been categorised as a proprietary interest, and the wrong is not that of theft or appropriation, but rather of some kind of deception.[63] The answer to the question of whether intellectual property in an image is recognised is therefore simply that it is probably not, at least not explicitly. The legal entitlement is not a right to property-in-the-self (and in personal attributes, such as an image), but rather a principle derived from the law of torts that prevents others from misusing one's image in certain circumstances. However, here as elsewhere,[64] it is important to remember that formal characterisation of a legal principle does not necessarily fully describe it. Saying that something is not *de jure* property does not mean that it does not assume many of the same practical characteristics of property. It only shows that the courts have not been willing to attach the nomenclature of property to this kind of object. As we will see, the difference between property in the person and the interest recognised by the law of passing off is difficult to define satisfactorily.

Some of the justifications used in support of defending a person's image from passing off rely upon the rationale, structure, and moral basis of private (intellectual) property. This strengthens our perception that the concept of property underpins the protection of images, even in Australia. The notion that a defendant should not reap where they have not sown is a simple reversal of the labour justification of private property. The separation of the celebrity's goodwill from their natural identity is an objectifying of the person, which is a condition precedent to any private property structure. And the moral condemnation of defendants using unauthorised images of a celebrity may indicate the existence of an assumption that the inviolability of the private person extends to their image.[65] It is hardly surprising that this should be the case. As we have indicated in previous chapters, the power of the property form resides in its ability to adapt to new situations: even where it is not formally adopted by law, it operates metaphorically within the broader culture and it supplies a context for legal decision-making.[66]

These matters can be illustrated with a few cases, which will be familiar to anyone with an interest in this area of law. *Henderson v Radio Corporation* was an early Australian case concerning the unauthorised use of a personal image.[67] The plaintiffs were a husband and wife team of professional ballroom dancers who had at different times outside Australia promoted several products, including beans, records, sunblock, and jewellery.[68] The defendants produced and distributed a gramophone record of ballroom dance music which had a picture of the plaintiffs on the cover. Although the plaintiffs were not identified by name, apparently they were easily recognisable by dancing experts. The plaintiffs' permission for the use of their image had not been sought by the defendants.

Similar fact situations had given rise to success in defamation actions, where the plaintiff could show that her or his reputation was damaged by an association with the defendant's product.[69] Here that was not seriously an issue.[70] Rather, the court determined in the plaintiffs' favour, using the law of passing off to justify the decision. The court held that because the defendant had falsely represented that the plaintiffs were in some way recommending the record, the action in passing off would succeed: 'In our view, once it is proved that A. is falsely representing his goods as the goods of B., or his business to be the same as or connected with the business of B., the wrong of passing-off has been established and B. is entitled to relief'.[71] The action itself was therefore based upon the existence of a deception, that is, a misleading association of the plaintiffs' name and reputation with the defendant's product. At common law, such a finding would lead either to nominal damages or to general damages if actual damage were proved. Understandably, the Hendersons did not ask for damages, but rather for an injunction to restrain the further production and dissemination of the record cover. As an injunction is an equitable remedy, the court applied equitable principles concerning damage to property. If 'he [the plaintiff] sues in equity, he takes advantage of the equitable principle that the Court will interfere by injunction *to restrain irreparable injury to property*'[72] (emphasis added). There had to be an actual or potential 'injury to property' for the court to award an injunction. In this case, Evatt CJ and Myers J were of the opinion that 'the appellant has appropriated the professional reputation of the respondents for its own commercial ends'.[73] Moreover,

> the wrongful appropriation of another's professional or business reputation is an injury in itself, no less, in our opinion, than the appropriation of his goods or money ... It is as much an injury as if the appellant had paid the respondents for their recommendation and then robbed them of the money.[74]

Although the basis of the claim was passing off, thus requiring the plaintiffs to show some deception or misrepresentation, the majority used the language of self-proprietorship in assessing the type of damage suffered. A clear analogy was drawn between the appropriation of personality to theft, and the court recognised property in the goodwill associated with a person's professional reputation.

With the traditional type of passing off, a defendant 'passes off' goods as having some association with the plaintiff's business, where both are operating within a 'common field of activity'. *Henderson* has normally been understood as a decision based upon an 'extended' action for passing off, that is, an action extended beyond this traditional form. Although the court in *Henderson* was critical of the need to show a 'common field of activity',[75] it held, nonetheless, that this requirement could be understood broadly. The Hendersons were 'in a real sense competing in the special area of providing gramophone records specially adapted to dancing and dance teaching'.[76] Presumably this was due to the fact that the plaintiffs had previously initiated negotiations with a record company aimed at producing such a record — a project which did not proceed, but which could have been revived at some future date.

The need to show some deception or misrepresentation is well illustrated by *Newton-John v Scholl-Plough*,[77] a case which also highlights the differences between Australian law, and the laws of the United States and Canada. The defendants had placed advertisements featuring an Olivia Newton-John look-alike. At the top of the advertisement were the words 'Olivia? No, Maybelline!' Olivia Newton-John sought an injunction to restrain further publication. It was alleged that the advertisement was in breach of sections 52 and 53 of the *Trade Practices Act* (misleading and deceptive conduct), and that it constituted a passing off. Both 'misleading and deceptive conduct' and the tort of passing off rely upon the existence of deception. In this case the judge was unable to find that any deception existed, since the advertisement clearly stated that the picture was *not* Olivia Newton-John. Although there was an appropriation of personality, in that the object of the advertisement was to draw attention to itself by creating an association with Olivia Newton-John, the judge indicated that any suggested connection between Newton-John and Maybelline cosmetics had been severed by the words of the advertisement. At the same time, the judge clearly disapproved of the advertisement, saying that the defendants were 'taking advantage of [Newton-John's] name and reputation'.[78] This case provides a clear expression of the legal position in Australia which is that mere appropriation of an image, without some form of deception, is not a legal wrong. At the same time, there is some judicial disapproval of what amounts to an immoral, rather than an unlawful, taking of personality.

By contrast, in the second of two cases concerning the Crocodile Dundee character,[79] even though there could have been no mistaking the imitation Dundee character used in a shoe advertisement for the real Paul Hogan, a passing off claim was successful, because of the (tenuous) misleading association of Hogan with the product. The trial judge, Gummow J, as well as Beaumont J on appeal, relied upon a perception that members of the public would believe that Hogan had authorised the use of the Dundee character for the purposes of the advertisement. Presumably a similar line of argument *could* have been successful in the Olivia Newton-John case: although the advertisement did not use her own image, members of the public might have assumed that she had authorised the use of a look-alike.[80]

In *Honey v Australian Airlines,* the plaintiff, long jumper Gary Honey, was unsuccessful in his claim because the unauthorised poster in which he featured was interpreted as having as its main purpose the promotion of sport. Northrop J said 'the poster should be described as promoting excellence in sport and the desirability of participating in sport'.[81] According to Northrop J, the poster was not a representation that Honey promoted the business of Australian Airlines,[82] even though their logo and name did appear at the base of the poster. Therefore the poster did not contravene sections 53 (c) and (d) of the *Trade Practices Act*,[83] which prohibits false representations about the sponsorship or approval of a company and its products. The claim for passing off was also unsuccessful, Northrop J finding that there was no implication that Honey endorsed Australian Airlines.

These and other cases based upon the *Trade Practices Act* and the tort of passing off[84] illustrate the essential point about Australian law on the unauthorised use of a person's image — that the wrong is that of misleading or deceptive conduct, or of falsely associating the image of the celebrity with a particular product or company. And yet, the language of self-ownership is never far away in these cases, and it is well recognised that the appropriation of a celebrity's goodwill constitutes damage. We have already quoted the court in *Henderson* saying that misuse of reputation is just like theft. More recently, in *Talmax v Telstra*, a case involving the swimmer Kieran Perkins, the Supreme Court of Queensland appeared to accept that '[i]n general terms ... it is disadvantageous to expend celebrity in promoting an entity, product, or service on a single occasion; each association to which a famous person *lends* himself or herself utilises a part of his or her "credibility" for advertising purposes'. (Emphasis added)[85] The assumption here is that credibility, if not image, is a limited commodity, and therefore misuse of a celebrity's credibility constitutes a taking. The 'diminution of opportunity' to exploit celebrity status is the damage, because the appropriator has taken away something of real commercial value to the celebrity. A failure to impose limitations on the exploitation of another's image would result in a real loss of property for that person.

Australian law has been criticised for refusing explicitly to acknowledge a proprietary interest in the image, while covertly proceeding on the basis that such an interest exists — at least in relation to those whose image has commercial value. For instance, in *Tot Toys v Mitchell*, Fisher J of the New Zealand High Court made the following comments:

It is not easy to escape the conclusion that on occasion the result in Australia may have sprung not so much from a finding of actual deception or independent damage as the tacit assumption that there should be a right of property in names, reputations and artificial images for character merchandising purposes. If the latter is the real aim, it might be questioned whether passing off is the best vehicle for achieving it. ... what of the credibility of the courts if they are seen to strain towards a particular finding of fact in order to adapt an ill-fitting cause of action? Is it really necessary to force the square peg of character merchandising into the round hole of passing off? [86]

The effect of the cases dealing with passing off and the *Trade Practices Act* is relatively straightforward: it is to delineate an area in which a person's reputation, image, or name can be protected. It is for individual celebrities to determine what they wish to endorse, and therefore they may be said to have an exclusive interest in the commercial exploitation of their personality. The limit of this recognition of self-ownership in Australian law is reached where a person's image is used for commercial purposes without any false implication of endorsement.

Conclusion

Had their actions been brought in the United States, Gary Honey and Olivia Newton-John would probably have been more fortunate in their claims. The US 'right of publicity' cases show that the person's 'persona' (including their name, face, and image) is their 'property'. A mere misappropriation for commercial purposes constitutes a wrong done to the person, in much the same way as if their personal property had been converted. In Australia, as we have seen, a celebrity is legally wronged only where there has been some deception or misrepresentation. However, the courts have in some cases been remarkably flexible in their willingness to find that a deception has occurred. They have also been willing to attribute a commercial and proprietary *value* to the persona.

We have seen in this chapter that it is possible to recognise self-ownership on a formal level. The 'right of publicity' cases recognise that a person owns their persona, and therefore has the right to exclude others from profiting from it. These cases provide a vivid example of the division of the person into a controlling subject or mind, and an object of property – in this case some material representation of a person's character or image. Such formal legal recognition of self-ownership protects personal integrity in a context in which personal images can be extremely valuable. The paradox observed in Chapter One, that the person must become the property of themselves in order to avoid being the property of others, is clearly evident here. The recognition of ownership of the persona is also said to reward the labour expended either in creating a particular image, or in achieving a position in which one's image may be of some value. Such rationales for regarding the persona as property demonstrate a strong legal commitment to the concept of self-ownership.

We have also seen that even where the persona is not formally owned by the legal person, the concept of self-ownership still informs the law in other respects. Even when the complaint is one of 'misleading conduct' rather than a 'right of publicity', the persona is regarded as having a value as property, diminution of which damages the person.

Notes

1   As we will see, 'persona' is not a clearly defined concept, but rather a term used generally to refer to the unique characteristics which give a person their public identity, in particular, the name and image. As *Midler v Ford Motor Co* 849 F 2d 460 (9th Cir 1988) indicates, 'persona' may also encompass other distinctive traits, such as the voice.

2   *Midler v Ford Motor Co* 849 F.2d. 460 (9th Cir 1988); *Estate of Elvis Presley v Russen* 513 F Supp 1339 (1981); *Martin Luther King Jr Ctr for Social Change v American Heritage Products* 694 F 2d 674 (11th Cir. 1983); *Onassis v Christian Dior New York* 472 NYS 2d 254 (Sup Ct 1984), aff'd 488 NYS 2d 943 (1st Dept 1985). Good overviews include Kathleen Birkel Dangelo 'How Much of You Do You Really Own? A Property Right in Identity' (1989) 37 *Cleveland State Law Review* 499 and Barbara Singer 'The Right of Publicity: Star Vehicle or Shooting Star?' (1991) 10 *Cardozo Arts and Entertainment Law Journal* 1.

3   See generally, Stephen Burley 'Passing Off and Character Merchandising: Should England Lean Towards Australia?' [1991] *European Intellectual Property Review* 227.

4   Thomas Hobbes *Leviathan* [1651] (Cambridge University Press, 1991), ch XVI 'Of Persons, Authors, and Things Personated', 112.

5   'Indeed, it is almost a truism that in intellectual property law the protected subject matter must be both reproducible and repeatable'. Brad Sherman and Lionel Bently *The Making of Modern Intellectual Property Law: The British Experience, 1760–1911* (Cambridge: Cambridge University Press, 1999), 51.

6   According to McKeough and Stewart, 'intellectual property is a generic term for the various rights or bundles of rights which the law accords for the protection of creative effort — or, more especially, for the protection of economic investment in creative effort'. Jill McKeough and Andrew Stewart *Intellectual Property in Australia* 2nd ed (Sydney: Butterworths, 1997), 1.

7   *Patents Act* 1996 (Australia); *Copyright Act 1968* (Australia) s33.

8   This factor does not serve as a sufficient condition for distinguishing between intellectual property and other forms of property. There are some conventional forms of proprietary interest, such as a lease, or a limited estate in land, which also expire with the passing of time. Fortunately, we are not interested here in drawing analytical distinctions between different forms of property.

9   *Sydney 2000 Games (Indicia and Images) Protection Act 1996* (Australia).

10   See Samuel Warren and Louis Brandeis 'The Right to Privacy' (1890) 4 *Harvard Law Review* 193; the first common law recognition of a full-blown right to publicity was in *Haelan Laboratories v Topps Chewing Gum* 202 F 2d 866 (1953).

11   See, for instance, *Midler v Ford Motor Company* 849 F2d 460 (9th Cir 1988). The Canadian position is clarified in *Krouse v Chrysler Canada* 40 DLR (3d) 15 (1973) and *Athans v Canadian Adventure Camps* 80 DLR (3d) 583 (1977). Barbara Singer traces the development of the right of publicity from the right of privacy in 'The Right of Publicity'.

12   *Estate of Elvis Presley v Russen* 513 F Supp 1339 (1981), 1353 (per Brotman, District Judge); see also Thomas McCarthy 'The Human Persona as Commercial Property: The Right of Publicity' (1996) 7 *Australian Intellectual Property Journal* 20. The Elvis Presley cases are usefully surveyed in David Wall 'Reconstructing the Soul of Elvis: The Social Development and Legal Maintenance of Elvis Presley as Intellectual Property' (1996) 24 *International Journal of the Sociology of Law* 117. Wall reports that, until 1994, 86 Elvis-related legal actions had been brought before US courts.

13   This was decided for Tennessee in *State ex rel Elvis Presley v Crowell* 733 SW 2d 89 (Tenn App 1987); see also *Lugosi v Universal Pictures* 603 P 2d

425 (Cal 1979); Barbara Singer 'The Right of Publicity', 20ff. In 1996 McCarthy reported that the 'postmortem right of publicity has been recognised as the law in 13 states'. McCarthy 'The Human Persona as Commercial Property', 21. The development of computer technology making it possible to digitally re-create moving images of dead people will make the post mortem transferability of the right to publicity all the more important. See Erin Giacoppo 'Avoiding the Tragedy of Frankenstein: The Application of the Right of Publicity to the Use of Digitally Reproduced Actors in Film' (1997) 48 *Hastings Law Journal* 601. Giacoppo points out that whereas the rights to protect the person through defamation and privacy laws terminate upon death, the descendability of the right of publicity makes it an avenue for controlling post mortem uses of image.

14   Article 6 *bis* of the Berne Convention states: 'Independently of the author's economic rights, and even after the transfer of the said rights, the author shall have the right to claim authorship of the work and to object to any distortion, mutilation or other modification of, or other derogatory action in relation to, the said work, which would be prejudicial to his honour or reputation'. At the time of writing the *Copyright Amendment (Moral Rights) Bill 1999* was still before the Australian Parliament. On the history of common law recognition of moral rights see Gerald Dworkin 'Moral Rights and the Common Law Countries' (1994) 5 *Australian Intellectual Property Journal* 5.

15   Other rights are also contained within the bundle of moral rights, but are not protected in every jurisdiction recognising moral rights. For example, moral rights may also include the right to determine if and when a creative work is disseminated publicly, the right not to have work falsely attributed to an author, and the right to withdraw work from the public. See *Parliament of Australia Bills Digest No. 99* (1999–2000); Claire Burke 'European Intellectual Property Rights: A Tabular Guide' [1995] 10 *European Intellectual Property Review* 466–476; Carolyn Jones 'Principles Versus Practicalities: Should Moral Rights Be Subject to Waiver?' (1995) 4 *Arts and Entertainment Law Review* 56.

16   *Discussion Paper Proposed Moral Rights Legislation for Copyright Creators* (Canberra: Commonwealth of Australia, 1994), 5.

17   See especially Justin Hughes 'The Philosophy of Intellectual Property' (1988) 77 *Georgetown Law Journal* 287; Peter Drahos *A Philosophy of Intellectual Property* (Aldershot: Dartmouth, 1996).

18   The distinction between mere idea and its expressive form is difficult. In a metaphysical sense, such a distinction relies upon a Platonic separation of idea from form or representation. We may ask how an idea can be

formless, and whether the form in which an idea is expressed is absolutely inseparable from the idea itself? However, the practical significance of the distinction is, in most cases, clear. See McKeough and Stewart *Intellectual Property in Australia*, 131–132.

19   Drahos *The Philosophy of Intellectual Property*. See also Felix Cohen 'Transcendental Nonsense and the Functional Approach' (1935) 35 *Columbia Law Review* 809.

20   Sherman and Bently *The Making of Modern Intellectual Property Law*, 51–52.

21   Sherman and Bently *The Making of Modern Intellectual Property Law*, 51.

22   For discussion of this question in relation to Elvis impersonators, see Wall 'Reconstructing the Soul of Elvis', 134.

23   *Midler v Ford Motor Co* 849 F 2d 460 (9th Cir. 1988).

24   Ibid, 463 (Noonan, Circuit Judge).

25   These issues are also raised in *White v Samsung Electronics America* 971 F 2d 1395 (9th Cir 1992). The case concerned an advertisement which parodied a television personality, Vanna White, in the form of a robot dressed in her characteristic style. See the discussion in McCarthy 'The Human Persona as Commercial Property', 24.

26   *Onassis v Christian Dior-New York Inc* (1985); cf Jane Gaines *Contested Culture: The Image, the Voice, and the Law* (Chapel Hill: University of North Carolina Press, 1991), 12–13.

27   A matter also raised by the Olivia Newton-John case. See *Newton-John v Scholl-Plough (Australia)* (1985) 11 FCR 233.

28   See Drahos *A Philosophy of Intellectual Property*, 54–55. Drahos states that 'One way in which to think about it [the intellectual commons] is to say that it consists of that part of the objective world of knowledge which is not subject to any of the following: property rights or some other conventional bar (contract, for instance); technological bars (for example, encryption) or a physical bar (hidden manuscripts). Our definition emphasizes the idea that the intellectual commons is an independently existing resource which is open to use.'

29   Roland Barthes 'The Death of the Author' in Roland Barthes *Image, Music, Text* Stephen Heath (trans.) (London: Fontana, 1977), 142.

30   Drahos *A Philosophy of Intellectual Property*, 56.

31   The English intellectual property law was strongly influenced by lobbying from commercial interests. See Drahos *A Philosophy of Intellectual*

Property, 22–32; Sherman and Bently *The Making of Intellectual Property Law*.

32   Attempts to control the image of the Princess of Wales after her death raise the question of whether it is in fact either possible or desirable to 'own' historical images.

33   Wall 'Reconstructing the Soul of Elvis'.

34   Shelley Wright 'A Feminist Exploration of the Legal Protection of Art' (1994) 7 *Canadian Journal of Women and the Law* 59, 62.

35   See Chapter One, above, for a further discussion of Locke. John Locke *Two Treatises of Government*, Peter Laslett (ed) 2nd ed (Cambridge University Press, 1967, first published 1690) *Second Treatise*, ch V.

36   Locke *Two Treatises, Second Treatise*, ss27–28.

37   See, for instance, the famous case of *Millar v Taylor* (1769) 98 English Reports 229. Discussed in Drahos *A Philosophy of Intellectual Property* at 24–25. See also Sherman and Bentley *The Making of Modern Intellectual Property Law*, ch 1 'Property in Mental Labour' especially 23–24. For an exposition of the 'natural rights' or libertarian interpretation of Locke in the context of intellectual property, see R. Anthony Reese 'Reflections on the Intellectual Commons: Two Perspectives on Copyright Duration and Reversion' (1995) 47 *Stanford Law Review* 707-747. On Locke and intellectual property generally, see Drahos *A Philosophy of Intellectual Property*, ch 3.

38   A detailed discussion is to be found in Drahos *A Philosophy of Intellectual Property*, ch 3, and in Hughes 'The Philosophy of Intellectual Property'.

39   Drahos *A Philosophy of Intellectual Property*, 48–49. The creation/discovery distinction in patent law is built upon the assumption that things in nature are simply 'there', and are not the product of human intervention.

40   And even among Western legal systems there have been significant variations in the role of the author, as the example of moral rights, discussed above, illustrates.

41   See Boyle 'A Theory of Law and Information: Copyright, Spleens, Blackmail, and Insider Trading' (1882) 80 *California Law Review* 1413, 1463–1469.

42   Justin Hughes suggests that persona is not normally a product of labour: 'While some politicians and rock stars may work on their public images, the world is full of famous athletes, heroes, and actors who do not labour to create their public images.' Hughes 'The Philosophy of Intellectual Property', 340, n218.

43   'For this *Labour* being the unquestionable Property of the labourer, no man but he can have a right to what that is once joyned to, at least where there is enough, and as good left in common for others'. Locke *Two Treatises, Second Treatise*, s27, 288.

44   Drahos *A Philosophy of Intellectual Property*, 49-50.

45   Locke *Two Treatises*, Second Treatise, ss31, 290.

46   Money makes the condition redundant because it is 'some lasting thing that Men might keep without spoiling' and enables exchange, meaning that a surplus of goods need not spoil, but can rather be sold. *Ibid*, s46, 300.

47   See Hughes 'The Philosophy of Intellectual Property', 327–329.

48   *Moore v Regents of the University of California* 793 P 2d 479 (Cal 1990).

49   For a discussion of this aspect of the case, see James Boyle 'A Theory of Law and Information'; John Frow 'Elvis' Fame: The Commodity Form and the Form of the Person' (1995) 7 *Cardozo Studies in Law and Literature* 131, 154–155.

50   James Boyle 'A Theory of Law and Information', 1519.

51   Ibid, 1520.

52   William Shakespeare *Twelfth Night* II, v, 144-146.

53   See above, Chapter Four.

54   Such as Crocodile Dundee was to Paul Hogan. We discuss some cases involving the Dundee character in the final section of this chapter.

55   Richard Dyer *Heavenly Bodies: Film Stars and Society* (Basingstoke and London: Macmillan, 1986), 5–6. For a good example of a detailed analysis of this process at work in relation to a particular celebrity (Esther Williams), see Catherine Williamson 'Swimming Pools, Movie Stars: The Celebrity Body in the Post-War Marketplace' (1996) 38 *camera obscura* 5, 9–10.

56   Williamson 'Swimming Pools, Movie Stars'.

57   Of course, fact that value derives from public perception does not, in the Western way of thinking, defeat or modify the argument that the celebrity has created and therefore 'owns' her or his image — the value of a painting may be attributable as much to the notoriety of the artist as it is to any intrinsic merit but that does not alter the perception that the artist is author, creator and therefore owner of the work.

58   *Factors Inc v Pro Arts* 440 US 908, as discussed in John Frow 'Elvis' Fame: The Commodity Form and the Form of the Person', 156–157.

59   *Elvis Presley Trademarks* [1999] RPC 567.

60   Jennifer Davis 'The King Is Dead: Long Live the King' [2000] *Cambridge Law Journal* 33, at 36.

61   See Barry King 'Articulating Stardom' (1985) 26 (5) *Screen* 27, 38–41; Jane Gaines *Contested Culture*, 33–35.

62   See s52 *Trade Practices Act* 1974 (Cth). *Wickham v Associated Pool Builders* (1988) 12 IPR 567; *Talmax v Telstra* (1996) 36 IPR 46.

63   See *Henderson v Radio Corporation* [1960] SR (NSW) 576; *Newton-John v Scholl-Plough (Australia)* (1985) 11 FCR 233; *Shoshana v 10th Cantanae* (1988) 18 FCR 285; *Wickham v Associated Press* (1988) ATPR 40-910; *Hogan v Koala Dundee* (1988) 20 FCR 314; *Pacific Dunlop v Hogan* (1989) 23 FCR 553–587; *Honey v Australian Airlines* (1989) 14 IPR 264; *Talmax v Telstra* (1996) 36 IPR 46.

64   See the discussion in Chapter Two, above.

65   For instance, in *Newton-John v Scholl Plough* (1986) 11 FCR 233, the judge condemned the defendants' behaviour, but decided in their favour.

66   See the discussion on the limitations of positivism in Chapter Three, above.

67   *Henderson v Radio Corporation* [1960] SR (NSW) 576–604.

68   Ibid, 579–580.

69   *Tolley v Fry* [1931] AC 333. In this case the damage in question was not so much the association of the amateur golfer with the defendant's chocolate, but rather that an inference could be drawn that he had accepted remuneration for promoting the product, therefore compromising his status as an amateur sportsperson.

70   Although a defamation-type claim does appear to have been pleaded, little weight was attached to it, and it had no impact on the final decision: see *Henderson v Radio Corporation* [1960] SR (NSW) 576, 584–585.

71   Ibid, 593.

72   Ibid, 594. The first instance judge had some interesting things to say about what 'property' means in this context. Ibid, 582.

73   Ibid, 595.

74   Ibid, 595.

75   Ibid, 593–594.

76   Ibid, 594.

77   *Newton-John v Scholl-Plough* (1986) 11 FCR 233.

78   Burchett J: 'accepting that the respondent, in a not particularly praiseworthy way, is taking advantage of her name and reputation to obtain attention to his message, it seems to me that, having got the attention, he is

79 making it perfectly clear that his product does not have any relevant association with the applicant'. Ibid, 235.

79 *Pacific Dunlop v Hogan* (1989) 23 FCR 553. A scene from Crocodile Dundee had been parodied in a shoe advertisement, using an actor dressed in the same style as Paul Hogan's character in the film. McMullan concludes that there 'seems little substantive difference' between the Olivia Newton-John case and the Crocodile Dundee cases. See McMullan 'Personality Rights in Australia' (1997) 8 *Australian Intellectual Property Journal* 86, 88. The first case was *Hogan v Koala Dundee* (1988) 20 FCR 314, and involved the sale of unauthorised merchandise based upon the Crocodile Dundee character.

80 It is true that the representation in the Newton-John case was of a real person, while the representation of Crocodile Dundee was of a fictional character, however closely associated with Hogan as an actor. Whether the public would be more prepared to assume that Hogan had agreed to the use of the character he created than to assume that Newton-John had agreed to the use of her 'real' persona is pure speculation, and shows the uncertain and disputable nature of this line of reasoning.

81 *Honey v Australian Airlines* (1989) 14 IPR 264, 278. The case is discussed at some length in Andrew Terry 'The Unauthorised Use of Celebrity Photographs in Advertising' (1991) 65 *Australian Law Journal* 587.

82 The second respondents in the case were the House of Tabor, which had — also without Honey's permission — reproduced the picture on the front cover of a religious book. For the purposes of our discussion the issues involved in relation to each respondent are substantially similar.

83 'A corporation shall not, in trade or commerce, in connection with the supply or possible supply of goods or services or in connection with the promotion by any means of the supply or use of goods or services: ... (c) represent that goods or services have sponsorship, approval, performance characteristics, accessories, uses or benefits they do not have; (d) represent that the corporation has a sponsorship, approval or affiliation it does not have'.

84 *Hogan v Koala Dundee Pty Ltd* (1988) 20 FCR 314; *Pacific Dunlop Ltd v Hogan* (1989) 23 FCR 553; *Wickham v Associated Pool Builders Pty Ltd* (1988) ATPR 40-910; *10th Cantanae Pty Ltd v Shoshana Pty Ltd* (1987) 79 ALR 279; *Talmax Pty Ltd v Telstra Corporation Ltd* (1996) 36 IPR 46.

85 *Talmax v Telstra* (1996) 36 IPR 46, 53.

86 *Tot Toys v Mitchell* HC (NZ) 25 IPR 337 at 379. See also Terry 'The Unauthorised Use of Celebrity Photographs in Advertising'; Howell

'Character Merchandising: The Marketing Potential Attaching to a Name, Image, Persona, or Copyright Work' (1991) 6 *IPJ* 197.

7 Owning the Building Blocks of Life

Introduction

We have seen in previous chapters that the rhetoric of self-ownership, and in particular the self-possession associated with the male subject, plays a major, though frequently unacknowledged, role in defining the legal person. For instance, the woman who deviates from the standard case of the self-owning masculine person — by having heterosexual relations, by becoming pregnant, or by being the victim of a rape — finds herself occupying a marginal category, in which she is neither fully a person nor a form of property. The foetus and the corpse are neither (self-owning) persons, nor the property of another. The potential person, the former person, and the gendered person, are all entities which stand as 'other' to the self-possessed person. As such, these marginal entities exist in the frontier zones between subject and object, between self-possessed person and the property of other self-possessed persons.

The concept of the *persona* in intellectual property is also ambiguous. It is the mask that mediates the relationship between the self and the world. As our public face, our persona is inherently visible and accessible to all. It can be construed as a mere object, common property, or as historical artefact. At the same time, it is uniquely ours, and intimately connected with our reputation, our commercial activities, and our identity. However, unlike the other aspects of the human self which we have discussed, one's personality or character can be separated from the physical person and partially commodified. An ability to control access to the image is regarded as a necessary attribute of the self-owning person and has a strong cultural resonance, which is reflected explicitly in the law of the United States, and implicitly in Australian law.

In this chapter we move to another area of law which both challenges and, in some ways, reinforces the concept of the self-possessed individual. The commercial exploitation of genetic science has generated large numbers of patent applications for 'inventions' associated with human genes. We will consider this phenomenon in the context of the law relating to patents, and also with regard to the broader debate about self-ownership and ownership of human beings. As we will see, the issue has provoked extreme reactions. Some regard the patenting of genes as a modern form of slavery, others argue that such patenting furthers the interests of the species by encouraging proper rewards for inventive effort, and therefore ensuring continued medical research in genetic disease. As we will see, the debate is strongly influenced by the language of self-possession.

Microbiologists are sometimes characterised as tackling the question of 'life itself'.[1] Because the primary resources of microbiologists are regarded as the 'building blocks' of life, it is thought that their concern is with the most elementary conditions of existence, including human life. The science of genetics claims more than an insight into the general characteristics of human life. The complete DNA pattern for an individual is thought of as a 'genetic fingerprint' (and is used as such by forensic science), and therefore genetics also provides one method of identifying individuals. Regardless of the view we take of the debate over how much of our identity is biological and how much is social, within the scientific paradigm, microbiology provides an apparently objective means of differentiating human beings, and therefore of fixing an 'identity' which is distinct from any other.

The medical advances made possible by genetic science have not been universally welcomed. Many critics express fears that insurance companies and employers will attempt to minimise their risks by discriminating on the basis of genetic characteristics.[2] Some efforts have been made to ensure that such discrimination is outlawed. For instance, UNESCO's *Universal Declaration on the Human Genome and Human Rights* (1997) states that 'no-one shall be subject to discrimination based on genetic characteristics that is intended to infringe or has the effect of infringing human rights, fundamental freedoms and human dignity'.[3] The problem of discrimination has also been taken seriously by at least one Australian politician, Natasha Stott Despoja, who in 1998 presented a private member's bill to the Senate designed to eliminate such discrimination. The long title of the *Genetic Privacy and Non-discrimination Bill* 1998 states that it intends to 'protect the genetic privacy of individuals, to prohibit genetic discrimination and to provide for the collection, storage, and analysis of DNA samples'. The Bill, however, was not passed.

Just as troubling as genetic discrimination is the prospect of a new eugenics, which would not only be capable of determining genetic make-up at the stage of conception, but also of eliminating unwanted genetic characteristics in live human beings.[4] Although most would welcome the development of techniques to minimise or eliminate serious illnesses which can be traced to defective genes, such as cystic fibrosis, Huntington's Disease, and Alzheimer's disease,[5] many critics object to the model of the 'perfect' human being which underlies efforts at improving our genetic stock. Other scientific and ethical dilemmas concern the means used to obtain the benefits of genetic research. The Harvard Oncomouse was a mouse genetically engineered to have a special susceptibility to cancer. It was therefore deliberately bred to suffer. Transgenic animals have been created by injecting human genes into non-human embryos. Such research raises the fear of the creation of transgenic part-human species.

Interesting and necessary as these debates are, our concern in this chapter is more focused. It is to consider whether there is 'property' in human genetic resources. As mentioned above, private enterprise and public research institutions have begun to exploit what is perceived to be the huge commercial potential of genetic science. Genetic 'inventions' consist mainly of (allegedly) vastly improved diagnostic and therapeutic procedures for some illnesses and more effective pharmaceutical products. Patent law relating to genetic science has become a battleground between those who oppose patenting and those who wish to exploit commercially the potential of genetic science or who view patents as encouraging investment in scientific progress. Can an individual be said to have 'property' in the information contained in her own genes? Does the fact that an 'inventor' can be granted a patent over a biotechnological process or product based upon a human gene interfere with the concept of proprietorship in the self? And how does law resolve these dilemmas?

Arguments against the patenting of human genes, and the biotechnology products derived from genes, have taken several forms. Some critics regard the patenting of the products of human biotechnology as a transgression of the norms of self-ownership.[6] As a general protest at the extreme commercialisation of the biotechnology industry and its patenting of products based upon human genes, a British poet, Donna

MacLean, has filed an application for a patent on herself, claiming that she is original, the product of much inventive effort, and highly useful.[7] MacLean's claim of self-ownership is a protest against the commercial appropriation of the human being. To organisations such as Greenpeace, biotechnology patents are an appropriation of the common heritage of humanity which could ultimately reduce the world's biodiversity.[8] Indigenous people and third-world activists around the world have reacted strongly against sampling and patenting specifically directed at their regional genetic characteristics, arguing that it is an act of 'bio-piracy' and a violation of cultural self-determination.[9] Finally, many within the scientific community, especially researchers within public institutions, believe that patents and patent applications destroy the traditionally free generation of scientific knowledge.[10]

The mostly commercial interests supporting patenting of human genetic resources do so because it allegedly encourages investment in research and scientific advancement. An unreconstructed commercial approach to genetic information is that it is an enormous deposit of raw material within a largely unexploited intellectual commons.[11]

The extent to which genetic resources remain common or become 'owned', and therefore monopolised by private enterprise, will be strongly influenced by the manner in which person and property are distinguished in scientific, legal, and commercial debates over genetics. Patents on genetic information and inventions are socially palatable and legally permissible only when the patented objects are separated from the human body. It is only when our genes become mere objects, and are no longer an intrinsic part of our subjectivity, that they are regarded as capable of being reduced to property. The legal characterisation of genetic knowledge and innovation is therefore critical to the struggle for control of genetic resources.

Beyond Corporeality

Genetic science poses a number of challenges to our thinking about our relationships with ourselves, and with the world of objects. Genetic 'information' is at once universal and particular. Genetic patterns are said to be 99.9% identical across the human species. On average, only one in a thousand of the 'base pairs' that make up our genes will be different from one person to the next.[12] Unlike our physical bodies, genetic material is shared. The human genome, the genetic pattern for the human species, consists of a vast amount of information held in common by members of the human species. The human genome is also very similar to those of the other higher primates.[13]

Yet each individual has their own genome and their own distinct processing of genetic information. The specific combination of genes ensures that each person is genetically distinct from every other individual. Susan Aldridge comments that '[y]our identity is written into your genome'.[14] 'Identity', in this context, should probably be confined to '*genetic* identity', given the complexity of a person's social, legal, or moral identity. Identical twins are the one exception to the rule of unique genetic identity. Like our social persona, therefore, human genetic 'identity' is a composite of shared characteristics, unique in its total composition, but not in its component parts. And, like our social persona, genetic identity is placed within a vast, complex, and dynamic system.[15] As Dorothy Nelkin and Susan Lindee illustrate, the DNA sequences which comprise genes are commonly represented in popular culture as 'building blocks' which define and even determine human life.[16] In reality, the links between genes and identity are much more complicated than such 'genetic essentialism' suggests.[17]

Genetic science depends upon an extreme fragmentation of our corporeal identity.[18] In a sense many of the case studies discussed in previous chapters also assumed a differentiation between various types of body. We have discussed human corporeality as gendered, as potential human being, as dead human being, and as mere image. As we saw in Chapter Five, in the eighteenth century the commodity-value of the body for medical research was as a whole entity which could be dissected and analysed as related physical parts. By contrast, modern geneticists are dissecting and analysing the body at the microscopic cellular level, reducing it to the minutest chemical structures, and attempting to discover, replicate, and manipulate the biochemical processes which produce life. The value of actual bodies is still as a source of information for science: but now, the information can be derived from a small tissue or blood sample, and can be extracted and altered in such a way as to change the biological make-up of the body or of other bodies. Yet the comparatively low levels of interference with actual bodies required by geneticists gathering information has not saved the scientists (in some contexts) from accusations that they are the modern equivalents of body-snatchers and pirates.

The science of genetics undermines some of the fundamental distinctions upon which philosophy, science, and law are based. For instance, genetics makes it possible to copy the most elementary biochemical processes, and thus tends to collapse the distinction between nature and culture. Science can replicate nature and will be able to reconstitute the body, purify it, and recreate it in a form that both reproduces and transcends 'nature'. Scientists claim to be able to eliminate or minimise the occurrence of some of the genetic variations which influence disease. Science may therefore 'improve' nature.[19] Genetics also challenges the distinction between mind and body. By relocating 'information' and the processing of information away from the conscious mind and placing it in the minutest fragments of the body (DNA and amino acids), it displaces the centrality of mind, and the dominance of mind over body. Every cell in the human body has its own intelligence, and is constantly processing its own information. Furthermore, the science of genetics defies the distinction between life and death by creating 'immortal' cell-lines from mortal persons,[20] and by its potential to recreate genetically-identical organisms with the technology of cloning. The individual person may die, but their genetic characteristics can live on. Moreover, the distinction between the whole body and its parts takes on a new meaning when each and every cell carries the information needed to reproduce the whole. Finally, and perhaps most crucially for our purposes, the distinction between person and thing begins to look different when the corporeal person can be reduced to a complex, very abstract set of data, and when a person's genetic characteristics can be reproduced in a form which is conceptually and physically separable from any individual. What is the relationship between Dolly the cloned sheep, and her original? Is she the same, or different, or both? What is the relationship of Mr Moore[21] to the cell-line derived from his tissue sample? Is the cell-line part of his identity, or does it stand in relation to him as a mere object? These questions are crucial because they frame the debate over whether ownership of genetic resources transgresses the norm of self-ownership. Is a cell-line produced in a laboratory person or property? Essentially, we must ask whether a patent over a product derived from a human gene diminishes the original donor of the gene and whether it diminishes the 'common heritage of humanity'.

Genes, the Genome, and Gene Technology

Research into genetics breaks the body into minute, very abstract bits of information. For genetic science, bodies are matter, and matter is composed of chemical structures which are capable of being understood by the most detailed analysis.[22]

At the risk of indulging in what Mosk J, the major dissentient in *Moore's Case*, called an 'amateur biology lecture',[23] it is necessary to attempt a brief summary of some of the basic ideas of genetics and biochemistry. With the exception of the zygotes (ova and sperm), each cell in the body contains a complete set of forty-six chromosomes, containing an estimated 50 000 to 100 000 genes.[24] A gene is a chemical pattern within a strand of deoxyribonucleic acid (DNA). A DNA strand is normally represented as a double helix or twisted ladder, which consists of a series of nucleotides, made up of a sugar molecule, a phosphate molecule, and one of four bases (A, T, C, G[25]). The sugar and phosphate molecules of each nucleotide are connected along the sides of the ladder, while each base connects to its complementary base to form the rungs. The pairs of bases (or 'base pairs') are arranged in sequences along the DNA strand. Genes are specific sequences of base pairs within the DNA strand, though most of the DNA is said to be 'junk', because it performs no function, or (perhaps more likely) no known function.[26] The gene for a specific biological characteristic or function may take many forms. These differences between forms of a gene account for human individuality.[27]

Research into the applications of genetics takes a number of forms. Two aspects of genetic research which are of significance here are the processes of isolating and recombining DNA. The process of isolating DNA involves taking a DNA sequence, isolating the useful information, discarding the non-coding information, and creating a clone which can be used for further purposes. Recombining DNA is the technique of cutting sections of DNA from different sources, and connecting them together. Both processes are said to take genetic material out of its natural state, making it into something different. As we will see, this removal of the gene from its natural state is important as far as patent protection is concerned, as patents are not granted for naturally-occurring substances or organisms. Scientists must be able to assert that they have produced something which is not 'natural', and in fact is an 'invention'.

Described by the Human Genome Project (HGP) internet site as the 'master blueprint' of an organism,[28] the 'genome' is the totality of the base pair patterns for that organism. There are apparently some three *billion* such base pairs in the human genome, and the aim of the Human Genome Project is to create a 'map' of the human genome by locating and describing all of the DNA sequences.[29] Significantly, it is a 'consensus' map, derived from the DNA samples of a small number of anonymous donors.[30] It does not map all of the variations in human genomes, but extracts a standard model. A draft map of the genome, announced in June 2000, places most of the human DNA in its correct sequence.[31] At the time of writing, nearly a quarter of the sequence is reportedly completely mapped, while the rest is in varying states of completion. The mapping has also included the identification of thousands of genes. A complete map is expected to be completed by 2003 or sooner.

Donna Harraway, a feminist philosopher of science, explains that the conventional emphasis upon DNA as information contained in a code which can be cracked, conceals the true complexity of genetic processes:

> Conventionally, the genome refers only to the nucleic acid that 'codes' for something and not to the dynamic, multipart structures and processes that constitute functional, reproducing cells and organisms. Thus, not even the proteins critical to nuclear chromosomal organization or DNA structures such as mitochondrial chromosomes outside the nucleus are part of the genome, much less the whole living cell. Embodied information with a complex time structure is reduced to a linear code in an archive outside time. ... DNA in this view is a master molecule, the code of codes, the foundation of unity and diversity.[32]

Haraway's suggestion is that the project of decoding *the* (representative) genome is reductive. However useful and interesting the mapping project might be, it tends to focus upon DNA, at the expense of other important elements of the information systems of an organism. It also represents a dynamic process as a linear code, and takes a 'consensus' human, rather than human diversity on a global scale, as its object of knowledge.[33]

This sceptical view of the Human Genome Project is shared by Richard Pollack, who casts doubt upon the very idea of a 'representative' genome.

Another lesson that must be drawn from this century's earlier, disastrous romance with applied eugenics is that we cannot possibly distil from the billions of evanescent drafts of the human genome a single, canonical text. 'The human genome' does not exist except as an abstract notion, and while one or even a few alleles [ie. gene variants] may one day be isolated and sequenced for every human gene, even this collection would be different in interesting and revealing ways from the particular human genome in you, in me, or anyone else who has ever lived or ever will live.[34]

Pollack points out that the human genome is not the genome of any person, but is rather an abstract construct. At the same time, any one gene variant identified by the project might be present in a large number of people, especially those in the same populations of the original sample group.

The Human Genome Diversity Project (HGDP) has been attempting to correct some of the deficiencies of the Human Genome Project by sampling, documenting, and storing the DNA of diverse human populations. Where the HGP is concentrating on similarity across the human race, and finds genetic variation as a by-product of its primary research, the HGDP takes diversity and variation as its starting point. To this end, its goal is to collect samples from indigenous populations and local communities around the world. However the HGDP has also found itself the target of criticism, especially from indigenous groups, who have on a number of occasions declared strong opposition to the project. The opposition is based upon several concerns: that the HGDP will allow patents on products derived from indigenous DNA, that the research treats samples from indigenous populations as exhibits to be stored in a research 'museum', and that the research does not sufficiently allow for the meaningful participation of the communities to be targeted.

These are but two public examples of the numerous research projects on human genetic patterns currently being undertaken. A multitude of private projects are also being conducted. The HGP stands out for its sheer scale and ambition in producing a whole genetic code, and for the rhetoric of mastery and control that tends to accompany the search for the secrets of life.[35] The HGDP stands out for its supposedly well-meaning, if clumsy, attempt to record diversity in human genomes.[36] Both projects will apparently result in a huge repository of information which can be used by research scientists, providing a springboard for the development of new therapeutic techniques and new drugs.[37]

A number of metaphors are commonly used to describe the human genome and human genome research. Each of these metaphors suggests a slightly different type of relationship between the human individual and their genes. As we noted above, the HGP refers to the genome as a 'blueprint', implying a close and symbiotic relationship between genes and human identity. It is impossible to say what *the* human genome is a blueprint for, as it is no one person's genome. DNA is also generally represented as information, or as a code,[38] metaphors that take the DNA out of its messy organic bodily context, and place it in the realm of 'bio-information' which can be stored on, and analysed by, a computer.

The notion of rendering the genome as a map is also metaphorical. Donna Harraway argues that 'mapping' is a trope which has a tendency to fetishise and essentialise what is in reality an irreducibly complex and dynamic process.[39] 'Mapping,' according to Harraway, gives the impression of a knowledge which is global. Moreover, the concept of a map is a preliminary to turning the mapped object into property: 'map-making is essential to enclosing entities (land, minerals, populations etc.) and readying them for further exploration, specification, sale, contract, protection, management, or whatever'.[40] To Harraway, the depiction of the genome as a map is a rhetorical strategy which objectifies genes. The idea of a 'map' helps to separate a genome from the dynamic processes of the human body, and reduces it to an object capable of being owned.

A metaphor suggesting the dynamic nature of genetic processes (absent from the notion of the map) has been developed by geneticist Richard Pollack.[41] Pollack argues that DNA is a 'text'. DNA is not simply a blueprint providing clear and unambiguous information for the growth of the human body. It is rather what literary critics might once have inelegantly called a 'readerly text', that is, a text which has multiple meanings, and many hidden meanings, expressed in complex ways. It is a text which means different things in different contexts. It cannot be fully understood, fully closed in its meanings, or controlled in its manifestations. The metaphor of the 'text' captures both the notion of DNA as information, as well as the complexity of the processes by which its meanings are manifested. Pollack is therefore critical of attempts to master the genome, pointing out that we are many inter-related genomes.

We can see from this brief overview of genetics and its commentators that some significant questions are raised by genetic science. There is the problem of the 'identity' of the individual: where liberal thought has tended to assume the absolute boundaries of the self-owning person, genetics breaks down the frontiers between one person and the next. In the end, we are all made from the same (or very similar) stuff. Our physical uniqueness is purely a consequence of our distinct combination of this common material. At the same time, the dominant interpretations of genetic knowledge tend to disembody it. Although it is inherently concerned with bodies, speaking of genetic patterns as 'sequences of data', 'maps', 'information' and even 'texts', turns our genes into objects. A gene is not a part of a person, but rather an abstraction or reproduction of a (fragment of a) person. These two factors — the lack of uniqueness of genes, and their removal from the body — are crucial elements of the process of turning them into private property. If genetic information is not specific to any one person, it must subsist within the 'intellectual commons',[42] and may, under certain conditions, be subject to appropriation. Because it is 'information' or 'invention' and not 'body' or 'persona', it is separate and objectifiable. It is not person, but it is potentially property. Indeed, as we will now explain, patenting of genetic resources has become quite common.

Patenting Genes

A patent is a form of intellectual property giving inventors and their assignees exclusive rights over inventions for a defined period, normally twenty years.[43] The requirements which must be satisfied before a patent can be granted are fairly uniform throughout the Western world, and have recently been prescribed by the international *Agreement on Trade-Related Aspects of Intellectual Property Rights* (TRIPS).[44]

The general requirements for patentability laid down by this agreement are enshrined in the Australian *Patents Act* (1990) and its counterparts in other countries.[45] The claimed subject matter must be an invention, not a discovery. It can be a process or a product, but it must involve an 'inventive step' and be novel when compared to the 'prior art base'.[46] The invention must have a defined purpose or use. Finally, it must not have been secretly used before the date the patent is claimed. The

TRIPS agreement lays down the general principle that patents 'shall be available' when the conditions of novelty, inventive step, and usefulness are met, and the Australian legislation reflects these general requirements.

Drawing upon all of these criteria, the British poet Donna MacLean, as mentioned above, filed a patent application in early 2000.[47] Her invention is simply titled 'Myself'. Claiming that she had discovered and invented herself with 'hard labour' over a period of 30 years, that she was new, not obvious, and had industrial applications, MacLean filed the application in protest at the exploitation of human genetic resources by biotechnology companies. MacLean's claim draws upon both the concept of self-ownership and the Lockean association of labour with new property claims.

The primary legal impediments to MacLean's application are the normal prohibitions on patenting of both human beings and naturally-occurring organisms. Without stating that there is a moral limit to patentable inventions, the TRIPS agreement allows (but does not require) member states to deny patent protection to certain types of inventions. These allowable exceptions include inventions which may cause a risk to '*ordre public* or morality',[48] 'diagnostic, therapeutic and surgical methods for the treatment of humans or animals',[49] and 'plants and animals other than micro-organisms, and essentially biological processes for the production of plants or animals other than non-biological and microbiological processes'.[50] Not all of these allowable exceptions are reflected in the legal regimes. Australian law does incorporate a general prohibition, derived from the *Statute of Monopolies*, on granting patents that are 'contrary to law, or mischievous to the state, by raising prices of commodities at home, or generally mischievous'.[51]

Importantly, the *Patents Act,* and its counterparts in other jurisdictions, limits the patentability of human beings: 'Human beings and the biological processes for their generation, are not patentable inventions'.[52] The precise implications of this exclusion for biotechnology are not at all evident. As McKeough and Stewart comment, 'it is not clear whether a stretch of DNA is a "human being" or an isolated part thereof which should be patentable'.[53] In practice, DNA coding sequences *are* often regarded as patentable. The Australian Patent Office has released a statement claiming that patentable inventions include the following: 'synthetic genes or DNA sequences; mutant forms and fragments of gene sequences; the DNA coding sequence for a gene'. In relation to the DNA sequence, the statement indicates that such patents must be claimed 'in either the isolated or recombinant state (otherwise it is claiming something which occurs in nature)'.[54] Although this statement sets out the practice of the Australian Patents Office, and reflects international practice in the area, it has not been tested in the courts. The precise meaning of the exclusion of human beings from the class of things that may be patented remains unclear. The European Directive on the legal protection of biotechnological inventions also makes a distinction between the unpatentable human body (including naturally-occurring genes) and patentable material 'isolated from the human body or otherwise produced by means of a technical process'.[55]

The obstacle to the success of Donna MacLean's patent application on herself is presumably that human beings and 'naturally-occurring organisms' are normally unpatentable. It may well be said that the concept of 'nature' is itself problematic: when is a human being 'natural' and when is she not? Feminists have grappled with this question for decades, and many have concluded that 'nature' is itself a construct. Surely, however, the concept of the 'human being' is sufficiently clear to prohibit a claim over the self. Or is it? What makes MacLean's claim an attempt to patent a human being, while the biotechnology patents are not? The formal answer is that biotechnology patents do not seek to control use and access to a whole person, just objectifiable fragments, information, or codes. In Kantian terms, such fragments are not ends-in-themselves, simply means to the ends of others. The dilemma is whether this is a sufficient legal and ethical response.

An English common law rule that methods of medical treatments are not patentable[56] was for a time adopted by the Australian courts.[57] (Importantly, drugs are regarded as patentable, even though they are closely connected with methods of medical treatment.) However, the medical treatment exclusion is not reflected in the Australian legislation, and has been disapproved by the Federal Court.[58] This omission of the traditional exclusion is significant, given that many of the biotechnology patents are for diagnostic and therapeutic procedures.

Despite much opposition to any patenting of human genetic information, the practice of granting such patents is well established. A study published in 1996 found that between 1981 and 1995, a total of 1,175 patents had been granted globally for DNA sequences derived from human tissue. Most of these patents were granted by the European Patent

Office, the US Patent Office and the Japanese Patent Office. About 70% of all patents were owned by US and Japanese organisations.[59] By 2000, the numbers had increased dramatically. Recent research has identified over 161 000 granted or pending patent applications on human genetic sequences.[60] It would seem therefore that human genetic 'inventions' are clearly regarded as appropriate subject matter for patents.

However well established the practice of granting patents for human genes may be, applying the broad principles of patent law to the patenting of genetic inventions has provided an endless source of debate for scholars of intellectual property. If an invention is to satisfy the requirement of originality, it must not be obvious. That is, it must not be something that an ordinary skilled person working in the area would think of trying.[61] Because knowledge of genetics is increasing at an exponential rate, processes and ideas which might have been original a few years ago might now be regarded as routine. Can all of the tens of thousands of patent applications relating to human genes really be said to be based upon an 'invention', especially where the gene has been identified by a computer?

In addition, there have been problems with the requirement of usefulness. A patent application must include specific information as to the claimed invention's industrial or commercial use, and should not be a 'land grab' with as yet unspecified applications. Some attempts have been made to patent isolated DNA sequences without specifying a precise application for the information. In 1991, the US National Institutes of Health filed a patent application for a large number of gene fragments that code for human brain functions. Although the precise significance of the genes was unknown, and no commercial or practical application was at that time envisaged, the decision was defended on the basis that it would keep open commercial options.[62] Most commentators regard any attempt to patent genes whose precise use and application is not known as dangerous: such practices could result in vast portions of the genetic terrain being appropriated and monopolised. Eventually, this particular patent application failed. The prohibition on patents which would be 'generally mischievous' or against public policy might also provide an obstacle to a patent application in certain cases.

The most important issue, from our point of view, is whether a gene is characterised as human. If a gene sequence is to be regarded as an 'invention', and not a mere discovery of a particular chemical pattern, it must have some artificial characteristics which take it out of the state of (human) nature. Similarly, if an invention is to avoid characterisation as a human being, or as the biological processes for the generation of a human being, it must be capable of being conceptually differentiated from an actual human being or actual human genes. In other words, it must become an 'object' which is clearly separated from the human subject, if patent protection is to be granted. This need to differentiate the object of the patent from any individual human being, and from human beings generally, is at the heart of our enquiry in this chapter.

Same or Different?

As we noted above, one of the most disputed issues in the area of biotechnology patents is whether or not such patenting amounts to ownership of life. We do not expect to be able to answer this question definitively, because it depends on irreconcilable accounts of what constitutes 'life', what constitutes 'human identity', and what exactly is being appropriated in the process of sampling, isolating, and reproducing DNA. The advocates for patenting clearly see the subject-matter of the patent as qualitatively different from the human body, while those who oppose patenting tend to see it as intimately connected to the human body.

Some of the methods for describing the research in genetics entrench the view that genes which have been identified and modified bear little resemblance to their source body. For instance, speaking of the genome as 'information', as a 'code', a 'blueprint', a 'map', a 'sequence', or a 'text' suggests that it is something different from the human body. It has an abstract quality. All of these metaphors are useful, particularly for the layperson with little or no knowledge of genetics. But these terms also perform the rhetorical function of separating genes and the genome from its bodily context. Emphasis upon the processes of isolating and recombining DNA also draws our attention to the novelty and distinctiveness of the material. It becomes a product with an application, rather than a merely cloned body part.

The view that the cloned gene is different from the human body, as well as the opposing view that it is the same, are both represented in *Moore v Regents of the University of California*. Although we have already considered this case in Chapter One, we wish now to reconsider it with specific reference to the relationship of Moore to his genetic information.

The majority in *Moore's Case* considered and rejected an argument that compared a person's cells to their persona or image. Counsel for Moore suggested that genetic information is even more significant to a person's identity than their image or name. If the image is regarded as property, as it is in many parts of the United States, then why should genetic information not have the same status?

> ...[i]f the courts have found a sufficient proprietary interest in one's persona, how could one not have a right in one's own genetic material, something far more profoundly the essence of one's human uniqueness than a name or a face?[63]

In a thoughtful and comprehensive analysis of the problem of property in one's own genetic information, Catherine Valerio Barrad has expanded upon this argument. As she says, 'If one's face, physical features, and voice are so intrinsic to the individual as to be protected as inviolate personality, then the genetic determinant of those attributes must be the true expression of the person's identity and also protectable against appropriation'.[64]

However, the majority in *Moore's Case* found such arguments completely unconvincing. In their view, the genetic material does not suggest unique identity, but rather commonality with others. It is not like an image, because it is shared. And the *purpose* of the research was to find a process for manufacturing a common biological substance, lymphokines:

> Lymphokines, unlike a name or a face, have the same molecular structure in every human being, and the same, important functions in every human being's immune system. Moreover, the particular genetic material which is responsible for the natural production of lymphokines, and which defendants use to manufacture lymphokines in the laboratory, is also the same in every person; it is no more unique to Moore than the number of vertebrae in the spine or the chemical formula of hemoglobin.[65]

The characterisation of the genetic material as common to all (or most) militates against its characterisation as property. Something which is common to all cannot be individual property, except with the intervention of some skill and effort, such as that of the defendants, to take it out of its natural condition. However, as James Boyle comments, '[t]his passage is remarkable partly because it is nonsensical'.[66] In emphasising the common nature of the material, the majority manages to gloss over the obvious fact that the researchers gained an advantage in their research specifically through the use of the plaintiff's cells. Not just anybody's cells had this potential. It was the plaintiff's cells that were of significance. Whether or not the information could have been found in another person's tissue sample, it was the information contained in Moore's cells that was crucial to the research.[67]

In relation to the subject-matter of the patent, the opinion of the majority was also clear: 'the patented cell line is both factually and legally distinct from the cells taken from Moore's body'.[68] On its face, the statement is ambiguous. In one sense, the cell line was 'factually distinct' from the plaintiff's cells because it contained different matter: the actual substance of the cells in the cell-line is by definition different from the substance of the cells upon which it was based. This difference is not, however, the one to which the majority referred. The aim of the researchers was to reproduce the *information* contained in the cells that gave them certain desirable and valuable characteristics. The researchers had changed the cells, by reproducing and immortalising them, as the majority point out in a footnote.[69] The cell-line was different in its composition from the original cells.

The claim that the cell-line is 'legally' distinct from the original cells is based upon the fact that the cell-line is the subject matter of a patent. Referring to the landmark U.S. case on biotechnology inventions, *Diamond v Chakrabarty*,[70] the majority reiterated the primary tenet of patent law, that patents are available for inventions, not for 'naturally occurring organisms'. Cell lines are considered patentable because they are developed and grown in an artificial environment, and involve the application of effort and skill. The labour involved justifies the recognition of property. Moreover, the fact that the patent was granted leads the majority to conclude that Moore's claim was unfounded. The majority thus argued that the patent legally contradicts any claim of competing ownership in the cell line. The problem with this line of argument is that it suggests that the granting of the patent puts a legal stop to all issues of ownership. It does not consider the possibility that the patent might have been inappropriately granted, but assumes that because the patent *was* granted, the plaintiff thereby has lost any right that he might otherwise have had.

Mosk J meets the assertion that the cell-line is 'factually distinct' from the plaintiff's body by pointing out that the important qualities of the original cells were preserved in the cell-line. In fact, the preservation of these qualities was the very reason for the production of the cell-line:

> For present purposes no distinction can be drawn between Moore's cells and the Mo cell-line. It appears that the principal reason for establishing a cell line is not to 'improve' the quality of the parent cells but simply to extend their life indefinitely, in order to permit long term study and/or exploitation of the qualities already present in them.[71]

Certainly the substance and the precise composition of the cells had changed, but they still contained the same information.

Mosk J also finds the claim that the cell-line is 'legally distinct' from the plaintiff's original tissue unconvincing. In the first place, the granting of the patent is completely irrelevant to any dealing with the cells that took place before the patent was granted. The patent does not retrospectively authorise improper appropriation. More interestingly, Mosk J also attempts to give Moore a more active role in the intellectual property that resulted from the research.

> I do not question that the cell line is primarily the product of the defendants' inventive effort. Yet likewise no one can question Moore's crucial contribution to the invention — an invention named, ironically, after him: but for the cells of Moore's body taken by defendants, *there would have been no Mo cell line.* (emphasis in original)[72]

As Debra Mortimer explains, the 'cell-line could not exist without Moore's primary cells'.[73] Although in no sense can Moore be regarded as an 'inventor', Mosk J considers that it would be completely unfair to bar him from a share of the profits of an invention which rested so clearly upon his unwitting contribution.[74] An analogous case might be that of Carol Jenkins, a medical anthropologist who collected blood samples from the Hagahai tribe in Papua New Guinea. When a patent application was (infamously) filed for a cell-line derived from the sample, Jenkins was named as one of five inventors. (The patent was later withdrawn.) Her role was crucial to the process, although she did not actively participate in the processing of the genetic material that led to the patent, and apparently saw herself as a 'disinterested intermediary'.[75] As Alain Pottage observes, the naming of Jenkins as one of the inventors of the cell-line 'indicates that the cell line was not conceived as an entirely "scientific" artefact'.[76] Similarly, it might be surmised that, although there was no intermediary party involved in Moore's case, the contributor of the sample might gain a share of the profits.

Mosk J concludes his judgement with a strongly-worded criticism of the majority's reliance on material not on the court record. These extraneous documents, he says 'bear solely or primarily on whether Moore's "genetic material" was or was not "unique"',[77] an issue which he regards as irrelevant to the case. Just because others might have shared aspects of Moore's genetic material does not mean that there was no property in it.

As we noted in Chapter One, the fear of commodification of the human body is reflected in all of the judgements in *Moore's Case*. The majority feared that the recognition of Moore's claim would reduce the body to mere property. It was felt that tort law was a more appropriate way of protecting personal integrity. Accordingly, the majority judges distinguished the property rights obtained by the defendants from Moore as a physical entity. The weaknesses of this argument have been identified. The concept of property deployed by the majority resembles complete or absolute ownership, rather than the flexible and contextual notion more commonly recognised by the common law, meaning that the fear of commodification is perhaps over-stated. Moreover, by emphasising the commonality of genetic information rather than its distinctiveness, the indebtedness of the researchers to Moore is understated by the majority. Undoubtedly the over-riding argument advanced is the utilitarian one: that recognition of property in the person in such a context would unduly inhibit research. And yet, the minority judgements regarded some form of self-ownership as necessary to protect the human body from exploitation. Property in the genetic person need not be absolute ownership consisting of all of the possible rights in the bundle, but could be more partial, for instance it could include the right to control access and use, but not the right to alienate.

Conclusion

The patenting of human genes is seen by some as a blatant transgression of the principle that persons should never be the object of another's property. If genetic information can be 'owned' by someone other than the individual from whom such information was taken, then, in this view, the person no longer has complete and exclusive control over the very attributes that make her a person. The person's genetic information becomes a mere natural resource, which may be appropriated on a first-possession basis. In this account, protecting the individual from such interference with their bodily autonomy demands recognition of their own prior property claim in their own genetic resources. But, as we have seen, both the patent law and genetic science present the opposite view: that the 'property' of a biotechnology patent for an 'invention' derived from human genes is not itself a person, or even part of a person. It can be compared to neither the personality, nor body part. It is simply information, which does not occur naturally, and which must be altered in order to be useful. From this perspective, there is therefore no need to protect individuals with anything more than the normal ethical and legal principles requiring informed consent and recognition of bodily autonomy.

Notes

1   See, for instance, Francis Crick *Life Itself: Its Origin and Nature* (London: MacDonald and Co, 1982).

2   The issue of discrimination on the basis of genetic characteristics is raised vividly by the film GATTACCA. See also Catherine M. Valerio Barrad 'Genetic Information and Property Theory' (1993) 87 *Northwestern University Law Review* 1037, 1045–1046; Onora O'Neill 'Insurance and Genetics: The Current State of Play' in Roger Brownsword, WR Cornish, and Margaret Llewelyn (eds) *Law and Human Genetics: Regulating a Revolution* (Oxford: Hart Publishing, 1998), 124.

3   *Universal Declaration on the Human Genome and Human Rights* (1997), Article 6.

4   Adam Nash, for instance, was born in the United States in August 2000 after pre-implantation genetic diagnosis. His embryo, fertilised *in vitro*, was selected from several viable embryos before being implanted. The purpose of the selection was to provide his sister Molly with a cell-donor

for her otherwise fatal illness, as well as to avoid the risk of the parents conceiving another child suffering the same illness. The case was highly publicised, many commentators expressing fears of 'designer babies', and of the commodification of children in the search for cures: *The Guardian*, 4 October 2000.

5   Barrad 'Genetic Information and Property Theory', 1037–1038, n31. Detailed information is to be found in Sunil Maulik and Salil Patel *Molecular Biotechnology: Therapeutic Applications and Strategies* (New York: Wiley-Liss, 1997), ch 1.

6   *Moore v Regents of the University of California* 793 P. 2d 479 (Cal. 1990) (*Moore's Case*) raises this very point, and will be discussed below.

7   This application (number GB0000180.0) is discussed further below. See the report in *The Guardian*, February 29, 2000.

8   See Alain Pottage 'The Inscription of Life in Law: Genes, Patents, and Biopolitics' in Brownsword, Cornish and Llewellyn (eds) *Law and Human Genetics: Regulating a Revolution*.

9   See *Ukupseni Declaration, Kuna Yala on the Human Genome Diversity Project* (1997); Jean Christie 'Biodiversity and Intellectual Property Rights: Implications for Indigenous People' in *Ecopolitics IX: Perspectives on Indigenous Peoples Management of Environmental Resources* (Darwin: Northern Territory University, 1995); Naomi Toht-Arriaza 'Of Seeds and Shamans: The Appropriation of the Scientific and Technical Knowledge of Indigenous and Local Communities' in Bruce Zeff and Pralima Rao (eds) *Borrowed Power: Essays on Cultural Appropriation* (New Brunswick, NJ: Rutgers University Press, 1997); Jill McKeough 'Patent Abuse: Rights in Genetic and Environmental Resources' (1997) 8 (1) *Polemic* 31; Vandana Shiva *Biopiracy* (South End Press, 1997).

10   Leslie Roberts 'Who Owns the Human Genome?' (1987) 237 *Science* 358; David Dickson 'UK clinical geneticists ask for ban on the patenting of human genes' (1993) 366 *Nature* 391; David Dickson 'Open access to sequence data "will boost hunt for breast cancer gene"' (1995) 378 (30) *Nature* 425.

11   See the discussion of this term in Chapter Six.

12   Robert Pollack *Signs of Life: The Language and Meanings of DNA* (London: Viking, 1994), 105.

13   The similarity of the human genome to the genome of the higher primates is one argument which is advanced on behalf of recognising legal personality in the Great Apes.

14   Susan Aldridge *The Thread of Life: the Story of Genes and Genetic Engineering* (Cambridge University Press, 1996), 159. Robert Pollack, in casting some doubt on the aims of the Human Genome Project, says 'There are as many human genomes as there are persons': Pollack *Signs of Life*, 37

15   Donna Harraway *Modest_Witness@Second_Millenium.FemaleMan©_ Meets_OncoMouse™ Feminism and Technoscience* (New York: Routledge, 1997), 142.

16   Dorothy Nelkin and M. Susan Lindee *The DNA Mystique: The Gene as a Cultural Icon* (New York: W.H. Freeman and Co., 1995), ch 3 'Sacred DNA'.

17   Authors who focus upon the dynamic and diverse nature of human genetics include Donna Harraway, Dorothy Nelkin, Susan Lindee, and Robert Pollack.

18   See Roxanne Mykitiuk 'Fragmenting the Body' (1994) 4 *Australian Feminist Law Journal* 63.

19   One concern about the environmental impact of genetically-modified food is that species which are 'improved', for instance which have superior growth rates to their natural counterparts, may escape into the wild. If this happens, they may outcompete those species reliant on evolution for improvement, and eventually replace them.

20   The most infamous example, perhaps, is the HeLa cell line created from Henrietta Lacks, an African-American woman who died of cervical cancer in 1951. Samples of the cancerous cells were taken by scientists, and developed into the HeLa cell-line, which proved to be far easier to cultivate than any previously used. The cell line was an important factor in the development of the polio vaccine. Because of the success of the cell line, it was used extensively throughout the world, and even took over other cell cultures because of its unprecedented strength. Henrietta Lacks' family only learnt of the extensive use of her cells in 1975. Undoubtedly the cells have had an enormous commercial application, but of course the family has not directly benefited from the use.

21   *Moore's Case* has been discussed in Chapter One, and will be considered further at the end of this chapter.

22   The brief information about genetics which follows is largely derived from the following sources: the Human Genome Project internet site 'The Science Behind the Human Genome Project' at http://www.ornl.gov /hgms/resource/info.html; Stuart Ira Fox *Human Physiology* 5th ed (Dubuque, IA: Wm. C. Brown, 1996), 58–62; Aldridge *The Thread of Life*;

Sunil Maulik and Salil Patel *Molecular Biology: Therapeutic Applications and Strategies*; Pollack *Signs of Life*.

23 'I dissociate myself completely from the amateur biology lecture that the majority impose on us throughout their opinion'. *Moore v Regents of the University of California* 793 P2d 479 (Cal. 1990), 521.

24 Aldridge *The Thread of Life*, 57.

25 Adenine, thymine, cytosine, and guanine.

26 Aldridge *The Thread of Life*, 57.

27 Pollack *Signs of Life*, 37.

28 Similarly, the *Universal Declaration on the Human Genome and Human Rights*, states that the human genome 'underlies the fundamental unity of all members of the human family' (Article 1).

29 The HGP is an international consortium of genetics research institutes, first established in 1988 under the auspices of the US National Institutes of Health and the Department of Energy.

30 According to the information provided in the Human Genome Project internet site, the sampling protocol involves gaining blood and sperm donations from numbers of anonymous donors. Only a few of the samples are actually processed, meaning that neither the donors nor the scientists are aware of the identity of the ten to twenty people whose DNA will eventually make up the 'human genome'. See http://www.ornl.gov/hgmis/faq/seqfacts.html#whose.

31 National Institutes of Health (US) Press Release, 26/6/2000.

32 Donna Harraway *Modest_Witness*, 245.

33 Harraway also critiques the notion that the HGP is a new scientific frontier: 'No wonder the Human Genome Project's apologists have called it biology's equivalent to putting a man on the moon. Where else could he go with all that thrust? The Human Genome Project is discursively produced as, once more, "one small step ..." At this origin, this new frontier, man's footprints are radioactive traces in gel; at the dawn of hominization, the prints were made in volcanic dust at Laetoli in Ethiopia; at the dawn of the space age, a white man, acting as surrogate for all mankind, walked in moon dust. All of these technoscientific travel narratives are about freedom; the free world; democracy; and, inevitably, the free market.' Harraway *Modest_Witness*, 167.

34 Pollack *Signs of Life*, 61–62.

35 See Sarah Franklin 'Romancing the Helix: Nature and Scientific Discovery' in Lynne Pearce and Jackie Stacey (eds) *Romance Revisited* (New York: New York University Press, 1995), 63, 65.

36   We acknowledge that, from the point of view of indigenous groups, the intentions of the HGDP researchers have not appeared at all 'well-meaning', but rather commercially motivated.

37   See Sunil Maulik and Salil Patel *Molecular Biotechnology*, ch 1.

38   Franklin 'Romancing the Helix', 67.

39   See Harraway *Modest_Witness*, see also Nelkin and Lindee *The DNA Mystique*.

40   Harraway *Modest_Witness*, 136.

41   Pollack *Signs of Life*.

42   We have discussed this idea in Chapter 6.

43   Twenty years is the minimum term laid down by the TRIPS agreement, Article 33.

44   *Agreement on Trade-Related Aspects of Intellectual Property Rights* (1993), Article 27.

45   See, for instance, *Patents Act* 1990 (Cth), s18 [Australia]; *Patents Act* 1977 (UK) s1; *Patent Act* (US) ss101–103.

46   *Patents Act* 1990 (Australia), ss7, 18. See *National Research Development Corporation v Commissioner of Patents* (1959) Commonwealth Law Reports 252.

47   *The Guardian*, February 29, 2000.

48   *Agreement on Trade-Related Aspects of Intellectual Property Rights*, Article 27, 2.

49   *Agreement on Trade-Related Aspects of Intellectual Property Rights*, Article 27, 3(a).

50   *Agreement on Trade-Related Aspects of Intellectual Property Rights*, Article 27, 3(b).

51   The words are from the *Statute of Monopolies* 1623, s6. The section is incorporated into the *Patents Act* in s18(1)(a).

52   *Patents Act* 1990 (Cth), s18(2) [Australia].

53   Jill McKeough and Andrew Stewart *Intellectual Property in Australia* 2nd ed (Sydney: Butterworths, 1997), 338.

54   Intellectual Property Australia 'Australian Patents for: Microorganisms; Cell lines; Hybridomas; Related biological materials and their use; and Genetically manipulated organisms' (1998). The *Patents Amendment Bill* (1990) proposed a revision of the *Patents Act*. If enacted, the revision would have specifically excluded naturally occurring genes, sequences, and descriptions of genes and their sequences, from being the subject of a patent

application. Arguably the proposed amendment does no more than elaborate upon the existing state of the law.

55 Directive 98/44/EC of the European Parliament and of the Council of 6 July 1998 on the legal protection of biotechnological inventions. Official Journal L213, 30/07/1998 p. 0013–0021.

56 The UK exclusion of medical treatment is based on the desirability of ensuring that medical treatments are as freely available as possible. See *Re C & W's Application* (1914) 31 RPC 235. The exclusion is now included in the *Patents Act 1977* (UK), and in the *European Patents Convention*, Article 52 (4).

57 *National Research Development Corporation v Commissioner of Patents* (1959) 102 CLR 252, at 270 (per Dixon CJ, Kitto J and Windeyer J); in *Joos v Commissioner of Patents* (1972) 46 ALR 438 Barwick CJ held that medical treatments are not patentable, but cosmetic processes are.

58 The medical exclusion, the distinction between treatments and drugs, and the distinction between cosmetic processes and medical treatment were all disapproved in *Anaesthetic Supplies v Rescare* (1994) 122 ALR 141. For a detailed discussion of this case and others relating to the medical treatment exclusion, see Dianne Nicol 'Should Human Genes Be Patentable Inventions under Australian Patent Law?' (1996) 3 *Journal of Law and Medicine* 231, 239–241.

59 SM Thomas, ARW Davies, NJ Birtwistle, SM Crowther, and JF Burke 'Ownership of the Human Genome' (1996) 380 *Nature* 387.

60 The research, conducted by Gene Watch UK, was commissioned by *The Guardian*, and reported on November 15, 2000. See James Meek 'The Race to Buy Life'.

61 *Patents Act 1990* (Cth), s7(2) [Australia]. For a discussion of the requirement of 'inventive step' see *Genentech's Patent* [1989] RPC 147 (Court of Appeal) and *Biogen v Medeva* [1997] RPC 1 (House of Lords). A much more generous approach from the perspective of the biotechnology companies was taken in a US case *In re Deuel* 51 F3d 1552 (US Federal Circuit 1995). The nature of an inventive step has not been tested in Australian courts in relation to human genetic inventions, but see *Coopers Animal Health v Western Stock Distributors* (1986) 67 ALR 390. The practice of the Australian Patent Office is apparently to grant patents on any isolated or cloned gene sequence. See generally Peter Montague 'Biotechnology Patents and the Problem of Obviousness' (1993) 4 *Australian Intellectual Property Journal* 3.

62   See Rainer Moufang 'Patenting of Human Genes, Cells and Parts of the Body? — The Ethical Dimension of Patent Law' (1994) 25 (4) IIC 487, 492–493; see also 'HUGO warning over broad patents on gene sequences' (1997) 387 *Nature* 326; 'MRC to limit patents on cDNA sequences' (1993) 366 *Nature* 6.

63   Argument for Moore, quoted in majority judgement, 490.

64   Catherine M Valerio Barrad 'Genetic Information and Property Theory'.

65   *Moore v Regents of the University of California* 793 P. 2d 479 (Cal. 1990), 490.

66   James Boyle 'A Theory of Law and Information: Copyright, Spleens, Blackmail, and Insider Trading' (1992) 80 *California Law Review* 1413, 1516.

67   Boyle adds 'Both Steve Timmons and I can jump and hit a volleyball. Only one of us, however, will be asked to endorse shoes, or to play on the US Olympic team. But by the court's logic, since both Steve and I are "playing volleyball" we are both "volleyball players" and are therefore "the same"'. Boyle 'A Theory of Law and Information', 1516.

68   *Moore v Regents of the University of California* 793 P. 2d 479 (Cal. 1990), 493.

69   Ibid, 492 n35.

70   *Diamond v Chakrabarty* 447 US 303 (1980). The case concerned a patent application for a genetically modified bacterium. The application was initially refused on the grounds that it related to a natural organism, but the appeal court upheld the application, stating that the bacterium was new and 'invented', not naturally occurring.

71   *Moore v Regents of the University of California* 793 P 2d 479 (Cal 1990), 511.

72   Ibid, 511.

73   Debra Mortimer 'Proprietary Rights in Body Parts: The Relevance of *Moore's Case* in Australia' (1993) 19 *Monash Law Review* 217, 225.

74   *Moore v Regents of the University of California* 793 P 2d 479 (Cal 1990), 512.

75   Alain Pottage 'The Inscription of Life in Law: Genes, Patents, and Biopolitics', 148.

76   Ibid, 160.

77   The documents in question were an appendix to the opening brief made by the defendant Golde. *Moore v Regents of the University of California* 793 P. 2d 479 (Cal. 1990), 522.

8 Persons Beyond Property?

The Inadequacy of Natural Law and Positivism

Throughout this book we have posed the question 'are persons property?' and discovered that there is no simple answer. Even to attempt an answer to the necessary antecedent questions, 'what is the person?' and 'what is property?' is to traverse vast areas of legal scholarship with significant conceptual and legal complexities and ambiguities, as we saw in Chapters Two and Three. Neither the concept of 'property' nor the concept of 'personality' possesses a unitary, stable meaning. They are multi-faceted concepts whose meaning has shifted over time and continues to change; they are not fixed legal categories. This makes it difficult to assert, with any degree of confidence, either that persons *are* property or that they are not. To provide a definite answer to our question, we would have to do one of two things: either we would have to attribute a core meaning to the concepts of person and property, or we would have to accept legal statements on the matter at face value. Both approaches, however, would result in a rather formalistic account of our subject, one that fails to reveal the intricacy of the various relationships between person and property.

These sceptical reflections about our principal question do not, however, reduce its legal and political significance. Nor do they render us incapable of offering some tentative comments on the nature of the relationship between these two great legal concepts. As we indicated in Chapter One, the dogmatic legal position is that persons are *not* property: we cannot be the property of another, and we do not own ourselves, at least not in any straightforward manner. And as we have seen, these dogmatic assertions that persons are not property are animated by good ethical instincts. Lawyers and lawmakers do not want to be party to the commodification of persons. Along with Kant, we do not want to reduce people to things. Slavery is too fresh in our minds. And surely there is something transcendent about persons, some moral force or spirit, which means that it is quite inappropriate to think of persons as property — as mere animals or things? This is the sort of thinking about persons we have consistently identified in our study. Certainly we have observed a great legal reluctance explicitly to recognise property in persons. (The 'right of publicity' recognised in the US is possibly the only area of law where self-ownership is explicitly recognised as such.)

However, to accept the dogmatic position would be to accept a misleadingly singular, positivist view of the law of this area. One important element of our research has been to scrutinise some of the many dimensions of the personality/property relation in order to reveal its complexity and thus to rebut the orthodox view of legal persons. We have found that there are many contexts — such as the maternity ward and the burial ground and the gene laboratory — in which the formal view of legal personality is contradicted both by legal practice and by background understandings of what it is to be a person. These implicit understandings of personality serve to justify and reinforce the practice.

In Chapters Two and Three we therefore questioned the adequacy of an approach to our problem which depended exclusively on formal law. To be sure, the concepts of both property and the person do assume a formal legal character: positivist jurisprudence in the twentieth century has in fact depicted such entities as legal constructs with an arbitrary content. Hans Kelsen, who thought that both property and the legal person are figments of the legal imagination, argued the extreme positivist position. These concepts, he said, do not have legal meaning outside the law, but are the product or effect of legal relations.[1]

Notwithstanding the inherent appeal of this positivist approach — after all, it allows lawyers to be the final arbiters of the meanings of their concepts — we have endeavoured to show that it undervalues the role played by social and philosophical constructs of person and property. In our view, it is quite impossible to disentangle the positive law from its surrounding ideology. The legal person may technically be a bundle of rights and responsibilities, which vary from case to case, but a culturally-specific model of a natural person, with natural capacities, and even natural rights, frequently gives shape and meaning to the legal concept of person. Similarly, although property may in a formal sense be nothing more than a bundle of 'disaggregated' and non-fixed legal relationships between persons, a strong cultural concept of absolute property rights continues to influence the law.

Our law's resistance to formal recognition of self-ownership (even while there is much tacit approval of this notion) is one consequence of the persistence of a relatively absolute concept of property. That is to say, courts and legal commentators have often failed to recognise that property itself is a malleable notion, which can be shaped to suit some very different contexts, according to the purposes desired. Because they have assumed that any explicit association of the person with property *inevitably* means commodification of the person, they have often produced decisions and legal analyses that seem unsatisfactory and unfair. For example, many have expressed dissatisfaction with the legal treatment of Mr Moore and the cells derived from his spleen. He was unable to assert any property rights in his cell line, but the scientists in question were allowed to derive enormous commercial benefit from his person.

The judgement in *Moore* prompts us to ask, 'Are judges right to be so nervous about the idea of property in persons?' '*Should* the person be their own property?' not only metaphorically but also in a formal legal sense. Or would we thereby enslave ourselves? What political and social arguments can be advanced in favour of the idea of the self-owning person, and should any right of self-ownership include a right of self-alienation?

Again, much depends on how the concepts of person and property are understood. For feminists, and others concerned with the interests of social groups poorly represented in traditional models of the legal person, such a question has a crucial political significance. It may be that in many respects the model of the self-owning individual is a *strategically* useful and defensible model of the person, precisely because it calls upon the deep liberal sensibilities of respect for privacy and property. On this view, the defence of property rights in the person, on the grounds that such rights strengthen and support the interests of the individual in a competitive world, might be a pragmatic method of maintaining some basic equality, at least at the level of bodily integrity.[2] However, as we have indicated throughout our book, we are sceptical of the self-owning person's enduring place in the socio-legal order. At the very least, if the self-owning person is to respond to feminist and communitarian demands that the person be recognised as a relational and contextualised being, it will need to draw upon a concept of property more oriented towards an ethical responsibility for the natural and cultural environments.

We have further observed that the descriptive question ('are persons property?') is not as distinct from the normative question ('should we be?'), as positivists would have us believe. Indeed our enduring concern has been to show how moral and cultural beliefs about persons and property inevitably shape perceptions and descriptions of the substantive law. As we have insisted throughout, the philosophy of self-ownership underpins the notion of the self, which is integral to the liberal legal tradition. The norm of self-ownership is supposed to be a statement, in the strongest possible terms, that the individual in principle ought to be free from the control of any other person. It is impossible to separate this liberal morality of autonomous personhood from the positive law: the person is (their own) property not because the positive law explicitly recognises such a principle, but because the model of the person which informs the law is a self-owning, bounded, self-determining individual.

Needless to say, our rejection of the positivist approach to persons and property does not lead to an acceptance of any natural law explanation. Far from it. Indeed, one of our avowed intentions has been to reflect upon the historical, contextual nature of models of the person. Any claim to universality which might be made on behalf of the notion of the possessive individual draws upon the power and pervasiveness of this idea of personhood in the liberal West (and especially in the English-speaking West) and not upon a natural form of the human being. We do not believe that there is anything inevitable about the possessive individual. Arguments from human nature only tend to divert attention from the historical and discursive processes which shape our socio-legal environment.

Beyond Possessive Individualism?

Although we have been unable to supply a definitive answer to the question 'Are persons property?' — and to be honest we doubt that there is one — we hope to have shed some light on the complex relationship between persons and property. We have shown some of the ways in which persons do become property, even when the courts say that they do not and must not. And we have shown some of the ways that persons seek to avoid becoming property, either of themselves or of other legal persons, but do not always succeed. If there is a general point to be drawn from all of this, it is to note the high degree of complicity between the concepts of person and property within the liberal legalism of the recent common law.

Jeremy Bentham said that 'Property and law are born together, and die together. Before laws were made there was no property; take away laws, and property ceases'.[3] We might also observe that property and the person are born together and die together. Without the (legal *or* natural) person there is no property: ownership is meaningless without an owner.

Bentham did not go so far as to say that without property there could be no law.[4] Nor have we given unqualified support to the controversial proposition that without property there is no person.[5] And yet the assertion that there is no person without property is perfectly reasonable, if it is understood as a reflection upon the plural manifestations of possessive individualism we have found in our law and in our legal culture. Our constant refrain has been that the legal person is born out of a quite particular way of dividing the world into subjects and objects. Both our self-relation and our relations with others are highly mediated by property or by metaphors of property.

This is not to say that the person and property are of necessity tied together in this particular manner. There are other understandings of the person, which presuppose neither the formal nor the metaphorical relation of person with property we have found in *our* law. Property, as we know it, denotes the ability to exclude others from an 'object': it is a form of control over access. Property is a hierarchical relationship, in which the owner has power over the owned, as well as over those who do not own. But the relationship between persons and themselves and between persons and the things of the world do not *have* to be one of power *over* self or over others. Rather, it may be understood, for example, as a partnership or custodianship or even an intermingling. So, although we accept that persons depend upon some relationship with things as well as with other persons, this does not of itself tie the person to property in the way that *we* know it and which we do indeed regard as highly problematic.

Similarly the person does not have to be viewed as a unitary bounded, self-possessing autonomous individual, always in command of his own being and always able to exclude all others. The relationship of the pregnant woman to her foetus reveals just some of the failings of this view. So too does the relationship of persons in the acts of sexual intercourse. Possessive individualism begins to appear very odd when one reflects on the varieties of human experience.

The possessive individual of our liberal Western law is a highly particular and peculiar being. The trouble is that lawyers, be they positivists or natural lawyers, have often had difficulty seeing this particularity, naively assuming that their understanding of persons is simply the way the world is. Without further discussion, indeed with very little reflection at all, they have taken their worldview to be uncontroversial because it is thought to be universal. But as the anthropologist Clifford Geertz has remarked:

> The Western conception of the person as a bounded, unique, more or less integrated motivational and cognitive universe, a dynamic centre

of awareness, emotion, judgement, and action organised into a distinctive whole and set contrastively against other such wholes and against a social and natural background, is, however incorrigible it may seem to us, a rather peculiar idea within the context of the world's cultures.[6]

We hope that we have conveyed some sense of this being's peculiarity and limitations and hinted at a few of the many ways we might think of her differently.

Notes

1   Hans Kelsen *Pure Theory of Law* (Berkeley: University of California Press, 1967), 131, 173–174.
2   Margaret Radin's work can be understood in this light.
3   Bentham *Theory of Legislation*, CK Ogden (ed) (London: Kegan Paul, Trench, Trubner and Co, 1931), 113.
4   Although Bentham did not say this, it is perfectly feasible to argue that the positivist model of law is just as reliant upon the metaphor of property as is the liberal person. See Margaret Davies 'The Proper: Discourses of Purity' (1998) 9 *Law and Critique*.
5   One reading of Hegel's *Philosophy of Right* might lead to such a conclusion, although this interpretation is by no means inevitable.
6   Clifford Geertz, 'From the Native's Point of View: On the Nature of Anthropological Understanding' in Paul Rabinow and William M Sullivan (eds) *Interpretive Social Science: A Reader* (Berkeley: University of California Press, 1979) 16.

Bibliography

Aldridge, Susan *The Thread of Life: the Story of Genes and Genetic Engineering* (Cambridge University Press, 1996).

Allen, Carleton Kemp *Duties and Other Essays in Jurisprudence* (Aalen: Scientia, 1931).

Andrews, Lori 'My Body My Property' (1986) 16(5) *Hastings Center Report* 28.

Arneson, Richard 'Lockean Self-Ownership: Towards a Demolition' (1991) 39 *Political Studies* 36.

Atherton, Rosalind 'Expectation Without Right: Testamentary Freedom and the Position of Women in 19th Century New South Wales' (1988) 11 *University of New South Wales Law Journal* 133.

Atherton, Rosalind and Prue Vines *Australian Succession Law* (Sydney: Butterworths, 1996).

Atherton, Rosalind 'Claims on the Deceased: The Corpse as property' (2000) (8)1 *Journal of Law and Medicine* 361.

Atiyah, Patrick *The Rise and Fall of Freedom of Contract* (Oxford: Clarendon Press, 1979).

Austin, John *Lectures on Jurisprudence* (London: John Murray, 1886).

Australia, Model Criminal Code Officers Committee *Model Criminal Code Chapter 5, Sexual Offences Against the Person: Discussion Paper* (Canberra: The Committee, 1996).

Baker, John H *An Introduction to English Legal History* 3rd ed (London: Butterworths, 1990).

Barrett, Michèle *Women's Oppression Today: Problems in Marxist Feminist Analysis* (London: Verso, 1980).

Barthes, Roland 'The Death of the Author' in Roland Barthes *Image, Music, Text* (London: Fontana, 1987), 142.

Bennett, Belinda 'Pregnant Women and the Duty to Rescue: A Feminist Response to the Fetal Rights Debate' (1991) 9(1) *Law in Context* 70.

Bennett, Belinda *Law and Medicine* (North Ryde: LBC, 1997).

Bentham, Jeremy 'Principles of the Civil Code' in John Bowring (ed), *The Works of Jeremy Bentham Volume I* (Edinburgh: William Tait, 1843).

Bentham, Jeremy *Theory of Legislation* CK Ogden (ed) (London: Kegan Paul, Trench, Trubner and Co, 1931).

Berlin, Isaiah 'Two Concepts of Liberty' in Isaiah Berlin *Four Essays on Liberty*, Oxford University Press, 1969).

Birkel Dangelo, Kathleen 'How Much of You Do You Really Own? A Property Right in Identity' (1989) 37 *Cleveland State Law Review* 499.

Birks, Peter 'The Unacceptable Face of Human Property' in Peter Birks (ed) *New Perspectives in the Roman Law of Property: Essays for Barry Nicholas* (Oxford: Clarendon Press, 1989), 61.

Blackstone, William *Commentaries on the Laws of England, A Facsimile of the First Edition of 1765-1769* (University of Chicago Press, 1979).

Bourianoff Bray, Michelle 'Personalizing Personalty: Toward a Property Right in Human Bodies' (1990) 69 *Texas Law Review* 209.

Boyle, James 'A Theory of Law and Information: Copyright, Spleens, Blackmail, and Insider Trading' (1992) 80 *California Law Review* 1413.

Bracton, Henry de *On the Laws and Customs of England* (Samuel Thorne (trans), Cambridge: Belknap, 1968).

Bray, M 'Personalizing Personalty: Toward a Property Right in Human Bodies' (1990) 69 *Texas Law Review* 209.

Burke, Claire 'European Intellectual Property Rights: A Tabular Guide' (1995) 10 *European Intellectual Property Review* 466.

Burley, Stephen 'Passing Off and Character Merchandising: Should England Lean Towards Australia?' (1991) *European Intellectual Property Review* 227.

Campbell, Courtney 'Body, Self, and the Property Paradigm', (1992) 22(5) *Hastings Center Report* 34.

Carter, Angela *The Sadeian Woman: An Exercise in Cultural History* (London: Virago, 1979).

Christie, Jean 'Biodiversity and Intellectual Property Rights: Implications for indigenous people' in *Ecopolitics IX: Perspectives on Indigenous Peoples Management of Environmental Resources* (Northern Territory University, 1995).

Christman, John 'Self-Ownership, Equality and the Structure of Property Rights' (1991) 19 *Political Theory* 28.

Cohen, Felix S 'Transcendental Nonsense and the Functional Approach', (1935) 35 *Columbia Law Review* 809.

Cohen, G A 'Self-Ownership, World-Ownership, and Equality', in Frank S Lucash (ed) *Justice and Equality Here and Now* (Cornell University Press, 1986), 108.

Cohen, Morris 'Property and Sovereignty' (1927) 13 *Cornell Law Quarterly* 8.

Coke, Edward *Institutes of the Laws of England Part III* (London: Thames Baset, 1680).

Crick, Francis *Life Itself: Its Origin and Nature* (London: MacDonald, 1982).

Daunton, MJ *Progress and Poverty: An Economic and Social History of Britain 1700–1850* (Oxford University Press, 1995).

Davies, Margaret *Asking the Law Question* (Sydney: Law Book Company and London: Sweet and Maxwell, 1994).

Davies, Margaret 'Feminist Appropriations: Law, Property and Personality' (1994) 3 *Social and Legal Studies* 365.

Davies, Margaret 'The Heterosexual Economy' (1995) 5 *Australian Feminist Law Journal* 27.

Davies, Margaret 'The Proper: Discourses of Purity' (1998) 9 *Law and Critique* 147.

Davies, Margaret 'Queer Persons, Queer Property: Self-Ownership and Beyond' (1999) 8 *Social and Legal Studies* 327.

Davis, Jennifer 'The King Is Dead: Long Live the King' (2000) 59 *Cambridge Law Journal* 33.

Derrida, Jacques 'Force de Loi: "Le Fondement Mystique de l'Autorité"' ['Force of Law: The "Mystical Foundation of Authority"'] (1990) 11 *Cardozo Law Review* 919.

Descartes, René *Meditations on First Philosophy* (Indianapolis: Bobbs-Merrill, 1960).

Devereux, John and Shaunnagh Dorsett 'Towards a Reconsideration of the Doctrines of Estates and Tenure' (1996) 4 *Australian Property Law Journal* 30.

Dias, Reginald WM *Jurisprudence* 5th ed (London: Butterworths, 1985).

Dickenson, Donna *Property, Women and Politics: Subjects or Objects?* (Cambridge: Polity Press, 1997).

Dickson, David 'Open access to sequence data "will boost hunt for breast cancer gene"' (1995) 378 (30) *Nature* 425.

Dickson, David 'UK clinical geneticists ask for ban on the patenting of human genes' (1993) 366 *Nature* 391.

Dinwiddy, John *Bentham* (Oxford University Press, 1989).

Diósdi, György *Ownership in Ancient and Preclassical Roman Law* (Budapest: Akadémiai Kiadó, 1970).

Donohue, Charles 'The Future of the Concept of Property Predicted from its Past' in J Roland Pennock and John Chapman (eds) *Property: Nomos XXII* (New York University Press, 1980) 28.

Drahos, Peter *A Philosophy of Intellectual Property* (Aldershot: Dartmouth, 1996).

Ducor, Phillippe 'The Legal Status of Human Materials' (1996) 44 *Drake Law Review* 195.

Duff, Patrick W *Personality in Roman Private Law* (Cambridge University Press, 1938).

Dworkin, Gerald 'Moral Rights and the Common Law Countries' (1994) 5 *Australian Intellectual Property Journal* 5.

Dyer, Richard *Heavenly Bodies: Film Stars and Society* (Basingstoke: Macmillan, 1986).

Edgeworth, Brendan 'Post-property? A Postmodern Conception of Private Property' (1988) 11 *University of New South Wales Law Journal* 31.

Edgeworth, Brendan 'Tenure, Allodialism and Indigenous Rights at Common Law: English, United States and Australian Land Law Compared After Mabo v Queensland' (1994) 23 *Anglo-American Law Review* 397.

Ehr-Soon Tay, Alice 'Law, the Citizen and the State' in Eugene Kamenka, Robert Brown and Alice Ehr-Soon Tay (eds) *Law and Society: The Crisis in Legal Ideals* (London: E Arnold, 1978) 10.

Eleftheriadis, Pavlos 'The Analysis of Property Rights' (1996) 16 *Oxford Journal of Legal Studies* 31.

Finucane, RC 'Sacred Corpse, Profane Carrion: Social Ideals and Death Rituals in the Later Middle Ages' in Joachim Whaley (ed) *Mirrors of Mortality: Studies in the Social History of Death* (New York: St Martin's, 1981) 40.

Fortin, Jane ES 'Legal Protection for the Unborn Child' (1988) 51 *Modern Law Review* 54.

Fovargue, Sara and Jose Miola 'Policing Pregnancy: Implications of the Attorney-General's Reference (No 3 of 1994)' (1998) 6 *Medical Law Review* 265.

Fox, Stuart Ira *Human Physiology* 5th ed (Dubuque: Wm C Brown, 1996).

Franklin, Sarah 'Romancing the Helix: Nature and Scientific Discovery' in Lynne Pearce and Jackie Stacey (eds) *Romance Revisited* (New York University Press, 1995) 63.

Frow, John 'Elvis' Fame: The Commodity Form and the Form of the Person' (1995) 7 *Cardozo Studies in Law and Literature* 131.

Fuller, Lon *Legal Fictions* (Stanford University Press, 1967).

Gaines, Jane *Contested Culture: The Image, the Voice, and the Law* (University of North Carolina Press, 1991).

Giacoppo, Erin 'Avoiding the Tragedy of Frankenstein: The Application of the Right of Publicity to the Use of Digitally Reproduced Actors in Film' (1997) 48 *Hastings Law Journal* 601.

Gittings, Clare *Death, Burial and the Individual in Early Modern England* (London: Croom Helm, 1984).

Godden, Lee 'Wik: Feudalism, Capitalism and the State. A Revision of Land Law in Australia?' (1997) 5 *Australian Property Law Journal* 162.

Goodrich, Peter *Reading the Law: A Critical Introduction to Legal Method and Technique* (Oxford: Basil Blackwell, 1986).

Graveson, RH *Status in the Common Law* (London: Athlone, 1953).

Gray, John Chipman *The Nature and Sources of the Law* 2nd ed (New York: Macmillan, 1921).

Gray, Kevin J 'Property in Thin Air' (1991) 50 *Cambridge Law Review* 252.

Gray, Kevin J and Susan Francis Gray 'Private Property and Public Propriety' in Janet McLean (ed) *Property and the Constitution* (Oxford: Hart Publishing, 1999) 11.

Gray, Kevin J and PD Symes *Real Property and Real People: Principles of Land Law* (London: Butterworths, 1981).

Grey, Thomas 'The Disintegration of Property' in J Roland Pennock and John Chapman (eds) *Property: Nomos XXII* (New York University Press, 1980), 69.

Grubb, Andrew 'Commentary on St George's Healthcare NHS Trust v S' (1998) 6 *Medical Law Review* 356.

Hale, Matthew *The History of the Pleas of the Crown, Volume I* (London: Professional Books, 1971).

Hannemann, Brian 'Body Parts and Property Rights: A New Commodity for the 1990s' (1993) 22 *Southwestern University Law Review* 399.

Hardiman, Roy 'Toward the Right of Commerciality: Recognising Property Rights in the Commercial Value of Human Tissue' (1986) 34 *UCLA Law Review* 207.

Harraway, Donna *Modest_Witness@Second_Millenium.FemaleMan©_ Meets_OncoMouse™ Feminism and Technoscience* (New York: Routledge, 1997).

Harris, Cheryl 'Whiteness as Property' (1993) 106 *Harvard Law Review* 1707.

Harris, JW 'Who Owns My Body?' (1996) 16 *Oxford Journal of Legal Studies* 55.

Hart, HLA *The Concept of Law* 2nd ed (Oxford: Clarendon, 1994).

Haskins, George '"Inconvenience" and the Rule for Perpetuities' (1983) 48 *Missouri Law Review* 451.

Hegel, Georg WF *The Philosophy of Right*, T M Knox (trans) (Oxford University Press, 1952).

Hobbes, Thomas *Leviathan* (Cambridge University Press, 1991).

Hohfeld, Wesley N 'Some Fundamental Legal Conceptions as Applied in Judicial Reasoning'(1913) 23 *Yale Law Journal* 16.

Hohfeld, Wesley N 'Fundamental Legal Conceptions as Applied in Judicial Reasoning'(1917) 26 *Yale Law Journal* 710.

Honoré, A M 'Ownership' in AG Guest (ed) *Oxford Essays in Jurisprudence* (Oxford University Press, 1961), 107.

Hughes, Justin 'The Philosophy of Intellectual Property' (1988) 77 *Georgetown Law Journal* 287.

Irigaray, Luce *Je, Tu, Nous: Toward a Culture of Difference* (New York: Routledge, 1993).

Jarrett, Bede, *Social Theories of the Middle Ages 1200–1500* (London: Ernest Benn, 1926).

Johnston, David *Roman Law in Context* (Cambridge University Press, 1999).

Jones, Carolyn 'Principles Versus Practicalities: Should Moral Rights Be Subject to Waiver?' (1995) 4 *Arts and Entertainment Law Review* 56.

Kant, Immanuel *Lectures on Ethics* L Infield (trans) (London: Methuen and Co, 1930).

Karpin, Isabel 'Foetalmania: Foetal Legal Identity and the Three Headed Monster' (1994) 5(1) *Polemic* 10.

Karpin, Isabel 'Reimagining Maternal Selfhood: Transgressing Body Boundaries and the Law' (1994) 2 *Australian Feminist Law Journal* 36.

Keeton, George W *The Elementary Principles of Jurisprudence* (London: Sir Isaac Pitman and Sons, 1930).

Kelley, Donald R *The Human Measure: Social Thought in the Western Legal Tradition* (Harvard University Press, 1990).

Kelsen, Hans *General Theory of Law and State* (New York: Russell and Russell, 1945).

Kelsen, Hans *Pure Theory of Law* (Berkeley: University of California Press, 1967).

Kelsen, Hans *General Theory of Norms* (Oxford: Clarendon, 1991).

Kelsen, Hans *An Introduction to the Problems of Legal Theory* (Oxford: Clarendon Press, 1992).

Kennedy, Ian 'Negligence: Interference with Right to Possession of a Body: Mackey v. U.S.', (1995) 3 *Medical Law Review* 233.

Kennedy, Ian 'Commentary on Re MB' (1997) 8 *Medical Law Review* 317.

King, Barry 'Articulating Stardom' (1985) 26 (5) *Screen* 27.

Kinley, David (ed) *Human Rights in Australian Law: Principles, Practice and Potential* (Sydney: Federation, 1998).

Kocourek, Alexander *Jural Relations* 2nd ed (Indianapolis: Bobbs-Merrill, 1928).

Lacey, Nicola *Unspeakable Subjects: Feminist Essays in Legal and Social Theory* (Oxford: Hart Publishing, 1998).

Lacey, Nicola, Celia Wells and Dirk Meure *Reconstructing Criminal Law: Critical Perspectives on Crime and the Criminal Process* (London: Weidenfeld and Nicholson, 1990).

Lawson, FH (ed) *International Encyclopedia of Comparative Law Vol VI: Property and Trust* (Tübingen: JCB Mohr, 1978).

Lee, RW *The Elements of Roman Law* 4th ed (London: Sweet and Maxwell, 1956).

Lindgren, Kevin E, John W Carter and David J Harland *Contract Law in Australia* (Sydney: Butterworths, 1986).

Linebaugh, P 'The Tyburn Riot Against the Surgeons' in Douglas Hay et al (eds) *Albion's Fatal Tree: Crime and Society in Eighteenth-Century England* (London: Lane, 1975), 65.

Locke, John *Two Treatises of Government* Peter Laslett (ed) 2nd ed (Cambridge University Press, 1967, first published 1690).

Lucy, William and Catherine Mitchell 'Replacing Private Property: The Case for Stewardship' [1996] *Cambridge Law Journal* 566.

MacKinnon, Catharine 'Reflections on Sex Equality under Law' (1991) 100 *Yale Law Journal* 1281.

Magnusson, Roger 'The Recognition of Proprietary Rights in Human Tissue in Common Law Jurisdictions' (1992) 18 *Melbourne University Law Review* 601.

Maine, Henry *Ancient Law: Its Connection with the Early History of Society and its Relation to Modern Ideas* (London: John Murray, 1930).

Maitland, Frederic and Frederick Pollock *The History of English Law Before the Time of Edward I* (Cambridge University Press, 1898).

Maitland, Frederic W and Francis C Montague *A Sketch of English Legal History* (New York: G P Putnam and Sons, 1915).

Marcus, Sharon 'Fighting Bodies Fighting Words: A Theory and Politics of Rape Prevention' in Judith Butler and JW Scott (eds) *Feminists Theorize the Political* (New York: Routledge, 1992), 400.

Matthews, Paul 'Whose Body? People as Property' (1993) *Current Legal Problems* 201.

Matthews, Paul 'The Man of Property' (1995) 3 *Medical Law Review*, 251.

Maulik, Sunil and Salil Patel *Molecular Biotechnology: Therapeutic Applications and Strategies* (New York: Wiley-Liss, 1997).

Mauss, Marcel 'A Category of the Human Mind: the notion of person; the notion of self' WD Hall (trans), in Michael Carrithers, Steven Collins and Steven Lukes (eds) *The Category of the Person: Anthropology, Philosophy, History* (Cambridge University Press, 1985), 15.

McCarthy, Thomas 'The Human Persona as Commercial Property: The Right of Publicity' (1996) 7 *Australian Intellectual Property Journal* 20.

McCauliff, CMF 'The Medieval Origin of the Doctrine of Estates in Land: Substantive Property Law, Family Considerations and the Interests of Women' (1992) 66 *Tulane Law Review* 919.

McHugh, James T 'What is the Difference Between a "Person" and a "Human Being" within the Law?' (1992) 54 *Review of Politics* 445.

McKeough, Jill 'Patent Abuse: Rights in Genetic and Environmental Resources' (1997) 8(1) *Polemic* 31.

McKeough, Jill and Andrew Stewart *Intellectual Property in Australia* 2nd ed (Sydney: Butterworths, 1997).

McLean, Janet (ed) *Property and the Constitution* (Oxford: Hart Publishing, 1999).

McMullan, John 'Personality Rights in Australia' (1997) 8 *Australian Intellectual Property Journal* 86.

McPherson, CB *The Political Theory of Possessive Individualism: Hobbes to Locke* (Oxford: Clarendon Press, 1964).

Meszaros, Istvan *Marx's Theory of Alienation* (London: Merlin, 1970).

Mill, John Stuart *Principles of Political Economy* 8th ed (London: Longmans, 1878).

Minogue, K 'The Concept of Property and its Contemporary Significance' in J Roland Pennock and John Chapman (eds) *Property: Nomos XXII* (New York University Press, 1980) 11.

Montague, Peter 'Biotechnology Patents and the Problem of Obviousness' (1993) 4 *Australian Intellectual Property Journal* 3.

Mortimer, Debra 'Proprietary Rights in Body Parts: The Relevance of *Moore's Case* in Australia' (1993) 19 *Monash Law Review* 217.

Moufang, Rainer 'Patenting of Human Genes, Cells and Parts of the Body? The Ethical Dimension of Patent Law' (1994) 25(4) *IIC* 487.

Munzer, Stephen 'Kant and Property Rights in Body Parts' (1993) 6 *Canadian Journal of Law and Jurisprudence* 319.

Mykitiuk, Roxanne 'Fragmenting the Body' (1994) 4 *Australian Feminist Law Journal* 63.

Naffine, Ngaire *Law and the Sexes: Explorations in Feminist Jurisprudence* (Sydney: Allen and Unwin, 1990).

Naffine, Ngaire 'Windows on the Legal Mind: Evocations of Rape in Legal Writing' (1992) 18 *Melbourne University Law Review* 741.

Naffine, Ngaire 'Possession: Erotic Love in the Law of Rape' (1994) 57 *Modern Law Review* 10.

Naffine, Ngaire 'The Body Bag' in Ngaire Naffine and Rosemary J Owens (eds), *Sexing the Subject of Law* (North Ryde: LBC, London: Sweet and Maxwell, 1997) 79.

Naffine, Ngaire 'But a Lump of Earth? The Legal Status of the Corpse' in Desmond Manderson (ed), *Courting Death: The Law of Mortality* (London: Pluto, 1999) 95.

Nedelsky, Jennifer 'Law, Boundaries, and the Bounded Self' in Robert Post (ed) *Law and the Order of Culture* (University of California Press, 1991).

Nedelsky, Jennifer 'Property in Potential Life? A Relational Approach to Choosing Legal Categories' (1993) 6 *Canadian Journal of Law and Jurisprudence* 343.

Nekam, Alexander *The Personality of the Legal Entity* (Cambridge, Mass: Harvard University Press, 1938).

Nelkin, Dorothy and M Susan Lindee *The DNA Mystique: The Gene as a Cultural Icon* (New York: W H Freeman, 1995).

Nicol, Dianne, 'Should Human Genes Be Patentable Inventions under Australian Patent Law?' (1996) 3 *Journal of Law and Medicine* 231.

Noyes, Charles R *The Institution of Property: A Study of the Development, Substance, and Arrangement of the System of Property in Modern Anglo-American Law* (London: Longmans, Green and Co, 1936).

Nozick, Robert *Anarchy, State and Utopia* (Oxford: Basil Blackwell, 1974).

O'Donovan, Katherine *Sexual Divisions in Law* (London: Weidenfeld and Nicholson, 1985).

O'Donovan, Katherine 'With Sense, Consent, or Just a Con? Legal Subjects in the Discourses of Autonomy' in Ngaire Naffine and Rosemary J Owens (eds) *Sexing the Subject of Law* (North Ryde: LBC and London: Sweet and Maxwell, 1997) 46.

O'Neill, Onora 'Insurance and Genetics: The Current State of Play' in Roger Brownsword, WR Cornish and Margaret Llewelyn (eds) *Law and Human Genetics: Regulating a Revolution* (Oxford: Hart Publishing, 1998) 124.

Ogden, C K *Jeremy Bentham 1832-2032: Being the Bentham Centenary Lecture, delivered in University College, London, on June 6th, 1932* (London: Kegan Paul, 1932).

Owens, Rosemary J 'Working in the Sex Market' in Ngaire Naffine and Rosemary J Owens eds *Sexing the Subject of Law* (North Ryde: LBC and London: Sweet and Maxwell, 1997) 119.

Pateman, Carole *The Sexual Contract* (Cambridge: Polity Press, 1988).

Penner, James E *The Idea of Property in Law* (Oxford: Clarendon Press, 1997).

Pierce Wells, Catherine 'Pragmatism, Feminism, and the Problem of Bad Coherence' (1995) 93 *Michigan Law Review* 1645.

Pollack, Robert *Signs of Life: The Language and Meanings of DNA* (London: Viking, 1994).

Posner, Richard *Sex and Reason* (Harvard University Press, 1992).

Pottage, Alain 'Instituting Property' (1998) 18 *Oxford Journal of Legal Studies* 331.

Pottage, Alain 'The Inscription of Life in Law: Genes, Patents, and Biopolitics' in Roger Brownsword, WR Cornish and Margaret Llewelyn (eds) *Law and Human Genetics: Regulating a Revolution* (Oxford: Hart Publishing, 1998), 148.

Pound, Roscoe *Jurisprudence Volume IV* (St Paul: West Publishing, 1959).

Purdy, Laura 'Are Pregnant Women Fetal Containers?' (1990) 4 *Bioethics* 273.

Radin, Margaret J 'Property and Personhood' (1982) 34 *Stanford Law Review* 957.

Radin, Margaret *Reinterpreting Property* (University of Chicago Press, 1993).

Radin, Margaret J 'The Colin Ruagh Thomas O'Fallon Memorial Lecture on Reconsidering Personhood' (1995) 74 *Oregon Law Review* 423.

Rattigan, W H *Roman Law of Persons* (London: Wildy and Sons, 1873).

Reed, Helen 'A Pregnant Woman's Rights Versus a Fetus's Rights: What is the Australian Position?' (1996) 4 *Journal of Law and Medicine* 165.

Reese, R Anthony 'Reflections on the Intellectual Commons: Two Perspectives on Copyright Duration and Reversion' (1995) 47 *Stanford Law Review* 707.

Reich, Charles 'The New Property' (1964) 73 *Yale Law Journal* 733.

Reich, Charles 'The Individual Sector' (1991) 100 *Yale Law Journal* 1409.

Richardson, Ruth *Death, Dissection and the Destitute* (London: Routledge, Kegan Paul, 1987).

Roberts, Leslie 'Who Owns the Human Genome?' (1987) 237 *Science* 358.

Rose, Carole 'Possession as the Origin of Property' (1985) 52 *University of Chicago Law Review* 73.

Rose, Carole *Property and Persuasion: Essays on the History, Theory, and Rhetoric of Ownership* (Boulder: Westview Press, 1994).

Ryan, Alan 'Self-Ownership, Autonomy and Property Rights' (1994) 11 *Social Philosophy and Policy* 241.

Salmond, John W *Salmond on Jurisprudence* 12th ed (London: Sweet and Maxwell, 1960).

Samuel, Geoffrey 'The Many Dimensions of Property' in Janet McLean (ed), *Property and the Constitution* (Oxford: Hart Publishing, 1999), 40.

Saussure, Ferdinande de *Course in General Linguistics* (New York: Philosophical Library, 1959).

Schroeder, Jeanne 'Virgin Territory: Margaret Radin's Imagery of the Inviolate Feminine Body' (1994) 79 *Minnesota Law Review* 55.

Schroeder, Jeanne *The Vestal and the Fasces* (University of California Press, 1998).

Scott, Russell *The Body as Property* (London: Allen Lane, 1981).

Seymour, John 'A Pregnant Woman's Decision to Decline Treatment: How Should the Law Respond?' (1994) 2 *Journal of Law and Medicine* 27.

Seymour, John 'Commentary: Unborn Child (Pre-Natal Injury): Homicide and Abortion, Attorney-General's Reference (No 3 of 1994)' (1995) 3(3) *Medical Law Review* 299.

Seymour, John *Childbirth and the Law* (Oxford University Press, 2000).

Sherman, Brad and Lionel Bently *The Making of Modern Intellectual Property Law: The British Experience, 1760–1911* (Cambridge University Press, 1999).

Shiva, Vandana *Biopiracy: The Plunder of Nature and Knowledge* (Dartington: Green, 1997).

Shnably, Stephen J 'Property and Pragmatism: A Critique of Radin's Theory of Property and Personhood' (1993) 45 *Stanford Law Review* 347.

Siepp, David 'The Concept of Property in the Early Common Law' (1994) 12 *Law and History Review* 29.

Simes, Lewis *Public Policy and the Dead Hand* (University of Michigan Law School, 1955).

Simpson, AW Brian *A History of the Land Law* 2nd ed (Oxford: Clarendon, 1986).

Singer, Barbara 'The Right of Publicity: Star Vehicle or Shooting Star?' (1991) 10 *Cardozo Arts and Entertainment Law Journal* 1.

Singer, Peter *Animal Liberation: A New Ethics for Our Treatment of Animals* (London: Jonathon Cape, 1976).

Smith, Bryant 'Legal Personality' (1928) 37 *Yale Law Journal* 283.

Tawney, RH *The Acquisitive Society* (Brighton: Wheatsheaf, 1982).

Terry, Andrew 'The Unauthorised Use of Celebrity Photographs in Advertising' (1991) 65 *Australian Law Journal* 587.

Thomas, JAC *The Institutes of Justinian* (Amsterdam: North Holland Publishing Co, 1975).

Thomas, JAC *Textbook of Roman Law* (Amsterdam: North Holland, 1976).

Thomas, SM, ARW Davies, NJ Birtwistle, SM Crowther and JF Burke 'Ownership of the Human Genome' (1996) 380 *Nature* 387.

Toht-Arriaza, Naomi 'Of Seeds and Shamans: The Appropriation of the Scientific and Technical Knowledge of Indigenous and Local Communities' in Bruce Zeff and Pralima Rao (eds) *Borrowed Power: Essays on Cultural Appropriation* (Rutgers University Press, 1997).

Tur, Richard 'The "Person" in Law' in Arthur Peacocke and Grant Gillett (eds) *Persons and Personality: A Contemporary Inquiry* (Oxford: Basil Blackwell, 1987) 123.

Turner, Michael *Enclosures in Britain 1750–1830* (London: Macmillan, 1984).

Valerio Barrad, Catherine M 'Genetic Information and Property Theory' (1993) 87 *Northwestern University Law Review* 1037.

Wagner, Danielle 'Property Rights in the Human Body: The Commercialisation of Organ Transplantation and Biotechnology' (1995) 33 *Duquesne Law Review* 931.

Waldron, Jeremy *The Right to Private Property* (Oxford: Clarendon Press, 1988).

Waldron, Jeremy 'Property, Justification, and Need' (1993) 6 *Canadian Journal of Law and Jurisprudence* 185.

Walker Bynam, Caroline *The Resurrection of the Body in Western Christianity, 200-1336* (New York: Columbia University Press, 1995).

Wall, David 'Reconstructing the Soul of Elvis: The Social Development and Legal Maintenance of Elvis Presley as Intellectual Property' (1996) 24 *International Journal of the Sociology of Law* 117.

Warren, M A 'The Moral Significance of Birth' (1990) 4 *Hypatia* 46.

Warren, Samuel and Louis Brandeis 'The Right to Privacy' (1890) 4 *Harvard Law Review* 193.

Watson, Irene 'Indigenous People's Law-Ways: Survival Against the Colonial State' (1997) 8 *Australian Feminist Law Journal* 39.

Watson, Irene 'Power Of The Muldarbi, The Road To Its Demise' (1998) 11 *Australian Feminist Law Journal* 28.

Waye, Vicki 'Rape and the Unconscionable Bargain' (1992) 16 *Criminal Law Journal* 94.

Wells, Celia and Derek Morgan 'Whose Foetus is it?' (1991) 18(4) *Journal of Law and Society* 431.

Williams, ?? 'Cohen on Locke, Land and Labour' (1992) 40 *Political Studies* 51.

Williams, Patricia 'On Being the Object of Property' (1988) 14 *Signs: Journal of Women in Culture and Society* 5.

Williamson, Catherine 'Swimming Pools, Movie Stars: The Celebrity Body in the Post-War Marketplace' (1996) 38 *camera obscura* 5.

Wood, Olive and G L Certoma *Hutley, Woodman and Wood: Succession: Commentary and Materials* 4th ed (Sydney: Law Book Company, 1990).

Wright, Shelley 'A Feminist Exploration of the Legal Protection of Art' (1994) 7 *Canadian Journal of Women and the Law* 59.

Index